Finding Statistics Online
How to Locate the Elusive Numbers You Need

Finding Statistics Online
How to Locate the Elusive Numbers You Need

Paula Berinstein

Edited by Susanne Bjørner

Information Today, Inc.

Medford, NJ
1998

Third printing, June 2000

ISBN 0-910965-25-0

For my research clients, who gave me the idea

Paula Berinstein

Table of Contents

About Links to Sites and Staying Current

With new software tools and Web sites appearing (and disappearing) every day, the challenge for the author of *Finding Statistics Online* is to offer you a way to keep abreast of new resources and developments. Our mission is to provide you with a book that not only retains but actually *increases* its value as technology moves forward, unpredictably, in leaps and bounds. Today, the Internet—and specifically the World Wide Web—makes this possible.

At the Berinstein Research Web site, beginning in April 1998 , you will find a regularly updated **DIRECTORY OF ONLINE STATISTICS SOURCES** that includes, wherever possible and practical, active links to sites (you must have an Internet connection and Web browser to utilize these links). The Directory is designed to help you find sites that offer statistical information and to keep you up-to-date on relevant trends and issues. It is being made available at no charge to you as a valued reader of *Finding Statistics Online*. Before using the Directory, please be sure to read the important disclaimer that appears at the bottom of this page.

To Access the DIRECTORY OF ONLINE STATISTICS SOURCES:

1. Go to the Berinstein Research Web page at: **www.berinsteinresearch.com**

2. Click on the **DIRECTORY OF ONLINE STATISTICS SOURCES** icon or the words, *Statistics Sources*.

3. Note that the Directory is organized alphabetically by subject area.

DIRECTORY OF ONLINE STATISTICS SOURCES

Please send feedback—including information about new or nonworking Web sites and other resources—by email to: *webmaster@berinsteinresearch.com*

DISCLAIMER (please read carefully)
Neither publisher nor author make any claim as to the results that may be obtained through the use of the DIRECTORY OF ONLINE STATISTICS SOURCES or any of the Internet sites it references. Neither publisher nor author will be held liable for any results, or lack thereof, obtained by the use of any links, for any third-party charges, or for any hardware, software, or other problems that may occur as a result of using links. The DIRECTORY OF ONLINE STATISTICS SOURCES is subject to change or discontinuation without notice at the discretion of the publisher and author.

Figures

Foreword

I had my first encounter with finding statistics online in 1981, when I was working as an information specialist for an educational consortium and had just discovered this thing called "online." My organization had invested in an Apple II+ microcomputer and 300 baud modem, and we had established a subscription with BRS (Bibliographic Retrieval Services), a now-defunct commercial online retrieval system. One of the key information sources on that system (as on all its competitors at the time) was the ERIC education database.

A teacher came to me in desperation when he had to find out about a "five thousand hour" study. He didn't know what the "five thousand hours" referred to, but he was sure that the statistic was significant. We were both in the dark about any other pointers to this alleged study. Author? No indication of one. A sponsoring organization, or publisher? No clue. When had the study been done? Anybody's guess.

I hopped onto BRS and found an answer in less than three minutes: ERIC had a reference to a 1979 book by Rutter et al. titled *Fifteen Thousand Hours: Secondary Schools and Their Effects on Children*. Even though the number was different, my requester agreed it was the one he was looking for. The "fifteen thousand" referred to the number of hours a typical student spends in school classrooms during a high school attendance.

Pretty impressive for a newbie at electronic database searching, but I soon found out that it was beginner's luck. Nevertheless, this experience demonstrated to me irrevocably the power of statistics and the power of online to find them. People remember statistics—even if they remember them incorrectly—and use them as important "hooks" to encapsulate information and present a point of view.

Finding statistics online can be fast and easy when everything goes right. Using a search string of four numbers (5000, for example) will quickly find a match even in all the documents now on the gigantic World Wide Web. It can get a bit dicier, however, when you have to consider all the text variations that can signify 5000—5000, 5,000, five thousand, 5 thousand, 5K, five grand, five thou, and more—and how the search syntax on today's multitude of online systems may or may not accommodate those variations. It gets worse still when you realize the ways statistics can be "hidden" in parts of online records—in tables, charts, graphs, captions, pictures, and other graphic elements—that require special ways of searching to identify them. And of course, when you don't know the precise numbers you're searching for—as you usually don't—it gets even more difficult.

That's where *Finding Statistics Online* comes in. If I had had this book during the years I've been searching online—since my initial lucky experience—I would have saved a lot of time, money, and frustration while trying to find a wide variety of numbers. This book helps you find statistics on all sorts of topics. Whether you're looking for company sales figures, industry market projections, the number of individuals who speak a particular language or attend a specific entertainment event, who favor a political candidate or are following the newest trend, how people—or companies or countries—spend their money, or a hundred other nagging questions, you can find help here.

Use *Finding Statistics Online* as both a how-to-do-it text and a desktop reference. If you managed to get through college without a course in statistics, you will find that Chapter 2 gives you the background you need. And if you haven't managed to avoid a course in statistics in your formal education, you will find that Chapter 2 and the Glossary of Statistics Terms are a palatable refresher course. Chapter 3 (The Sources—Who Generates and Publishes Statistics?) and the subject-specific chapters (5 through 18) will tell you much more than you could have learned in college about specific sources in all disciplines that include statistics. Read two or three of those chapters to become familiar with the most important sources in the fields you need to know about.

Chapters 1 and 4 address the online resources that can help you find statistics. Comparison charts evaluate the capabilities of 12 different proprietary and Web-based information services as they relate to statistics and will help you decide whether it's worthwhile adding a service to your toolkit. Chapter 4 (General Search Tips) is full of information about what to do and what not to do when you are looking for elusive numbers. Then, 23 down-to-earth case studies let you in on Paula Berinstein's thought processes as she uses the knowledge she has detailed in this book to show how she found statistics ranging from the population of a city to airline fatalities.

But this is not a book that you will read once and then put away on a top shelf. The detailed directory of hundreds of subject-specific sources, databases, and Web sites—arranged by subject in each chapter—will make you reach for it over and over again when you need to find a statistic and don't know exactly where to turn. Use the directories as a "first-place-to-look" brainstormer, especially when you need to venture into an area where you haven't been before. I certainly will.

Susanne Bjørner
Franconia, New Hampshire
February 1998

Susanne Bjørner has spent hundreds of hours searching for statistics, facts, and research online. She has worked as a search specialist at MIT's Computerized Literature Search Service and for more than ten years in her own research and consulting business. Susanne has been a columnist and editor of ONLINE *magazine, a columnist for* Link-Up, *and now serves as Special Projects Editor for online efforts at* Choice *magazine. She continues to write about electronic information issues for a number of leading industry publications.*

Acknowledgments

John Bryans, driving force behind CyberAge Books, is the absolute best! John enthusiastically embraces 90% of my wacky but winning ideas and 100% of my unwacky ones, and makes me feel like a million bucks (even if my books do fall ever so slightly short of that figure when it comes to royalties).

Thank you to Susanne Bjørner, my editor, who believed in and pushed for this book as soon as she heard about it. Her suggestions have made the book infinitely better than it would have been without their institution. So what if my Word for Windows files were significantly less than 100% readable with her Word for the Mac?

A number of people at Information Today, Inc. (ITI) worked very hard on this project, especially Heide Dengler and her staff including Lisa Boccadutre and Erica Oehler. Thanks also to ITI's president, Tom Hogan, Sr., and to Rhonda Forbes, John Yersak, Heather Rudolph and Tom Hogan, Jr.

Once again, Lori Lathrop has produced an excellent index—in this case under extreme pressure. Thanks Lori!

At Online Inc., special thanks are due to editorial manager Christine Watts and copyeditor Kathy Kane, and to Troy Santi for a stunning cover. I also want to thank Jeff, Jenny and Adam Pemberton and Nancy Garman, who have been most supportive of me and my work.

No book like this one could have been written without the enthusiastic support of database producers and vendors, who graciously allowed me to play with their systems, patiently answered all of my questions (no matter how dumb), and helped me brainstorm about how best to get at numeric data. Special thanks to:

Nadine Benton and Jeff Steinman from Congressional Information Service

Ed Dodds, editor of the ADRIS Newsletter (Association for the Development of Religious Information Systems)

Christopher Gavigan from Questel•Orbit, Inc.

Adelaide Hulbert from Information Access Company (IAC)

Christopher Karwowski from Profound

Jerry Mastey from UMI

Maria Pastino from NewsNet (NewsNet was originally included in this book, but was removed when the company folded. NewsNet's terrific resources and the gracious help of Maria and her colleagues will be sorely missed.)

Doug Peacock from UMI

Rod Pinkston and Fred Winer from STN

Dara Schechter from Dow Jones Interactive (*formerly Dow Jones News/Retrieval*)

Vibeka Sisodiya, Catherine Jennings, and Louise Dagit of The Dialog Corporation (*formerly Knight-Ridder Information, Inc.*)

Lesley Sprigg and Allan Huber from LEXIS-NEXIS

Julie Stich from International Foundation of Employee Benefit Plans

C. Edward Wall from Pierian Press

Thank you also to the following organizations/individuals for their gracious permission to publish their data and/or illustrations:

ABC-CLIO

American Demographics

A.C. Nielsen

Copper Development Association

Alex Gibson, Scottish Economic History Database

Inso Corporation (*Information Please Almanac*)

The Roper Center for Public Opinion Research

World Almanac

Dan Forbush of ProfNet offers a great service for writers and journalists. Thanks, Dan, for broadcasting my request for help. And thanks to Gary Shultz of SMU News and Information and Andrew Lavin at A. Lavin Communications for responding to Dan's query.

My gratitude, as always, to my cheering section, who send me jokes by email, feed me, and provide relief when I get too intense: my sister Jan Berinstein, my parents, Jim Cornelius, Patricia (Lead) Barnes-Svarney, Barbara and Marina Javor, Howard and Karen Resnick, Kathy and Scott Watters, Sue Rugge, Barbara Quint, Buddy Evans, Mark Marcus, Gary and Barb Cooper, Péter Jacsó, Rohn Engh, and Despina, the best cat in the whole world. And to Stanzi, who would have been there.

Introduction

Any researcher will tell you that statistics are just plain intractable. Because they tend to be highly specific, statistics are among the hardest types of information to find, yet their ubiquity leads us to expect their ready availability on just about any topic. No wonder we find them frustrating!

Many business, scientific, and personal decisions are based on statistics, or would be if people had access to them. But numbers-seekers face the following problems:

- In order for statistics to exist, someone has to gather them. This implies a reason to do so, as well as the manpower. No reason or resources, no statistics.

- Statistics are hard to find. They're often buried within articles, reports, books, and transcripts, with no indexing or guide that points to them. Even if you find figures on your subject, much of the time they're not "cut" the way you want to see them (what you want counted isn't counted). And there are so many sources from which to choose that only those who deal with statistics on a regular basis know who generates them and where to look.

- Validity is often questionable. Even when you can find statistics, they may mislead you—often without your realizing it.

But help is on the way. The online world is exploding with statistics, and computer power can help people find them faster than ever. Using that special ability that computers possess to pinpoint a character, a word, or a pattern of words, a searcher can zero in on figures almost unfindable in hard copy. *Finding Statistics Online* will explain how to harness that computer power and help you avoid some of the pitfalls lying in wait for the unwary. You'll learn what to expect when looking for statistics, who created them, how to find them even when they're mentioned only in passing, and what to consider in evaluating their validity. With this book in hand, a researcher will be able to save time and money. It may also reduce your frustration, and who couldn't use a little less frustration?

WHO SHOULD READ THIS BOOK

Finding Statistics Online is aimed at business people, journalists, information professionals, marketing professionals, association and advocacy group staff, and anyone who needs to find statistics or numeric information. Whether you are a constant or occasional searcher, there is something for you here. This book includes techniques for effective numbers hunting regardless of field or topic and a myriad of resources to get you started, with a choice of systems from the user-friendly to the complex.

Because there are so many ways to search online and to learn how to do it, the book does *not* attempt to teach online or Internet searching. Rather, it assumes a basic familiarity with online retrieval techniques, whether on the Internet or through a private service.

You will find this book useful if you need numbers for:

- Decision-making
- Writing press releases
- Writing articles and books
- Preparing proposals
- Conducting market research and competitive analysis
- Putting together presentations
- Drafting white papers
- Researching and writing dissertations
- Assessing a situation
- Learning about a topic
- Conducting scientific or technical research
- Interviewing others or being interviewed yourself

WHAT'S IN THIS BOOK
The book flows from the general to the specific. It goes like this:

Chapter 1. Quick Start
This section enables you to jump in without reading the entire book. You'll find:

- A list of statistically-rich online systems, with brief descriptions
- A chart showing the subjects covered by each system, and the relative strength of that system for each subject
- A chart showing the types of sources covered by each system
- A chart comparing the usability, effectiveness, and cost of each system
- A list of the top ten statistical sources you should know
- A subject guide to the best Web sites for statistics
- A few quick tips on strategy.

Chapter 2. Statistics Basics
This primer covers:

- The various types of statistics, with explanations of terms
- Methodologies used for gathering and calculating statistics

- Ways of reading and evaluating the data
- Pitfalls: Red flags to watch for

Chapter 3. The Sources—Who Generates and Publishes Statistics?

This chapter introduces the players. It gives several examples of government agencies, associations, institutions, and other organizations that produce specific statistical sources. Knowing who produces statistics will enable you to make educated guesses when looking for a starting place.

Chapter 4. General Search Tips

This chapter offers advice for choosing a place to look and for formulating a strategy once you get there. The heart of the chapter is a set of figures illustrating the various forms statistical data can assume. You'll also find techniques for searching specific systems.

Subject-Specific Chapters

The remainder of the book is divided into chapters devoted to finding statistics in particular subject areas:

- Demographics and Population Statistics
- Industry, Market, and General Business Statistics
- Financial and Economic Statistics
- Health and Medical Statistics
- Scientific, Agricultural, and Environmental Statistics
- Historical Statistics
- Public Opinion and Trend Statistics
- Political and Government Statistics
- Sports, Entertainment, and Arts Statistics
- Legal and Crime Statistics
- International Statistics
- Technology Statistics
- Education Statistics
- Transportation Statistics

Each subject-specific chapter includes sections for:

- Common types of data available on the subject
- Key producers
- The types of sources most likely to cover the subject (such as statistical compendia, trade journals, and so on)

- Best places to look

- Case studies

The case studies, which highlight individual online systems, producers, and sites, illustrate specific problems and suggest techniques to solve them. Each case study is drawn from real-life questions; in constructing them, I did not work backwards from the answer, but forward from the question. The case studies demonstrate hands-on search techniques and conclude with a list of lessons learned.

These case studies are meant as guidelines rather than strict prescriptions, presenting ways of thinking and analyzing that should remain valid despite constant system and content changes. Because system mechanics and content do vary over time, however, it is unlikely that your results will be identical to mine. Nor do the case studies present the *sole* approach or solution to the problem—they illustrate only one of many that might work. Finally, as mentioned previously, even though some commands are included for clarity, I have not endeavored to teach the systems in detail; there are many other fine sources for that.

Because it's impossible to cover every subject or situation in detail, be sure to pay special attention to Chapter 4: General Search Tips, which will give you a foundation for searching on any topic. If your area of concern is not covered in a chapter of its own, you'll nevertheless benefit from reading one or two of the related subject-specific chapters; these should spark ideas about the *types* of sources that might help you.

A **concluding chapter: Now You're Ready!** summarizes in brief form what you have learned throughout the entire book.

Finding Statistics Online also includes a lengthy section of appendixes for easy reference:

Appendix A. Vendor Information
Here you'll find contact information for all the vendors of online systems mentioned in this book.

Appendix B. Case Studies Table
The table of case studies provides easy access to search examples by listing the topics covered and the systems, files or Web sites used as source material in the case studies.

Appendix C. Glossary of Terms
The glossary of statistics terms is arranged alphabetically for quick referral.

Appendix D. Bibliography
This includes sources used in the preparation of this book that may be used for further reading.

NOTES ABOUT ORGANIZATION AND SELECTION CRITERIA

One of the difficulties in organizing a work of this kind is that statistical information doesn't always fall into neat categories. Hence, you will find overlap among the categories. For example, information about the telecommunications industry in Japan might appear in several sections: markets/industries (Chapter 6), international (Chapter 15), and technology (Chapter 16). Likewise, demographics can show up in the demographics chapter (Chapter 5), the international chapter (Chapter 15), the market chapter (Chapter 6), and the history chapter (Chapter 10). Therefore, be sure to consult more than one chapter when deciding where to look.

Although I have included many sources and systems to get you started in your quest, the list is not exhaustive. In selecting general systems, I've focused on those that seem to be most commonly used or available. There are other less well-known systems, or more specific systems, that are superb as well (the DRI/McGraw-Hill databases come immediately to mind, for example). As far as sources are concerned, I have examined as many as reasonable for inclusion in a book of this size.

I have also endeavored to provide accurate names for specific sources and locations. However, both are subject to change. I will keep this data as up to date as possible at the Web site for the book. Because of the pace and volume of change, there will inevitably be information that is less than perfect. I ask your indulgence. If you subscribe to the service in question, consult the documentation—preferably that which is online— if my data is incorrect. And please drop me an email so I can inform others.

Be sure to visit the Web site for *Finding Statistics Online* (http://www.berinstein research.com). It features a directory of statistics sources—hyperlinked and ready for clicking! You'll also find semiannual online updates, reviews, and a few other surprises. And please, let us know what you like and don't like about the book and the Web site. We want this to be *your* resource!

Paula Berinstein
Agoura, California
March 1998
pberinstein@worldnet.att.net

Quick Start

This book explains and demonstrates how to locate statistics through the use of "traditional" online systems and the World Wide Web. Basic online search proficiency is assumed, though familiarity with statistics and statistical sources is not. You don't have to know *every* online system. In fact, if all you know is a single system or the Web, you will still be able to find lots of useful information.

For experienced and new statistics searchers alike, this chapter will get you started looking for statistics in a hurry (and who among us isn't in a hurry these days?). It is not meant to be comprehensive, but rather to distill the best wisdom from the rest of the book. Here you'll find:

- Lists of online systems rich in statistics

- Comparison charts showing various characteristics of those systems, including subject strengths, types of sources, rough costs, ease of use, whether you can search by industry or individual source, and the like

- Lists of the top ten statistical sources you should know, and a subject guide to the best statistics Web sites

- Tips on strategy, including how to use the Web most effectively

You will also find this chapter helpful as a reference, especially when selecting a system to search.

GENERAL ONLINE SERVICES RICH IN STATISTICS

Most of these systems started out as dial-up information services. Many of them are now available through the Web as well, and some are accessible only that way. Some aim strictly for business from information professionals; others either have end-user options or are specifically designed for end-user searching. While not the only general online systems rich in statistics, these systems are among the most well-known throughout the information community. If you are unfamiliar with a service, see Appendix A: Vendor Information for full addresses and other contact information for these systems.

BrainWave. This end-user system, available only on the Web, includes important business, technical, and popular sources also found on DIALOG and other professional systems. Less powerful than such systems, its pricing structure makes it seem less expensive but, in practice, it may not be so. Search charges are low, but full record displays are no bargain. Still, its accessibility and rich content make BrainWave well worth considering. (http://alpha.n2kbrainwave.com)

DataStar. Primarily emphasizing European business and technical resources, this sister to DIALOG is now available on the Web as well as through dial-up. (http://www.dialog.com)

DIALOG. DIALOG is and has been for three decades a vast supermarket of excellent scholarly, business, popular, technical, and reference databases. It's now available on the Web as well as through dial-up. (http://www.dialog.com)

Dow Jones News/Retrieval. Now available on the Web as well as through dial-up, Dow Jones News/Retrieval is the pre-eminent source for online business and financial information, including journals, newswires, newspapers, and directories. This is the *only* system that provides a full-text archive of the *Wall Street Journal*, although recent marketing agreements with UMI also make it available to selected UMI markets. (bis.dowjones.com)

Electric Library. Electric Library is a sleeper. Priced for the consumer (with school and library options), it includes a variety of important journal and news sources as well as almanacs and encyclopedias. Electric Library is available only on the Web. (http://www.elibrary.com)

IAC InSite. This end-user system on the Web is rich in business, computer, and consumer sources familiar to users of the Information Access Company databases available on many online and CD-ROM services. Divided into five databases that can be purchased separately or in combination, this system sports a typical end-user interface. Pricing is by site license. The databases are: Business InSite, Consumer InSite, Computer InSite, Market InSite, and Newsletter InSite. (http://iac-insite.com)

IAC InSite Pro. InSite Pro, available on the Web, is the information professional version of IAC InSite. The content is exactly the same, but InSite Pro offers more search power. Pricing is by site license. (http://www.insitepro.com)

LEXIS-NEXIS. LEXIS-NEXIS is *the* source for *full-text* news, trade, legal, and financial information. Still available at this writing only through dial-up (a graphical interface), the system will probably have set up shop on the Web by the time you read this book. (http://www.lexis-nexis.com)

Profound. A system oriented toward end-users, Profound excels at market research, company reports, industry information, and country research. (http://www.profound.com)

ProQuest Direct. ProQuest Direct covers popular and scholarly sources and, in many cases, includes tables and images not available on other systems. Geared toward the end-user, the system offers enough power and flexibility to satisfy the demands of information professionals, as well. Available on the Web or through a Windows dial-up client. Graphically intensive. (http://www.umi.com)

Questel•Orbit. Strong in science and technology resources, Questel•Orbit is currently available only through dial-up. Numeric information is primarily in the area of physical properties of substances and materials. (http://www.questel.orbit.com)

STN. STN International is Chemical Abstracts Service's online scientific and technical information system. Numeric information includes chemical, physical, and other properties of substances. While this system requires a great amount of expertise to use, its end-user subset, STN Easy, may be searched effectively by those less familiar with the complexity of the mother system. Available by dial-up. (http://www.cas.org)

Wall Street Journal Interactive Edition. This Web-based newspaper is much more than it seems. It also houses the entire Dow Jones News/Retrieval Publications Library: a warehouse of general business, news, and industry-specific journals; newspapers; and wires. Pricing is extremely reasonable. The interface is "end-user graphical." (http://interactive.wsj.com)

SERVICES AND/OR DATABASES
PROVIDING SPECIALIZED STATISTICAL SOURCES

NOTE: These specialized services are not included in the following comparison charts of general online systems.

Cognito! and Encarta Online Library. Originally separate services, Cognito! and Encarta have now merged. Both are notable for their almanacs, including Information Please Almanac, Information Please Sports Almanac, and Information Please Environmental Almanac. They also feature Collier's Encyclopedia and Columbia Encyclopedia. (http://www.encarta.com/library/intro.asp)

Gale Business Resources. This useful collection includes well-known business reference sources such as *Ward's Business Directory of U.S. Private and Public Companies, Business Rankings Annual, Market Share Reporter*, and more. (http://galenet.gale.com)

A Matter of Fact. This database from Pierian Press, composed entirely of statistical material and short facts, is excellent for public policy topics, including economics, politics, health, environment, and social issues. Found primarily on library automation systems, this gold mine is also available to the individual and/or small business using SilverPlatter's Search by Search system. (http://www.silverplatter.com) Search by Search requires a rather hefty deposit of $500, but its pay-as-you-go pricing is extremely reasonable at $.25 per search plus $.30 per record for A Matter of Fact. (And the deposit authorizes you to search its other 15 to 20 databases in the same way.) A Matter of Fact is also available through Autographics, Brodart, COMPanion Corp., Endeavor Information, FirstSearch, Gateway Library Management Systems, Innovative Interfaces, NISC, Vista II, and Winnebago Software, and on CD-ROM and in print. The electronic version is updated each quarter. The print version comes out twice a year. With good luck, by the time you read this, other pay-as-you-go vendors will have made the database available so that non-institutional users can benefit from its superb information.

STN Easy. STN Easy features a subset of STN International databases and an end-user (but not consumer) Web-based interface. Numeric information includes properties of chemicals and chemical industry statistics. (http://stneasy.cas.org)

TableBase, a database composed solely of numerical tables (with associated full text available but not searchable), from Responsive Database Services, Inc. Find TableBase on the Web at http://www.tablebase.com, on Dialog, DataStar, and .xls. Coverage of business and industry is heavy, but you will also find macroeconomic data, health statistics, and general reference.

TOP TEN STATISTICAL SOURCES YOU SHOULD KNOW

There are thousands of online sources that include statistical information in many areas. This book lists hundreds of them. However, if you know only the following ten sources, you will probably be able to answer a large portion of your statistical questions.

A Matter of Fact (available from multiple vendors—see this page, above). A database from Pierian Press composed of statistical material drawn from newsletters, magazines, Congressional hearings, Web sites,

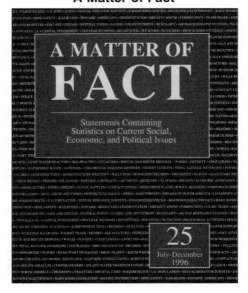

FIGURE 1-1
A Matter of Fact

FIGURE 1-2

COMPARISON CHART: Subjects Covered, By System

The following table summarizes the subject strengths of each system as they relate specifically to statistics, not the subject in general.

	BrainWave	DataStar	DIALOG	DJN/R	Electric Library	IAC InSite/ InSite Pro	LEXIS-NEXIS	Profound	ProQuest Direct	Questel-Orbit	STN	WSJIE
Agriculture	✓	No	No	No	✓	✓✓	✓✓	✓	✓	No	No	No
Biotechnology	✓	✓✓✓	✓✓✓	✓✓	✓	✓	✓✓	✓✓✓	No	✓	✓	✓✓
Business	✓✓	✓✓✓	✓✓✓	✓✓✓	✓	✓✓✓	✓✓✓	✓✓✓	✓✓✓	✓	✓	✓✓✓
Communcations/ broadcasting/ publishing industries	✓	✓	✓	✓✓✓	✓	✓	✓✓✓	✓✓	No	No	No	✓✓✓
Company financials	✓✓	✓✓✓	✓✓✓	✓✓✓	No	✓	✓✓✓	✓✓✓	✓	✓✓	✓	✓✓
Computer industry	✓✓	✓	✓✓	✓✓✓	No	✓✓✓	✓✓	✓✓	✓	✓	✓	✓✓✓
Crime	✓	No	✓✓	✓	✓	No	✓✓	No	✓	No	No	✓
Demographics/ population	✓	✓	✓	✓	✓	✓	✓	✓	✓	✓	✓	✓
Economy	✓	✓✓	✓✓✓	✓✓✓	✓	✓✓✓	✓✓✓	✓✓✓	✓✓✓	✓	No	✓✓✓
Education	✓	✓	✓	✓	✓	✓	✓	✓	✓	No	No	✓
Energy	✓✓	✓	✓	✓✓✓	No	✓✓	✓✓✓	✓✓	✓	✓	✓	✓✓✓
Entertainment industry	✓	No	✓	✓✓✓	✓	✓	✓✓✓	✓✓	✓	No	No	✓✓✓

COMPARISON CHART: Subjects Covered, By System (continued)

	BrainWave	DataStar	DIALOG	DJN/R	Electric Library	IAC InSite/ InSite Pro	LEXIS-NEXIS	Profound	ProQuest Direct	Questel-Orbit	STN	WSJIE
Environment	✓	✓	✓	✓✓✓	✓	✓	✓✓✓	✓✓	✓	No	✓	✓✓✓
Finance and financial services	✓	✓	✓✓✓	✓✓✓	✓	✓✓	✓✓✓	✓✓✓	✓✓	No	No	✓✓✓
Government-related	✓	✓	✓	✓	✓	No	✓✓✓	✓	✓	No	No	✓
Health and health care industry	✓	✓	✓✓	✓✓✓	✓	✓✓	✓✓✓	✓✓✓	✓	✓	✓	✓✓✓
Industries (other)	✓✓	✓✓	✓✓✓	✓✓✓	✓	✓✓✓	✓✓✓	✓✓✓	✓✓	✓	✓	✓✓✓
Market research	✓	✓✓✓	✓✓✓	✓✓	✓	✓	✓✓✓	✓✓✓	No	✓	✓	✓✓
Physical and earth sciences	✓	✓	✓	No	✓	No	No	No	No	✓	✓✓✓	No
Politics and election	✓	No	✓	✓	✓	No	✓✓✓	✓	✓	✓	No	✓
Public opinion	✓	✓	✓	✓	✓	No	✓✓	✓	✓	No	No	✓
Religion	No	No	✓	✓	✓	No	✓	No	No	No	No	✓
Sports	No	No	✓	No	✓	✓	✓	No	✓	No	No	No
Transportation	✓	✓	✓	✓✓✓	✓	✓✓	✓✓	✓✓	✓	No	No	✓✓✓
Weather	No	No	No	No	✓	No	No	No	No	No	No	No

Key

No= No coverage
✓ = A little coverage
✓✓ = Pretty good coverage
✓✓✓ = Outstanding coverage

FIGURE 1-3

COMPARISON CHART: Types of sources covered, by system

	BrainWave	DataStar	DIALOG	DJN/R	Electric Library	IAC InSite InSite Pro	LEXIS-NEXIS	Profound	ProQuest Direct	Questel-Orbit	STN	WSJIE
Almanacs/yearbooks	No	No	No	No	✓✓	No	✓	No	No	No	No	No
Business journals (general--full text)	✓	✓✓	✓✓✓	✓✓✓	✓	✓✓✓	✓✓✓	✓✓	✓✓	✓	✓	✓✓✓
Directories	✓	✓✓✓	✓✓✓	✓✓	No	No	✓✓✓	✓✓✓	No	✓✓	✓	No
Encyclopedias	✓	No	✓	✓	✓	No	✓	No	No	✓	No	No
Handbooks	No	No	✓	No	No	No	No	No	No	✓	✓✓✓	No
Newspapers (full text)	✓✓	✓	✓✓✓	✓✓✓	✓✓✓	No	✓✓✓	✓✓✓	✓✓✓	✓	No	✓✓✓
Popular journals (full text)	No	No	✓✓✓	✓✓	✓✓	✓✓✓	✓	No	✓	No	No	No
Scholarly journals (full text)	No	No	✓✓✓	✓✓	✓	No	No	No	No	No	✓✓✓	✓
Statistical compendia/factbooks	No	✓	✓✓	✓	✓	✓✓	No	No	No	No	✓✓✓	✓
Time series	No	✓	✓✓	✓	No	No	✓	✓	No	No	No	No
Trade- or industry-specific journals (full text)	✓	✓✓✓	✓✓✓	✓✓✓	✓	✓✓✓	✓✓✓	✓✓✓	✓✓	No	✓	✓✓✓

Key

No= No coverage
✓ = A little coverage
✓✓ = Pretty good coverage
✓✓✓ = Outstanding coverage

FIGURE 1-4

COMPARISON CHART: System Usability, Effectiveness, and Costs

	BrainWave	DataStar	DIALOG	DJN/R	Electric Library	IAC InSite/ InSite Pro	LEXIS-NEXIS	Profound	ProQuest Direct	Questel-Orbit	STN	WSJIE
Ability to set up account "on the fly?"	Yes	No	No	No	Yes	No	No	No	No	No	No	Yes
Subscription fee? (Annual fee not credited against searching)	No	No, but there is a charge for the manual	Yes, for setup; doesn't cover searching	Yes	No; monthly or annual, or site license for schools and libraries for unlimited searching	No; fee is flat annual for unlimited searching	Yes	Yes	Custom pricing makes it impossible to say "Yes" or "No"	Yes	No, but there is a one-time setup fee of $50	Yes
Charge to search?	Yes	Yes	Yes	No	No	No	Yes	No	No	Yes	Yes	No
Charge for full text/ full record?	Yes	Yes	Yes	Yes	No	No	Yes, if download; No if screen capture	Yes	Yes if pay-as-you-go; No if flat fee plan	Yes	Yes	Yes
Cost range	$ - $$	$$$	$$$	$ - $$	$/Individuals	$$$	$$$	$$$	$ - $$	$$$	$$$	$ - $$
Search by individual source?	No	Yes	Yes	Yes	Yes	Yes	Yes	No	Yes	Yes	Yes	Yes if you use codes, otherwise major papers category is as fine as you can go
Search by industry?	Yes, some	CROS groups can be broken down into some industries	Some ONESEARCH categories and/or databases are limited to particular industries; some databases have their own codes	Yes	No	Yes	Some libraries and/or files cover specific industries	Yes	Yes	Some databases cover specific industries	Some databases cover specific industries	Yes
Level of difficulty	End-user	Expert	Expert	End-user	End-user	IAC InSite is enduser. With InSite Pro, user chooses interface; all levels available	Expert	End-user	End-user	Expert	Expert	End-user

Nota Bene: Costs are variable, and often negotiable. Don't take them at face value. Haggle!

NOTE: No system includes all tables supplied with an article. Nor is there any way to predict whether tables will be included or not except on ProQuest Direct. There, if either full-page image or Text+Graphics format is available, everything is there—guaranteed. With other systems and even PQD's complete-text format, you may find one table within an article included and another excluded, or all excluded.

Key

NOTE: Cost ranges are ballpark only due to variations in pricing structures between services and database fees within a service.

$ = Low cost. Searching hourly rate $20 or less *or* monthly rate is $20 or less *or* per document is $4 or less.

$$ = Medium cost. Searching hourly rate averages between $21 and $50 *or* monthly rate between $21 and $30 *or* per document is $5 to $10.

$$$ = High cost. Searching hourly rate averages more than $50 *or* monthly rate more than $30 *or* per document more than $10.

and other resources. Focus is on issues that relate to public policy, such as economics, politics, health, environment, and social issues.

Statistical Abstract of the U.S. (http://www.census.gov/stat_abstract). The premier American statistical source, published annually. Includes the following: vital statistics, population, health, education, law enforcement, courts, prisons, geography and environment, recreation and travel, elections, government finances and employment, defense, social and human services, labor, income, wealth, spending, prices, banking, finance, insurance, business, communications, energy, science, transportation, agriculture, natural resources, mining, construction and housing, manufacturing, trade, foreign aid, and comparative international statistics.

The World Almanac (Electric Library, FirstSearch) or **Information Please Almanac** (Cognito!, Encarta Online Library). The scope of these almanacs is similar to that of the *Statistical Abstract of the U.S.* In addition, you'll find entertainment, astronomy, aviation, space travel, and information on famous people, states, and countries.

FIGURE 1-5
Statistical Abstract of the U.S.

FIGURE 1-6
The World Almanac and Information Please Almanac

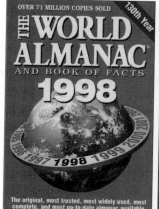

FIGURE 1-7
The U.S. Census Bureau's Web Site

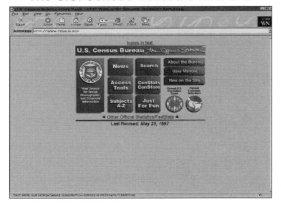

FIGURE 1-8
The CIA World Factbook Web Site

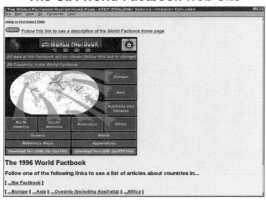

FIGURE 1-9
The FEDSTATS Web Site

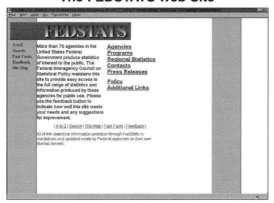

Fortune, Forbes, Business Week (available in several databases through DIALOG, Dow Jones News/Retrieval, Electric Library, LEXIS-NEXIS, Pro-Quest Direct, Wall Street Journal Interactive Edition. Also at http://www.fortune.com, http://www.forbes.com, and http://www.businessweek.com, respectively). These essential U.S. business magazines cover everything from business in general to specific industries, companies, products, and trends.

U.S. Bureau of the Census (http://www.census.gov). The Census Bureau reports not only on population and demographics, but also on other topics such as aging, ancestry, agriculture, business, child care, education, commuting, disability, the economy, finance, income, insurance, journey to work, living arrangements, migration, prices and inflation, retail and wholesale sales, state and local area profiles, service industries, manufacturing, voting and registration, and more.

The World Factbook (Electric Library, http://www.odci.gov/cia/publications/pubs.html). *The* source for information on countries around the world, from the CIA.

FEDSTATS (http://www.fedstats.gov). FEDSTATS is the central locator for U.S. federal government statistics provided by more than 70 agencies.

Newspapers. Newspapers cover just about every topic you can think of, from the economy to social issues to various industries to religion to the arts. Major papers like the *New York Times* and *The Washington Post* are essentially national papers, covering national and international issues. Smaller (regional) newspapers, including regional business papers, excel at covering local economies, companies, and issues.

American Demographics (Dow Jones News/ Retrieval, Electric Library, LEXIS-NEXIS (BUSFIN, MARKET, and NEWS Libraries), ProQuest Direct, Wall Street Journal Interactive, (http://www.demographics.com)). This wide-ranging journal covers issues related to consumer demographics, especially what people are thinking, doing, and purchasing.

Bureau of Labor Statistics (http://stats. bls.gov/). Everything about U.S. labor, employment, earnings, prices, the economy in general—even foreign labor statistics.

A SUBJECT GUIDE TO THE BEST WEB SITES FOR STATISTICS

There are thousands of sites on the World Wide Web that can be used as statistical sources. The following are some of the best sites that I have found for the subjects covered. Remember that Web sites change very quickly; if you have trouble connecting to a particular site, use a search engine to find a possible new location for the site by the name or sponsor indicated here.

Agriculture

Foreign Agricultural Service (non-U.S. food market overviews, world agricultural production, world markets for selected commodities)
http://www.fas.usda.gov.
Mann Library Index by Subject: Agriculture (agricultural economics, production, food consumption and expenditures, pesticides and fertilizer, crops and livestock, international)
http://www.mannlib.cornell.edu/cgi-bin/subj.cgi?ag
National Agricultural Statistics Service (agricultural census, crops and commodities, including historic)
http://www.usda.gov/nass/#NASS

FIGURE 1-10
American Demographics

FIGURE 1-11

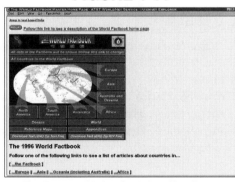

The Bureau of Labor Statistics offers figures dealing not only with the world of work, but also with prices and the economy in general.

Business/Economy

Beige Book of Current Economic Conditions (monetary, economic, and banking topics)
  http://www.clev.frb.org/research/index.htm
  http://www.bog.frb.fed.us/fomc/bb/current
Bureau of Economic Analysis. (National, regional, and international economic topics such as GDP, personal income, population, employment, balance of payments, investment abroad and foreign investment in the U.S. The Bureau's *Survey of Current Business* reviews the U.S. economic situation on a regular basis)
  http://www.bea.doc.gov
Census of Manufactures
  http://www.census.gov/econ/www/ma0100.html
Census of Retail and Wholesale Trades
  http://www.census.gov/econ/www/retmenu.html
County & City Data Book
  http://www.lib.virginia.edu/socsci/ccdb
County Business Patterns (county and state economic profiles)
  http://www.census.gov/epcd/cbp/view/cbpview.html
Current Industrial Reports
  http://www.census.gov/pub/cir/www/index.html
Survey of Current Business (Gross Domestic Product (GDP), personal income, gross product by industry, balance of payments, U.S. investment abroad, foreign investment in the U.S., state and county personal income, gross state products)
  http://www.bea.doc.gov
U.S. Global Trade Outlook (formerly *U.S. Industrial Outlook*)
  http://www.tradeport.org/ts/ntdb/usgto/
World Trade Organization
  http://www.wto.org

Crime

Crime Statistics Site by Regina Schekall
  http://www.crime.org
Sourcebook of Criminal Justice Statistics
  http://www.albany.edu/sourcebook/

Education

National Center for Education Statistics
  http://nces.ed.gov/

Energy

Energy Information Administration. (fuels, usage, prices, environmental effects of energy generation and use, economics)
  http://www.eia.doe.gov

Government and Politics

Federal Election Commission (campaign finance, elections)
  http://www.fec.gov

The Green Book Overview of Entitlement Programs
  http://aspe.os.dhhs.gov/

Office of Management and Budget: Budget Publications and Economic Report of the President (includes historical expenditures back to the 1920s)
  http://www.access.gpo.gov/su_docs/budget/index.html

Health

World Health Organization Statistical Information System (WHOSIS) (global health situation)
  http://www.who.org/whosis/

International

Library of Congress Country Studies
  http://lcweb2.loc.gov/frd/cs/cshome.html

Statistics Canada (Canadian analog of the U.S. Census Bureau)
  http://www.statcan.ca/

Transportation

Bureau of Transportation Statistics (aviation, ground and water transportation)
  http://www.bts.gov

Weather

National Climatic Data Center (historical weather statistics)
  http://www.ncdc.noaa.gov/ncdc.html

TIPS ON STRATEGY

Searching online and World Wide Web sources for statistical information requires practice, practice, and more practice. There are lots of differences from source to source. These tips represent the best of the best. For more complete information on strategy, see Chapter Four: General Search Tips.

When searching full text:

• Use terms like *study*, *survey*, *report*, and *research* to find statistics on your topic.

• Use codes and descriptors, if available.

Vendor-specific tips:

• Use the Wall Street Journal Interactive Edition Publications Library for general business, specific industries (it covers trade publications nicely), and major newspapers.

- Use LEXIS-NEXIS and Profound for financial information and market research. Both systems are especially strong on international coverage.
- Use DIALOG for full text of newspapers, company financials, and trade and industry information.
- Use Electric Library, Encarta Online Library, and Cognito! for almanacs.
- Use STN and Questel•Orbit for properties of substances and materials.
- Use TableBase for business, industry, technology, transportation, and health.

On the Web:
- Steer clear of Web search engines to look for the statistic itself but do use them to find the site of the producer or publisher.
- Use the U.S. Census Bureau and other government statistical agencies as starting points. Follow links from there.
- Use Web site rating services, categorized lists, and "town criers" to find good Web sites to search.

Rating services include:
- Magellan (http://www.mckinley.com)
- Excite (http://www.excite.com)
- Lycos (http://www.pointcom.com)
- Money$earch (http://www.moneysearch.com)
- NetFinder (http://www.aol.com/netfind/)
- NetGuide (http://www.netguide.com)
- WebCrawler (http://www.webcrawler.com)
- Wired Source (http://www.wired.com/cybrarian/)

The best categorized lists include:
- The BUBL Information Service (http://bubl.ac.uk)
- Infoseek (http://guide-p.infoseek.com)
- Librarians' Index to the Internet (http://sunsite.berkeley.edu/InternetIndex/)
- World Wide Web Virtual Library (http://vlib.stanford.edu/Overview.html)
- Yahoo! (http://www.yahoo.com)

Town criers are:
- Scout Report (archives are at http://www.scout.cs.wisc.edu/scout/report/archive/)
- Net-Happenings (http://scout.cs.wisc.edu/scout/net-hap/)

Statistics Basics

When we hear the term *statistics* most of us think of numbers, often associated with complicated analyses and dry-sounding terminology. Some people insist that statistics are all lies and should be ignored. Not many of us are clear about what statistics really are, how they come into being, and how to evaluate them. When we hear that "Forty-five percent of Americans are online" or "There has been a 12% drop in the crime rate," we know what our emotional reaction is, but many of us don't think beyond that to examine whether the reaction is justified by the facts.

This chapter is a statistics primer. Read on, and you will learn what statistics are, how they're arrived at, and what to watch for when assessing their validity. The concepts and issues treated here will arise again and again in the case studies in this book and in your own searches: questions of definition, methodology, currency, and bias. Knowing what to look for doesn't mean that you have to read every word of every methodology discussion or contact every researcher whose data you're considering, though you may wish to do so. This chapter helps you develop a foundation for asking the right questions. You decide how far to go.

TYPES OF STATISTICS

Statistics can take a variety of forms. Here are the types you'll encounter:

Raw Numbers. Raw numbers are pure data—they represent counts or measures. Population counts and company financials are both examples of raw numbers. Sometimes raw numbers are reworked before release; you'll recognize such data by phrases like "adjusted for seasonal variations" or "in 1986 dollars." Counts of items that cannot be subdivided, such as people or cars, are said to represent *discrete data*, while *continuous data*, such as weights, heights, and other scaled data, can always be subdivided just a little more.

Percentages. Percentages express the relationships between a part and the whole and help make sense of raw data. Percentages are easy to work with because they reduce counts to one common scale, based on a hundred.

For example, if I say that 47,401,185 people voted for Bill Clinton in 1996 as opposed to 39,197,469 for Dole, you can instantly recognize that more people voted for Clinton, but you can't tell how significant the difference is. However, when you convert the numbers into percentages (49.24% vs. 40.71%, respectively), you can appreciate the significance of the raw numbers and compare them to the total.

However, percentages can overstate or understate the significance of the raw numbers, so they should be supplemented with a consideration of the actual data. How accurate a picture percentages convey depends on where you start and the nature of the thing being counted. For example, we often hear that there has been a large increase in this or that undesirable thing, and good grief, isn't that scary! Sometimes alarm is warranted, and sometimes not, depending on the actual numbers and what the thing is. If the price of a taco has jumped 43% from 35 cents to 50 cents, that 43% is less significant than if it represented the increase in the price of a car from $17,000 to over $24,000. The next time you hear about percent increases or decreases in numbers of plane crashes, murders, or disease cases, look for the raw numbers before you decide whether to be alarmed, relieved, or unimpressed.

Indexes. An index is one number that summarizes multiple measurements. Because an index expresses those multiple measurements in terms of a common base, it enables us to compare apples to apples. An index may represent measurements or counts of many things, or different aspects of one thing. An example of the former is the consumer price index, which aggregates prices of many products and services. An example of the latter is gymnastic scoring, where many different attributes of gymnastic performance are being measured. An index may represent objective measurements, such as prices, or subjective ones, such as attitudes, feelings, and judgments.

Indexes are used as general indicators of the state of something. For example, the consumer price index says something about the state of the economy in general, as well as about prices of consumer goods. Familiar indexes include baseball player batting averages, IQ (Intelligence Quotient) scores, and crime rates.

Rankings. Ranking means placing something at various points on a scale. Two kinds of numbers are involved in ranking: the raw data, and the rank or rating number. A searcher might seek the rank number, the raw data, or both.

For example, if you were to rank countries according to the amount of money they spend on foreign aid, you'd have to start with the actual amounts of money. That would be the raw data. Then, you'd rank the countries by amount, either the largest to the smallest, or vice versa. You'd have two numbers: the actual amount and the rank.

Or, rather than using the dollar amount, you might calculate percent of national budget represented by foreign aid. This process would require that you find two raw numbers: the amount spent on foreign aid and the total national budget. Note that because some countries have more money than others, a list based on percent of national budget would look different from a list based on raw numbers alone.

Averages. There are three common types of averages: mean, median, and mode. These are often different for any given group and they denote different things, so it's important to know which average is being used.

Mean. The mean is the arithmetic average of a group of numbers. The mean is arrived at by adding up all the values and dividing by the number of measurements. For example, the mean age in a family of four, with ages of 42, 40, 10, and 4, is 24 (the sum of the ages divided by four). Notice that the mean in this example does not reflect any real person's age. Means are what give us silly-sounding statements such as "The average family includes 2.3 children." Because it may result in hypothetical rather than real values, the mean can be an unattractive measure in certain situations.

The mean can be skewed so that it is less than representative of reality if it includes one or a few numbers at either the high or low extreme. Using the family example, the inclusion of a 90-year-old grandparent could raise the mean substantially to a little over 37; the addition of a one-year-old baby would affect the mean far less (without the grandparent, the mean would be 19.4 rather than 24). When you see a mean figure that doesn't look quite right, consider what and who might have been counted.

Median. The median is the midpoint of a group of numbers; half the numbers in the group fall above the median and half fall below the median. For example, the median home price in an area might be $250,000, with half the homes valued at less than $250,000 and half valued at more than $250,000. It could very well be, however, that there are no houses actually priced at $250,000 (just as there was no one in the family aged 24 in the mean example above).

The median tells nothing about the range or distribution of the data. We don't know the high and low extremes, and we don't know how many houses might sell around $180,000 as opposed to $60,000. The mean will probably be different for each of two or more neighborhoods with a median price of $250,000, depending on how the data is clustered.

Let's look at means and medians with a detailed example. Neighborhood A is structured as follows:

100 houses at	$120,000
10 houses at	$250,000
30 houses at	$260,000
30 houses at	$270,000
30 houses at	$280,000
5 houses at	$350,000
5 houses at	$400,000

Neighborhood A includes 210 houses. The median (midpoint) home price is $250,000: ten homes cost $250,000, 100 homes cost less than $250,000, and 100 homes cost more than $250,000. Neighborhood A features a mean home price of $212,750; this number was computed by adding the price of each of the 210 houses and dividing by 210.

Neighborhood B is structured this way:

20 houses at	$210,000
20 houses at	$220,000
20 houses at	$230,000
20 houses at	$240,000
20 houses at	$250,000
20 houses at	$260,000
20 houses at	$280,000
20 houses at	$300,000
10 houses at	$350,000
10 houses at	$500,000

Neighborhood B is made up of 180 houses and also has a median home price of $250,000. However, the mean price for Neighborhood B is $287,777.

Even though the median and the mean taken together tell us something about each neighborhood, they don't tell us the high and low values, and we still don't know how many houses are priced at any particular level.

To illustrate this point, let's say you had $230,000 to spend on a house. Which neighborhood would you choose, based on the median and the mean?

Neighborhood B looks too expensive, but in fact, it isn't; there are 60 houses in or near your price range. Neighborhood A theoretically offers houses within your price range, but in reality, there aren't any—the 100 houses lower than $250,000 are all at $120,000, far below your budget. So remember that means and medians are just guides; they don't necessarily tell the whole story.

Mode. The mode is the most frequently-found number in a group. There can be more than one mode. For example, in the same residential neighborhood, there might be several modes, such as $180,000, $240,000, and $350,000. These figures indicate that the supply of houses valued at those three prices is higher than the supply at any other price. One positive attribute of the mode is that it reflects *real* values, unlike the mean and median, which may be theoretical ones.

Sometimes the three averages are close together, or even the same, and sometimes not, depending on whether the distribution of all possible values is even or not. (The well-known bell curve exemplifies an even, or *normal*, distribution.)

Dennis G. Haack, in his book *Statistical Literacy: A Guide to Interpretation*, presents guidelines for the use of the three averages. The choice depends on the distribution of the data. The mean is best when the data is evenly distributed and there is only one mode (for example, when housing prices run the gamut, but may cluster around a particular price, such as $350,000). The median is best when there is only one mode, but the data is skewed (when there are a few houses in the over $5 million price range, but almost everything else is $750,000 or lower, and there is no clustering around a particular price). If we are interested in categorizing the data and there is more than one mode, the mode is best (as when describing characteristics of people, e.g., females with higher education degrees, and there are large concentrations of English, history, and political science degree-holders).

Always check to see which kind of average is being presented. If the documentation doesn't say, you can't assume that it's the mean. The producer may have chosen the average that best supports his or her agenda and, though technically accurate, that average may mislead.

When evaluating whether the type of average accurately represents the data, try to determine the range of values in the study. Are there any houses priced at $100,000? $2,000,000? Knowing the range will give you a better idea of the character of the area. Two completely different areas might exhibit the same median, for example, but one might range from $80,000 to $350,000, and another from $150,000 to $3,000,000, The former community is less affluent than the latter, or else the standard of living in the area is computed on a different scale.

Standard deviation. When considering averages, watch for the term "standard deviation." Standard deviation is a unit that measures how variable the data is. An item is said to be one or more standard deviations away from the mean. The farther away, the more unique and rare. The closer, the more common. Standard deviations are the most accurate when the data is distributed fairly evenly, as in a bell curve. In a bell curve, 68% of the data is within one standard deviation of the mean; 95% of the data is within two standard deviations of the mean; all of the data is within three standard deviations of the mean.

Percentiles. Percentiles indicate how data is distributed. A percentile is a number below which a certain percent of the data falls. For example, the 80th percentile is a number below which 80% of the values occur. If a selling price of $350,000 is the 80th percentile, then 80% of the houses in the area sell for under $350,000. However, if a selling price of $750,000 is the 80th percentile, you're going to have to make a lot more money to afford to live in the neighborhood. Note that, in either case, the median value could be the same, though in reality that's unlikely.

Rates. A rate is expressed as so-many items per larger number. For example, parts per million, used to measure pollutants, is a rate.

Ratings. A rating is neither a rate nor a ranking. It is a subjective measure of something that has been assigned a numerical value. For example, consider the familiar strain "On a scale of one to ten, where would you rate such-and-such a movie?" Scales such as "agree strongly," "agree," "agree somewhat," "disagree somewhat," "disagree," "strongly disagree" are examples of ratings (once the values are converted to numbers). This kind of data is also called *ordinal data.*

Nominal Data. Nominal data overlaps to some degree with ratings. Nominal data represents categories that are *not* assigned numerical values. In the above example, "agree," etc., is an item of nominal data. The results of nominal counts are usually expressed as either percentages or raw numbers.

Probabilities. Probability is the likelihood that something will occur. Probability is calculated based on the number of times an event occurs when a random experiment is run many times.

Ratios. A ratio is the relationship between two numbers. Ratios only make sense if the relationship between the numbers means something. For example, it makes no sense to draw a ratio between two high temperatures of 101 and 106. (The ratio 101:106 or vice versa doesn't provide meaningful information.) However, it may make sense to construct a ratio of one Richter scale value to another because each increment represents a tenfold increase in energy measured in ground motion (10:1). Sometimes ratios are given without presentation of the raw numbers behind them. In that case, interpreting ratios requires the same caution as interpreting percentages: the situation can be overstated if small actual numbers are involved.

Interval Data. Interval data represents the difference between two measurements. Interval data is best used when that difference presents a meaningful picture of the situation. For example, "I am three inches taller than you are" depicts a meaningful interval, while "I generally go to bed an hour later than he does" does not, unless we know at which time "I" or "he" retires.

METHODOLOGIES FOR GATHERING AND CALCULATING STATISTICS

How do people count things? How can they say how many people approve of the President's performance—they never asked *me*! And how do they know how many miles per year I drive, or how many students play basketball after school? Following are common methodologies used for counting things:

Censuses. A census is a complete count of the thing or population to be measured. In theory, a census counts every single thing. However, in practice, a census can miss items. In the U.S. Census of Population and Housing, some people slip through the cracks. It is particularly difficult to count the homeless population, for example.

Surveys and Questionnaires

Samples. A sample is a representative "taste" of a group. A sample is a valid way of conducting a survey as long as it represents the group *without bias*, but not if it skews the characteristics found in the group. Samples may be used when censuses are too expensive or impossible to implement.

A well-known, oft-questioned sample is that of the Kinsey report on human sexuality. Some people argue that anyone who would respond to such a survey will probably be less inhibited and more experimental than the population at large.

Random samples are selected by chance. According to Darrell Huff in *How to Lie with Statistics*, the true test of whether a sample is random or not is whether any person or item in the group has an equal chance to be chosen. But, he explains, true random samples are so difficult and expensive to obtain that often variations on the random sample are used.

The larger the sample, the more precise the results. However, as the sample gets larger, the increase in rate of precision slows down. There comes a point at which increasing the size becomes more expensive but only minimally more effective. The *precision* of a sample is proportional to the square root of the sample size. See the chart (Figure 2-1).

FIGURE 2-1
Sample Sizes and Precision Rates

Sample size (number of people)	Precision rate	Increase over the previous value of precision
100	10	N/A
200	14.14	41.4%
400	20	39.3%
600	24.49	22.5%
800	28.28	15.5%
1000	31.62	11.8%

As the sample gets larger, the increase in rate of precision slows down. There comes a point at which increasing the sample size becomes more expensive but only minimally more effective.

Notice that the largest increases in precision occur when the size of the sample is small. As you increase sample size, precision grows at a slower rate. Somewhere there is a point of diminishing returns; the trick is to find it and size the sample accordingly.

Panels. A panel is an ongoing survey. Panels are advantageous to the researcher because they provide more data than a one-shot survey, and they allow follow-up. For example, if panelists say they intend to do something, such as vote for a particular candidate or purchase a certain brand, the researcher can follow up to see if they really performed the action. Did those who said they were going to buy a new car within six months really do so?

Panels are good methods for measuring changes and time-dependent phenomena, such as turnover. For example, you can measure the change in attitude regarding a particular government policy from one year to another *on an individual basis*. If a person approves of the President's welfare policy at the time the welfare reform bill was signed, does he still approve a year later? The measurement is not how many people approved then and approve now, but of those who initially approved, how many still do and do not and what is the net change.

Panels may introduce distortion through the "re-interview" process. If a person has been asked about a topic before, he may become self-conscious when interviewed again. Sometimes panels and one-shot surveys are conducted in tandem to see if there's any re-interviewing distortion occurring.

One pitfall of panels is dropouts due to death, personal resistance, moving, or other unavailability. This phenomenon may or may not affect the reliability of the study, depending on the magnitude of the loss and its effect on the thing being measured.

Observation. Observation involves looking at something in its natural setting.

Experiments. An experiment involves the use of both a special study group upon which the experiment is conducted, and a control group where "business as usual" occurs. If the results obtained from the two groups differ, the experiment *may* have produced credible results. An experiment differs from a survey in that the latter has no control group, and an experiment is usually constructed around an hypothesis, whereas a survey is not.

Tests. A test measures the way something or someone performs compared to a standard. It may be a procedure designed to see if a piece of equipment works, or it may be a set of scorable questions. A test differs from a *questionnaire* in that the latter does not measure against a standard. Rather, a questionnaire produces a snapshot of attitudes, behavior, or experience.

Measurements. In the context of statistics, measurement means the use of instruments or devices to gather data.

Forecasting/Estimation. Forecasting is the use of known measurements to predict the value of unknown measurements, which will be discernible at some future time. An estimate is an approximation of an unknown value based on an extrapolation from a known value. Forecasting applies only to the future, while estimation may apply to current or future measurements.

Derivation. Derivation involves extracting or reformatting information from the raw data. Index construction is one form of derivation. Changing units is another, as when you calculate a daily rate by dividing a yearly rate by 365.

Analysis. Analysis makes sense of the data and puts it in some context. One method of analysis is *correlation*, in which the relationship between two measurements is explored. One consideration when analyzing the data is whether or not a cause and effect relationship exists between measurements. A relationship between measurements may or may not imply cause and effect.

READING AND EVALUATING DATA
Here are some factors to consider when looking at data with a critical eye:

The "Normal" Range for the Thing Being Counted
Are you counting something that normally occurs in high numbers? Low numbers? The production of two offspring by a rare animal is a lot more significant than the production of thousands of offspring by a common animal. On the other hand, the death of a thousand people from a hurricane is a lot more significant than the death of two people from a hurricane.

The Starting Point
When dealing with increases and decreases, consider the location of the starting point. For example, if the price of a taco increases 43% from 35 cents to 50 cents, that sounds like a lot. However, the 35 cent price might have been a special offer or loss leader, and the jump may represent only a return to the regular price, which is the real starting point.

Retailers often advertise prices at 50 percent off. That sounds like a great deal, and it may be, but consider that markups on retail goods are enormous, so 50 percent off still could represent an adequate or substantial profit for the retailer.

Possible Rates of Change
To appreciate the significance of a number or percent, consider what's possible and/or likely for the thing being counted. For example, startup companies often log phenomenal rates of growth. However, mature companies do not, and probably cannot, rival those rates. If I say that a startup grew 400% in its first two years, and a mature company grew 5%, that doesn't necessarily mean that the mature company is doing poorly. Nor does it mean that the startup is making a lot of money.

Factors Behind the Numbers
The numbers alone may not tell the story. For example, there might be spikes and precipitous drops due to uncommon events. The 1996 increase in America Online's membership was astonishing and seemed to indicate that AOL was way out in front of other online services. However, when you consider that AOL changed its pricing so that it is taking in less revenue under the new plan, the numbers aren't nearly so impressive.

Self-reports
Any time people report facts or opinions about themselves or others, there may be distortion. (For a particularly interesting example of this phenomenon, see the case

study in Chapter Eleven: Finding Public Opinion and Trend Statistics.) Sometimes distortion occurs because the respondent doesn't understand the question. Sometimes the person exaggerates for effect or to avoid embarrassment or to give a "positive" answer, and sometimes the person's memory is poor. And sometimes the interviewer can skew the results by affecting the subject's comfort level.

The accuracy of self-reports also depends to some extent on how the *questions* are phrased. Requests for exact information are less likely to be accurate than requests for ranges of information. For example, if you are asked how many hours per month you log on the Internet, you might take a stab that may or may not be accurate. But if you're given ranges, such as 0-10, 11-20, 21-30, and more than 30 hours, your answers are more likely to represent your actual practice.

Misunderstood or hazy definitions can also skew results. What do "often," "sometimes," and "seldom" mean? Do they mean the same things to everyone? I can guarantee you that ASAP means an hour to some people and a week to others, and the meaning may vary with the situation.

Phrasing of the Questions

Assumptions. The assumptions behind the questions must be valid for the results to be valid. Watch out for the old "When did you stop beating your wife?" type of question. It's one thing to ask, "If you have a favorite color, what is it?" and another to ask, "Do you prefer pink or green?" The former acknowledges the possibility that you may not have a favorite color and lets you specify any color you want, while the latter circumscribes your choices and changes the definition and scope of the thing being measured. If you hate both colors, is expressing a preference valid?

Look at the question and/or categories carefully, and if there seem to be skewed assumptions behind them, be suspicious, especially if there is no "none of the above" or "not applicable" alternative.

Leading questions. The phrasing of questions may lead the respondent in a particular direction by pressuring him/her to answer a certain way or to fail to consider other alternatives. Consider the following choices:

Do you favor a socialist-type, government-run health care program?

Do you favor a universal health care program administered by the government?

In the U.S. in the 1990s, the use of the word "socialist-type" is extremely loaded and is likely to produce a "No" response, whereas the concept of universal coverage implies equality and justice, concepts with which more people will agree.

Don't know. The answer "Don't know" should not represent a large proportion of the answers. If it does, the questions weren't worded properly.

Self-reports by self-selected respondents are particularly suspicious. Those who volunteer for a study are unlikely to represent the characteristics of the general population. They may have a particular agenda to further or may be more outgoing and/or assertive than the average person. When you see that a study was composed of volunteers, be skeptical.

Definitions of Categories

Categories should not overlap. Ranges such as 0-5 and 5-10 are invalid, since 5 is included in both.

Degree of Significance, Probable Error, Standard Error

Degree of significance indicates the chances that the data is correct. Probable error and standard error tell you the chances the data is incorrect. All are expressions of how well the survey measures what it's supposed to measure.

PITFALLS

Look out for:

Specious or Biased Sources. Both researchers and respondents are sources, but in different ways. Either may be biased or unreliable. When evaluating the statement, "Four out of five doctors recommend....," one must consider both producer and respondent. Which doctors are being cited? Doctors on the payroll of the company advertising the product? Doctors of philosophy? Doctors who belong to the American Medical Association? Who chose these doctors for the survey? According to what methodology were the doctors chosen?

Authority. Consider whether the source is authoritative for the thing being measured. Just because doctors supposedly chew a certain kind of gum doesn't necessarily make that gum better than others. And just because a reliable source produces the data doesn't mean that the conclusions drawn by the presenter are necessarily accurate.

Bias. Consider the possible bias of the producer. Can you trust a study of the safety of a product conducted by its manufacturer, or is an independent testing agency likely to be more reliable? Are figures put forth by a lobbying organization likely to be unbiased or presented in a neutral way?

In addition to ideological or personal-interest-based bias, there is also "unconscious bias" which may stem from personal or cultural assumptions. Until recently, most medical studies concentrated on men and had little or no female participation. It's not that the researchers were trying to snub women—they were simply unaware that many health conditions are gender-related.

Flabby Use of Words, Trick Words. These practices involve the use of undefined terms, half-truths, and unfinished comparisons. Advertisers and producers who are honest and have nothing to hide will define their terms and give *complete* information.

Undefined terms. Using the example of the doctors, what does "recommend" mean? Recommend such-and-such medicine compared to using no medicine at all? Or compared to similar medicines? And what constitutes a recommendation? A prescription? A statement within the confines of the examining room?

Half-truths. Would you consider it fully truthful to refer to a single product as "recommended" when a doctor has listed a number of acceptable alternatives, such as "either Bufferin, Tylenol, or plain aspirin?"

Unfinished comparisons. Beware of "more," "fewer," or "less" when not followed by "than...." "More doctors recommend...." means nothing without qualification. More doctors than cab drivers? More doctors recommend aspirin than chicken fat for headaches? Always ask "...than what?"

Emphasizing the wrong part of the comparison. If I say that 5% of teenagers are drug addicts, that sounds pretty awful. But if I say that 95% of teenagers are *not* drug addicts, the situation sounds a lot more hopeful.

Watch out for these red flags:

Only, just, but. These words editorialize on the facts. If I say, "Only seven people in my high school class went on to become doctors," I make it sound as though not very many people with whom I graduated became physicians. But when you consider that my class numbered fifty people, there's no "only" about it. If I wanted to be more accurate, I could have said "Seven people in my high school class of fifty went on to become doctors."

Fully. "Fully" is the opposite of "only," "just," and "but." Its use implies that a figure is unexpectedly high, as in, "Fully 86% of my high school class did *not* become doctors." This statement sounds intense, but 86% is actually on the low side when compared to the average. In most high schools, the percent of students who do not go on to become doctors is much higher than that. My use of "fully" misleads the reader into thinking there's something wrong with my class.

(Twice) as many. While technically accurate, this type of talk can be misleading. If I say "Twice as many of my friends bought new cars this year as last year," it sounds as though the auto manufacturers are cleaning up. However, last year *one* friend bought a car. This year, *two* people bought cars. Big deal!

(Twice) as likely. See "Twice as many," immediately above.

Superlatives. "Most," "least," "fastest-growing," and the like may exaggerate the significance of the data.

Changing Definitions or Base Numbers (Comparing Apples to Something Other Than Apples).

Definitions are critical. Counts don't mean a thing if the entity being counted conforms to one definition one time and another definition another time. For example, we've heard much recently about changing the method of calculating the consumer price index (CPI). If the definition of consumer price index were changed, any table or chart showing the CPI over time would *have* to include a footnote explaining when and how the definition changed. If such a footnote were absent, the data alone would make it appear, falsely, that the cost of living dropped at the time the method of calculation changed.

The same precept holds true for base numbers. Inflation affects any number dealing with dollars, for example. When inflation is high, historical tables and charts presenting prices or expenditures make it appear as though spending and prices are high. The reverse is true for periods of low inflation. Therefore, statisticians use something called "constant dollars" to compensate for inflation. See Figure 2-2 on page 26 (Social Security: Average Monthly Benefit Payments to Retired Workers: 1970 to 1986) for a dramatic illustration of this concept. The bar chart on the left shows benefits paid in unadjusted dollars. The chart on the right shows benefits paid in constant dollars. The chart on the left exaggerates the rise in payments, while the constant dollar chart shows the increase to be far more even. What if the constant dollar chart were missing?

This pitfall—comparing apples to oranges or something else—can affect presentation of statistics or can even infect the methodology itself. Watch out in both areas.

Flawed Analysis

Attributing causality where none exists. Here's one of my favorites. The assumptions are: "The higher the GDP (Gross Domestic Product), the healthier the economy" and "High GDPs mean prosperity." Not necessarily so, especially when you consider that subsumed under GDP are all kinds of negative exchanges of money, such as rising health care costs (and not necessarily a concomitant rise in the good health of the people), rebuilding costs from devastating natural disasters, rising costs of administering the criminal justice system and law enforcement due to rising crime, etc. People may be spending lots of money, but that doesn't necessarily mean they're enjoying a rising standard of living.

Assuming a rise in something itself when the real rise is in the reporting of the thing. Rape statistics might fall into this category. It is entirely possible that the incidence of rape itself has not increased, but that women are more willing to report

FIGURE 2-2

Social Security: Average Monthly Benefit Payments to Retired Workers: 1970 to 1986

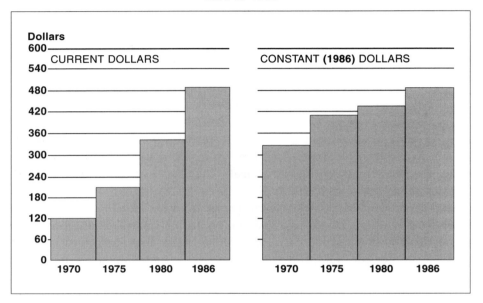

rapes than they were in the past. However, the statistics alone might imply that the rape *rate* has increased more than it has.

False extrapolation. It is misleading to extrapolate survey results to a population that was not measured. A survey of attitudes about social issues in Massachusetts cannot be inferred to apply to Oklahomans as well.

It may also be dangerous to extrapolate based on historical statistics. Past performance is not *necessarily* an indication of future performance.

Throwing numbers out of proportion. Small differences between and among numbers may not be significant because of the degree of error contained in the survey. Don't let analysts exaggerate significance, and don't inflate importance based on your own perusal of the data.

Lack of Context

Misleading graphs and time series. Graphs that don't start at zero and graphs that aren't proportional are old tricks. Rises and falls can be exaggerated by extracting a range of numbers and making that range look like the whole picture. Dips and spikes also can be exaggerated if you count off measures in smaller units than normal. For example, a graph in which each square represents ten is going to look far more dramatic than a graph in which each square represents fifty.

The same caveat goes for time series that don't present information over a long enough span of time. While values may be accurate, the proper context is lacking.

Lack of information about the study and the conditions under which the study was performed. You won't be able to look for signs of flawed methodology if you don't have access to information about the study. See Chapter 11: Finding Public Opinion and Trend Statistics for a case study dealing with the issue of incomplete information about the study.

Flawed Methodology

Samples that are too small. Even if the producer doesn't misuse language, he or she may not have followed rigorous statistical methodology. A sample that is too small may yield just the results the surveyor wants to see, but those results may be invalid. Clue: high nonresponse rates are red flags.

Samples that are nonrepresentative. A sample must accurately represent the population being studied. It wouldn't be accurate to survey attitudes of blacks by talking only to black people in South Central Los Angeles.

Contact methods that skew results. Telephone surveys may be suspect because they exclude people without access to phones, people who are rarely home, people who screen their calls, people with unlisted numbers, and so on. Door-to-door in-person surveys conducted on weekends are likely to exclude active people, or people who work on weekends, such as police officers, retail workers, and people in the performing arts.

Bad timing. Surveys should be taken at times when no influencing event has just occurred. For example, measuring investor sentiment right after the chairman of the Federal Reserve has expressed concern over the state of the economy is unlikely to yield a fair picture.

Gathering, presenting, and evaluating statistics accurately are essential if we are to avoid the "all statistics are lies" mentality. As a searcher for statistical information, you should note the red flags above and watch for pitfalls in the methodologies and presentation styles used by statistics gatherers. And you should be careful to evaluate the data and language used in describing statistics, so that you do not fall into errors of misinterpretation.

The Sources— Who Generates and Publishes Statistics?

The savvy sleuth makes educated guesses based on familiarity with the landscape. Even if you don't know for sure who might produce the statistics you need, you'll be ahead if you can recognize a likely starting place. This chapter maps the landscape for you by introducing *types* of statistics generators and publishers. The subject-specific chapters that follow, beginning with Chapter 5, fill in by highlighting specific producers in particular fields.

To get a good feel for some of the participants, pick up any general almanac, such as *World Almanac* or *Information Please Almanac*, and look at the credits with the tables. You'll see names like Bureau of Labor Statistics; *Variety*; National Cancer Institute; National Climatic Data Center; *Yearbook of American and Canadian Churches*; *Uniform Crime Reports*, FBI; and International Game Fish Association (they track the largest fish of each type ever caught).

Overlap among types of generators is common. For example, universities and government may team up, as in the case of the National Archive of Criminal Justice Data, which operates under the joint auspices of the Inter-university Consortium for Political and Social Research and the Bureau of Justice Statistics, which is part of the U.S. Department of Justice. Publishers often draw from other sources, though some generate their own statistics. Broadcast and print media may cooperate with each other, especially when conducting polls (such as ABC News and the *Washington Post*). Private companies often process and add value to government and other statistics.

While such line-blurring may cause some confusion, it's still important to know who tends to generate what. Statistics producers and publishers may be classified in the following broad and not mutually exclusive categories:

- Government agencies
- Special commissions and task forces
- International organizations
- Think tanks
- Independent survey, polling, market research, and data organizations
- Economists and banks
- Corporations

- Chambers of Commerce and economic development organizations
- Associations, industry groups, and labor unions
- Interest groups; advocacy, religious, and nonprofit organizations
- Universities
- Research centers
- Publishers and media
- Historical societies
- Individual researchers

This chapter takes a look at each of the categories and identifies some of the major players within each, as well as the types of statistics that they may generate. Knowing these types of producers gives you a logical starting point in your quest. With this knowledge and the search tips presented in Chapter 4, you will be well-positioned to find just about any numerical fact.

GOVERNMENT AGENCIES AT ALL LEVELS

Government agencies are perhaps the best-known and most prolific sources of statistics. Because information is so vital to policy planning and decision-making, not to mention daily operations, government agencies collect, tally, and analyze data on everything from demographics to traffic flow. Government's areas of interest are so catholic that you will find information on government statistics-generators in almost every chapter of this book.

Every level of government generates statistics. In the past, U.S. federal government statistics were the easiest to come by, since agencies published them and made them available at depository libraries throughout the country. State and local governments, with smaller budgets, were not able to disseminate their information so widely or so easily, and obtaining statistics from them was often a frustrating task.

With the advent of the World Wide Web, statistics from all levels of government are widely available. Much is in the public domain and easy to acquire, though some information remains offline. However, the WWW tidal wave is engulfing even the smallest cities, which can now "compete" with larger entities in the new level online playing field.

Diversity and inconsistency remain, however. While researching this book, I was fascinated by the differences in the kinds of statistics each state gathers and publishes. Some states provide detailed health- and disease-related information, for example, while others have mounted no online health statistics whatsoever. Be prepared for uneven coverage.

Governments may collect statistics through special surveys and censuses, or they may do so as a byproduct of other activities. For example, trade data is generated when customs forms are filled out. The decennial U.S. census was originally created to serve a constitutional function: to apportion the membership of the House of Representatives according to populations and distributions of people throughout the states. Now census data is used for just about every government function, and lots of business, health, environmental, and other applications, too.

National government

At the national level, statistics are generated by cabinet- or ministry-level agencies, independent agencies, and/or national statistical agencies that cover multiple areas. Often there are agencies within agencies, or bureaus within agencies, or other subdivisions, which can be confusing if you do not understand government organization. (You may wish to look at current or historical copies of the *U.S. Government Manual* to understand U.S. hierarchy.) Some organizations use each other's data to produce their own byproducts or analyses. By sharing resources, they are able to save money.

Following is a directory of the major U.S. federal agencies that generate statistics and their particular areas of concern. Agencies are grouped by their department name and the URL for the agency's WWW site is noted, if available.

Department of Agriculture

Agricultural Marketing Service (http://www.usda.gov/ams/titlepag.htm). This service offers statistics on:

- Commodity prices
- Demand
- Movement volume
- Quality

Economic Research Service (http://www.econ.ag.gov). The scope of the ERS includes:
- Supply, demand, and performance of domestic and international agricultural and food markets
- Indicators of food and consumer issues
- Economic and environmental indicators relating to agricultural production and resource use
- Socioeconomic indicators of the farm sector and rural economies

Foreign Agricultural Service (http://www.fas.usda.gov). This rich resource includes:
- Trade data
- Foreign market research
- Food aid

National Agricultural Statistics Service (http://www.usda.gov/nass). Scope includes:
- Production, supply, and prices of crops and livestock
- Farm wages and employment
- Growing conditions
- Farm acreage

Department of Commerce

Bureau of Economic Analysis (http://www.bea.doc.gov). In addition to the following, the BEA assembles various economic data series and publishes the monthly Survey of Current Business, online in PDF format:

- National and regional income and wealth
- GDP
- Corporate profits
- Sales and inventories
- National and state personal income
- Products by industry
- Balance of payments
- Direct investment abroad
- Foreign investment in the U.S.
- Trade

Bureau of the Census (http://www.census.gov). This agency is the major statistical outlet of the U.S. federal government, covering the people and economy of the country. Scope includes:

- Population and vital statistics
- Housing
- Agriculture
- Industry
- Trade
- Wealth and poverty
- Transportation
- Manufacturing
- Health care
- Tax revenues
- Migration/immigration

International Trade Administration (http://www.ita.doc.gov). Covers:

- Goods and services trade
- State exports
- Global trade outlook
- Trade for various countries
- Statistics for various industry groups, including employment, wages, capital expenditures, and trade

National Institute of Standards and Technology (http://ts.nist.gov/). This agency provides:

- Standard reference manuals and data
- Weights and measures
- Physical constants
- Spectroscopic data
- Thermodynamic data

National Oceanic and Atmospheric Administration (http://www.noaa.gov). NOAA is responsible for describing and predicting changes in the earth's environment and managing coastal and marine resources. Within its purview are these agencies:

- National Climatic Data Center (http://www.ncdc.noaa.gov)
- National Geophysical Data Center (http://www.ngdc.noaa.gov)
- National Oceanographic Data Center (http://nodc.noaa.gov)
- National Weather Service (http://www.nws.noaa.gov)

Patent and Trademark Office (http://www.uspto.gov). The USPTO provides intellectual property statistics.

STAT-USA (formerly Office of Business Analysis) (http://www.stat-usa.gov). STAT-USA is a subscription-based online system covering major areas such as:

- GDP
- Housing
- Construction
- Personal income and spending
- Home sales
- Economic indicators
- Durable goods
- Trade
- Interest rates
- Bank and consumer credit
- Reserves
- Foreign exchange
- Bond rates
- Productivity
- Consumer and producer price indexes
- Industrial production and capacity

- Gross product by industry
- Gross state product
- Employment
- National trade data bank
- Foreign market research reports

Department of Defense

Department of Defense (http://www.dtic.mil/defenselink). Includes these departments:
- Department of the Air Force (http://www.af.mil)
- Department of the Army (http://www.army.mil)
- Department of the Navy (http://www.navy.mil)
- U.S. Marine Corps (http://www.usmc.mil)

Department of Education

Department of Education (http://www.ed.gov)

National Center for Education Statistics (http://nces.ed.gov). *The* department for education statistics, it covers:
- Social and economic status of students and other demographics
- High school completions and dropouts
- Student progress and achievement
- School safety
- Education finance
- Student aid
- Characteristics of the education workplace
- Enrollments
- Attainment
- Characteristics of teachers

Department of Energy

Department of Energy (http://www.doe.gov)

The Energy Information Administration (http://www.eia.doe.gov). Provides a wealth of statistical information on:
- Energy trends and economic effects of those trends on regional and industrial sectors
- Energy resource reserves

- Production
- Demand and consumption
- Energy distribution
- Technology

Department of Health and Human Services

Department of Health and Human Services (http://www.os.dhhs.gov)

Health Care Financing Administration (http://www.hcfa.gov). Tracks:
- Medicare and Medicaid
- Health care expenditures
- Health care utilization
- Prices
- Employment
- Immunizations
- Mammography
- Managed care

National Institutes of Health (http://www.nih.gov). Includes these agencies:
- National Cancer Institute
- National Center for Nursing Research
- National Eye Institute
- National Heart, Lung, and Blood Institute
- National Institute of Allergy and Infectious Diseases
- National Institute of Arthritis and Musculoskeletal and Skin Diseases
- National Institute of Child Health and Human Development
- National Institute of Dental Research
- National Institute of Diabetes and Digestive and Kidney Diseases
- National Institute of Environmental Health Sciences
- National Institute of General Medical Sciences
- National Institute of Neurological and Communicative Disorders and Stroke
- National Institute on Aging
- National Library of Medicine. (Doesn't generate statistics, but does make them available.)

Agency for Toxic Substances and Disease Registry (http://atsdr1.atsdr.cdc.gov:8080/atsdrhome.html):

- Assesses public health hazards caused by waste sites
- Conducts health surveillance and keeps registries
- Keeps data on hazardous materials
- Tracks hazardous substance incidents

Centers for Disease Control and Prevention (http://www.cdc.gov)

Food and Drug Administration (http://www.fda.gov)

National Center for Health Statistics (http://www.cdc.gov/nchswww/nchshome.htm). Provides information on:

- Health and health care system utilization
- Vital statistics

Substance Abuse and Mental Health Services Administration (http://www.samhsa.gov)

Department of Housing and Urban Development

Department of Housing and Urban Development (http://www.hud.gov). The scope of this agency includes:

- U.S. housing market
- Housing survey
- Homelessness
- Market conditions for home loans and construction funding

Department of the Interior

Department of the Interior (http://www.doi.gov). This department includes the following agencies:

- Bureau of Indian Affairs (http://www.doi.gov/bureau-indian-affairs.html)
- Bureau of Land Management (http://www.blm.gov)
- Bureau of Mines (http://www.usbm.gov)
- Bureau of Reclamation (http://www.usbr.gov)
- Geological Survey (http://www.usgs.gov)
- Minerals Management Service (http://www.mms.gov)
- National Park Service (http://www.nps.gov)
- Office of Surface Mining Reclamation and Enforcement (http://www.osmre.gov)
- U.S. Fish and Wildlife Service (http://www.fws.gov)

Department of Justice

Department of Justice (http://www.usdoj.gov)

Bureau of Justice Statistics (http://www.ojp.usdoj.gov/bjs/). Provides information on:
- Crime perpetrators and victims
- Operation of justice systems at all levels of government
- Prison populations
- Court case processing
- Administration of law enforcement and corrections agencies

    Subagencies of the BJS include:
        Federal Bureau of Prisons (http://www.bop.gov)
        Drug Enforcement Administration (http://www.usdoj.gov/dea/)
        Federal Bureau of Investigation (http://www.fbi.gov)
        Immigration and Naturalization Service
        (http://www.ins.usdoj.gov/index.html)

Department of Labor

Department of Labor (http://www.dol.gov). Important statistical information comes from:
- Bureau of Labor Statistics, which provides some of the major U.S. economic indicators, such as:
    Employment
    Prices
    Consumer expenditures
    Compensation
    Working conditions
    Productivity

- Mine Safety and Health Administration (http://www.msha.gov)

- Occupational Safety and Health Administration (http://www.osha.gov)

Department of State

Department of State (http://www.state.gov). This agency monitors political situations in countries around the world.

Department of Transportation

Department of Transportation (http://www.dot.gov). DOT includes these agencies:
- Bureau of Transportation Statistics (http://www.bts.gov)
- Federal Aviation Administration (http://www.faa.gov)
- Federal Highway Administration (http://www.fhwa.dot.gov)
- Federal Railroad Administration (http://www.fra.dot.gov)

- Federal Transit Administration (http://www.fta.dot.gov)
- Maritime Administration (http://marad.dot.gov)
- National Highway Traffic Safety Administration (http://www.nhtsa.dot.gov)
- Research and Special Programs Administration (http://www.rspa.dot.gov)
      Office of Emergency Transportation
      Office of Hazardous Materials Transportation
      Office of Pipeline Safety
- U.S. Coast Guard (http://www.dot.gov/dotinfo/uscg/)

Department of the Treasury

Department of the Treasury (http://www.ustreas.gov). This department is home to these agencies:
- Bureau of Alcohol, Tobacco, and Firearms (http://www.atf.treas.gov)
- Bureau of Public Debt (http://www.publicdebt.treas.gov)
- Internal Revenue Service (http://www.irs.ustreas.gov)
      Statistics of Income Division reports on income finance and taxes.
- U.S. Customs Service (http://www.ustreas.gov/treasury/bureaus/customs/customs.html)

Department of Veterans Affairs

Department of Veterans Affairs (http://www.va.gov). This department is responsible for veterans and veterans' benefits.

Independent Agencies of the U.S. Federal Government

Independent Agencies of the U.S. Federal Government. These include:
- Central Intelligence Agency (http://www.odci.gov/cia/)
- Commission on Civil Rights (http://www.usccr.gov/index.html)
- Consumer Product Safety Commission (http://www.cpsc.gov)
- Environmental Protection Agency (http://www.epa.gov)
- Federal Communications Commission (http://www.fcc.gov)
- Federal Election Commission (http://www.fec.gov)
- Federal Emergency Management Agency (http://www.fema.gov)
- Federal Reserve System (http://www.bog.frb.fed.us)
- Federal Trade Commission (http://www.ftc.gov)
- International Trade Commission (http://www.usitc.gov)

- Interstate Commerce Commission
- National Aeronautics and Space Administration ((http://www.nasa.gov)
- National Archives and Records Administration (http://www.nara.gov)
- National Endowment for the Arts (http://arts.endow.gov)
- National Endowment for the Humanities (Web site not available at time of publication)
- National Science Foundation (http://www.nsf.gov)
- National Transportation Safety Board (http://www.ntsb.gov)
- Nuclear Regulatory Commission (http://www.nrc.gov)
- Postal Service (http://www.usps.gov)
- Securities and Exchange Commission (http://www.sec.gov)
- Selective Service System (http://www.sss.gov)
- Small Business Administration (http://www.sbaonline.sba.gov)
- Social Security Administration (http://www.ssa.gov)

Other U.S. government entities with statistical information include:
- General Accounting Office (http://www.gao.gov)
- Congressional Budget Office (http://gopher.cbo.gov:7100/)
- Library of Congress (http://www.loc.gov)
- Office of Management and Budget (http://www.whitehouse.gov/WH/EOP/omb

A number of WWW metasites have been created to facilitate access to government Web sites. For links to some government Web sites at all levels, see Policy Street at http://www.policy.com. Also check out an extensive list at LSU Libraries' U.S. Federal Government Agencies Page at http://www.lib.lsu.edu/gov/fedgov.html and a stark but utilitarian list of Executive Branch Servers at http://www.fie.com/www/exec.htm.

To read more about each agency and to see where it fits into governmental structure, see the key source, the *U.S. Government Manual.* You can get to the Manual from federal depository library gateways to Government Printing Office (GPO) Access. The gateways are listed at and can be linked to from http://www.access.gpo.gov/su_docs/aces/aaces002.html.

State Governments
State data centers team up with federal agencies to distribute U.S. data relating to the region in question. To link to state data centers, visit http://www.census.gov/sdc/www/.

State-level agencies that generate statistics often parallel federal government functions, with some exceptions, such as defense. Areas normally dealt with at the state level include:

Business and financial

- Banking
- Commerce
- Corporations
- Economic development
- Employment
- Insurance
- Licensing of professionals
- Real estate
- Taxes

Legal and law enforcement

- Civil rights
- Corrections
- Criminal and civil justice
- Law enforcement

Physical services

- Agriculture
- Conservation
- Emergency services
- Environment (including pollution, water and air quality, hazardous materials, forestry, fish and game, deserts, etc.)
- Housing
- Parks and recreation
- Public utilities
- Transportation and highways

Social services

- Consumer affairs
- Education
- Health and mental health
- Substance abuse
- Veterans
- Welfare

Other

- Elections

In some cases special agencies also exist, such as those dealing with women's issues, aging, lotteries, mining, horse racing, fairs, sports, alcoholic beverages, political practices, arts and culture, and boating and waterways. States also deal with matters such as hunting and fishing and guns.

Local Governments

City, town, county, and parish functions include:

Legal and law enforcement

- Police and sheriffs
- County and municipal courts

Physical services

- Airports
- Harbors
- Hospitals and clinics
- Fire control
- Traffic and roads
- Sanitation
- Utilities

Social services

- Welfare

Other

- Public welfare issues such as noise and smoking

SPECIAL COMMISSIONS AND TASK FORCES

Various levels of government mandate *ad hoc* commissions and task forces to study and make recommendations regarding problems of interest to the public. Such studies almost always produce statistics.

Examples of U.S. government-mandated commissions are the National Commission on Sleep Disorders Research, created by Congress in 1988; and the Christopher Commission, headed by former Secretary of State Warren Christopher, which has studied Los Angeles' police problems.

INTERNATIONAL ORGANIZATIONS

Many international organizations, such as the United Nations and the International Monetary Fund, are quasi-governmental ones and generate statistics in the same ways that governments do. While the United Nations and its agencies are major international statistics-makers, international chambers of commerce and associations also count things and track business conditions. (For a helpful set of links to international chambers of commerce, see http://www.worldchambers.com/chambers.html.) International alliances such as the European Union and the Organization of American States also produce statistics.

Usually, international organizations and governments generate statistics to support public policy decisions and planning. However, sometimes goals are even loftier. For example, UNESCO, the United Nations Educational, Scientific and Cultural Organization, defines part of its mission as "to promote collaboration among nations through education, science, culture, and communication in order to further universal respect for justice, law, human rights, fundamental freedoms...."

THINK TANKS

Think tanks generate statistics because they seek to contribute to the public good, or to promote (or defeat) arguments in favor of a particular point of view. The Brookings Institution, for example, seeks "to improve the performance of American institutions, the effectiveness of government programs, and the quality of U.S. public policies." The Economic Policy Institute "seeks to broaden the public debate about strategies to achieve a prosperous and fair economy."

Think tanks may be politically neutral or partisan. Some are private, some are associated with universities (Center for the Study of American Business at Washington University, St. Louis), and some are government-sponsored, such as the Competitiveness Policy Council, a federal advisory commission. Well-known think tanks include:

- American Enterprise Institute (conservative) (http://www.aei.org/)
- Brookings Institution (http://www.brook.edu/default.htm)
- The Carter Center (http://www.emory.edu/CARTER_CENTER/homepage.htm)
- Cato Institute (libertarian) (http://www.cato.org)
- Center for National Policy (http://www.access.digex.net/~cnp/index.html)
- Center for the New West (nonpartisan) (http://www.newwest.org)
- Economic Policy Institute (nonpartisan) (http://www.epinet.org/)
- Heritage Foundation (conservative) (http://www.heritage.org/)
- Hoover Institution on War, Revolution & Peace (http://www-hoover.stanford.edu/)
- Progressive Policy Institute (liberal) (http://www.dlcppi.org/)
- Rand Corporation (http://www.rand.org)

- Urban Institute (http://www.urban.org/)
- Woodrow Wilson Center for Scholars (http://wwics.si.edu/)

For lists of think tanks (mostly U.S., but also Canadian and UK), consult the following:

- Magellan (http://www.mckinley.com) (search reviewed and rated sites for "think tanks")
- NIRA 1996 World Directory of Think Tanks (http://www.nira.go.jp/ice/tt-info/nwdtt96/)
- Policy Street (http://www.policy.com/)
- Yahoo! (http://www.yahoo.com/social_science//political_science/public_policy/institutes/think_tanks/)

INDEPENDENT SURVEY, POLLING, MARKET RESEARCH, AND DATA ORGANIZATIONS

Survey and Polling

Everyone has heard of Gallup polls and Nielsen ratings. Companies like Gallup and Nielsen are private survey organizations that conduct demographic and attitude research for a fee. Newspapers and broadcast media, such as *The Los Angeles Times* and CNN, often conduct polls, frequently about political life but also on topics of interest to the public, such as smoking, crime, race, and even standards of beauty. Examples of polling organizations include:

- The Gallup Organization (http://www.gallup.com)
- Louis Harris and Associates (http://www.techsetter.com/harris/html/home.html)
- The Pew Research Center for the People and the Press (http://www.people-press.org/)
- Roper Center for Public Opinion Research (http://www.lib.uconn.edu/RoperCenter/)
- The Washington Post (http://www.washingtonpost.com)

Market Research

Market research organizations play a critical role in supporting business by providing information on actual and potential demand for products and services.

Market research may include major industry studies, customer satisfaction surveys, "would you buy this?" research, demographics, technological trends, and studies of the economy and business environments in general. Comparative pricing may also be involved. Some market research organizations are:

- Consumers Union
- Datamonitor

- Freedonia
- Frost & Sullivan
- J.D. Power & Associates (automotive—customer satisfaction)
- Jupiter Communications (Internet, online technologies)
- Simba Information (Internet, online technologies)

Some companies, such as Data Resources Inc., publish raw data, which you may purchase and analyze for yourself.

ECONOMISTS AND BANKS

Following the economy is critical to banks, brokerage houses, and other financial institutions. Researchers, usually professional economists, follow trends and often derive useful statistics from them.

CORPORATIONS

Private and public companies conduct their own market, scientific, and technical research. Rarely do they make such information public, however, unless it's the case of a scientist publishing a paper or giving a presentation at a conference. Sometimes private research comes out during litigation, such as in the case of the Dow Corning breast implants and lawsuits involving the tobacco companies. However, sometimes companies publish such information in annual reports and messages to shareholders, and sometimes you can even find such data in trade magazine articles or newspapers, especially in feature articles.

CHAMBERS OF COMMERCE AND
ECONOMIC DEVELOPMENT ORGANIZATIONS

Chambers of commerce may be international, national, or local. They produce demographics and economic information, which may or may not be found online. For a great example of a chamber that provides local statistics, see the Greater San Diego Area Chamber of Commerce economic bulletins at http://www.sddt.com/~chamberofcommerce/.

Other economic development organizations may use words like *advancement*, *development*, *small business*, *commerce*, *leadership*, and *industry* in their names.

ASSOCIATIONS, INDUSTRY GROUPS, AND UNIONS

Associations exist for all kinds of reasons, but always to look out for the interests of their members. Trade associations and industry groups exist to advance the business and financial interests of those working within a particular business or industry. Professional associations contribute to the body of knowledge necessary for practicing a particular profession, attempt to keep members' skills and expertise up-to-date, and try to promote a positive image of the profession. Sometimes the lines between trade and professional association blur, as in the case of the American Hospital Association. Many medical associations work to fund research into various diseases and to educate the public about them.

Ethnic and religious associations promote the cultures of the groups involved, provide education within and outside the association, and give members a place to meet. Public interest associations conduct educational programs and attempt to protect and promote the general welfare.

Statistics help associations monitor the environment within which they operate, identify trends, and conduct strategic planning. Many associations lobby, and statistics help persuade. Sometimes statistics are kept in-house; sometimes they appear in the association's journal (often as part of an article) or as a separate publication; increasingly, they are posted on Web sites.

Examples of various types of associations include:
- Academy of Motion Picture Arts and Sciences (professional)
- American Association for the Advancement of Science (professional)
- American Hospital Association (trade)
- The League of Women Voters (public interest)
- International Bottled Water Association (trade)
- National Association of Arab Americans (ethnic)
- Society of Automotive Engineers (professional)

To identify associations online, consult:
- Associations on the Net (http://ipl.sils.umich.edu/ref/AON/)
- The Encyclopedia of Associations (DIALOG file 114)
- Policy Street (http://www.policy.com)

For Canadian associations, see Canadian Almanac's Canada Info (http://www.clo.com/~canadainfo/associations.html)

Unions track developments that affect their members, such as health insurance coverage, interest rates, corporate profits, use of prison labor, and so on. Some unions and their Web sites are:
- AFL-CIO (LaborWEB) (http://www.aflcio.org) (For links to AFL-CIO unions, see http://www.aflcio.org/unionand.htm#cat1)
- International Association of Machinists (http://www.iamaw.org)
- United Auto Workers (http://www.uaw.org)
- United Mine Workers of America (http://www.access.digex.net/~miner)
- United Steel Workers of America (http://www.uswa.org)

INTEREST GROUPS; ADVOCACY, RELIGIOUS, AND NONPROFIT ORGANIZATIONS

Interest and Advocacy Groups

Interest groups exist to promulgate a particular point of view through the political process and, to support their arguments, they conduct surveys and compile statistics. You'll find everyone from the Sierra Club to the National Rifle Association measuring things. Advocacy organizations such as Americans for a Balanced Budget and the League of Conservation Voters are not the only groups that lobby or recommend political action. Many associations pursue political action as well, such as the American Medical Association and the American Library Association. For a list of advocacy organizations, consult Policy Street at http://www.policy.com.

Religious Organizations

You might not think of religious organizations as statistics-generators, but someone has to count the flocks. Sometimes religious organizations also track political and social issues such as abortion and civil rights. The National Council of Churches of Christ publishes the best source of statistics on American religious institutions: The Yearbook of American and Canadian Churches, partly available at http://www.dnaco.net/~kbedell/yearbook.html. Some of this work finds its way into the *Statistical Abstract of the United States*.

Nonprofit Clubs and Societies

People come together for all kinds of reasons, not just for politics and religion. You'll find everything from comic book clubs to the Japan Center for Intercultural Communications generating statistics for the use of their members and the public.

UNIVERSITIES

What would we do without scholars? University-related producers include professors who conduct research and publish reports, papers, and books; graduate students; libraries and librarians; and special organizations, such as the Office of Population Research at Princeton University and the Inter-university Consortium for Political and Social Research (ICPSR). Increasingly, universities and scholars are producing databases that are being made available to the public. University-related research runs the gamut from anthropology to zoology. Sometimes universities team up with other entities, such as governments, hospitals, and private companies, to compile and publish statistics.

RESEARCH CENTERS

Research centers, like universities, are a rich source of statistics in many of the same ways. While most are connected with universities and government agencies, some are independent. For example, there's the Deep Foundations Institute, an independent nonprofit engineering research center composed of practitioners, educators, and suppliers involved in deep-foundation building. In Singapore, there's a group called Asian Mass Communications Research & Information Centre (http://irdu.nus.sg/amic/), which provides country-specific statistics on broadcasting, publishing, film, and advertising as well as basic demographics and economic and social indicators.

To identify research centers, consult Research Centers and Services Directory (file 115 on DIALOG), or the hardcopy version, *Research Centers Directory*, published by Gale Research.

PUBLISHERS AND MEDIA

Many journals, encyclopedias, almanacs, databases, and other publications contain articles, tables, or chapters that cite statistics. Examples include: *American Demographics*; Asian Demographics Ltd. (http://asiadata.pacificnet.com/); *Harper's* magazine (available on Electric Library), which compiles the well-known Harper's Index of miscellaneous facts ("Percentage change since 1989 in the number of federal prison inmates over the age of forty-nine: +88"); *Variety*, which publishes financial information relating to entertainment; and newspapers like the *New York Times*. In many cases, these sources compile and cite statistics generated by others, but often they report on their own original work, including that of journalists, consultants, private companies, and scholars.

New online-only media are springing up such as Sportsline USA, which furnishes information as well as entertainment and merchandising. Sometimes it's hard to know whether to call such outfits media or online services, but at any rate, many do have statistics.

HISTORICAL SOCIETIES

Historical societies include some of the most dedicated and enthusiastic information-gatherers around because they're pursuing a labor of love. Not that professional historians do not involve themselves—they do—and not that professional historians are not dedicated and enthusiastic—they are. However, if you have ever attended an event sponsored by an historical society or have visited an historical society's museum, you'll know what I'm talking about.

The problem with historical societies from an online point of view is that many of them are not—online, that is. However, increasingly you'll find them on the Web, and some articles written by members find their way into computerized databases.

INDIVIDUAL RESEARCHERS

This category includes but is not limited to medical and psychological practitioners, and consultants. While many studies are conducted by individuals, most fall under the auspices of some other organization. However, a few are truly independent and, increasingly, they are making at least some of that data available on the Web.

With so many different entities generating statistics, it's natural to think that just about every numerical fact must be available somewhere. Unfortunately, that isn't so, but to increase your chances of success, you should attempt to determine who might have collected that information. This chapter gives you a framework with which to determine possible sources to find statistics. The next chapter will give some tips on how to ferret them out once you've decided on a source.

General Search Tips

You know that statistics are hard to find or you wouldn't be reading this book. But what is it about statistics that makes them so elusive? Perhaps it is that they are:

- Needles in haystacks. A numerical fact may be just one sentence in an article, and less than a speck within an entire database or library.

- Unobtrusive. Sometimes there's nothing distinctive about a sentence that includes statistics. There may simply be a number or two and a keyword, as in "There are 900,000 lawyers in the United States."

- Scattered about. Statistics are so common that they might appear anywhere, and often do, but in seemingly illogical places, some of which may not be indexed in databases.

- Buried in non-ASCII parts of documents and Web pages. Figures are often found in pictorial material and tables, which may be formatted as nonsearchable graphics.

- Taken for granted. We're numbers-weary. We hear statistics all day long, so we don't think much about them. (But just try to find that specific one.)

- Just plain scary. Many people find numbers and statistics boring, complicated, too hard to find, or otherwise unpleasant.

However, you *can* find the little devils if you follow sound methods and use your knowledge of the desired subject. There are three steps involved in statistics-hunting:

1. Selecting the right place to look
2. Choosing an effective strategy
3. Evaluating the data

Chapter 2: Statistics Basics addressed evaluation. Chapter 3: The Sources gave an outline of places to look. This chapter begins with tips and techniques for choosing a place to look and concludes with a plan to develop a winning strategy.

THE IDEAL SOURCE

If you and I were designing the ideal statistical database, it would probably exhibit these characteristics:

All Statistics. The database would consist of statistics, and only statistics. That way you wouldn't have to tell the system to pick out numerical information, and you wouldn't have to wade through full text.

Fields for Describing Characteristics of the Data. We'd start with the subject, indicated by keywords, and maybe codes for concepts like market share. Then we'd define our own categories, which would give us the ability to break down the numbers by criterion, such as age, race, educational level, company size, and so on.

There would be a field for units, such as people, or VCRs, or dollars; a field for the type of measurement, such as percent, or ranking, or nose-count. We'd include a field to indicate whether the numbers were comparative and, if so, whether they indicate more or less than something else. (For example, "Industry so-and-so has grown larger than it was last year" or "This number represents a decrease in the percentage of U.S. adults who attend baseball games when compared with a decade ago.") These concepts would be stored in compressed form, but would expand to full sentences upon display. One could find the source of the statistics, with contact information (and be able to link to it, or send email), and a complete description of the methodology. If we were really being spiffy, we could cite other sources for the same or similar data, so users could compare.

A Variety of Display and Formatting Options. A user would have the option to look at the data graphically (line graph, histogram, pie chart, 3-D graphs), or as tables, in ASCII, HTML, PDF, TIFF, or whatever format. He or she could request a spreadsheet or other database-compatible format.

Thesaurus and Online Classification Codes. Not only could you browse through a hierarchy of terms and codes (and link to related, broader, and narrower ones), you could also request "more of the same" when looking at an answer. In other words, if you found a good record covering school expenditures in Los Angeles, you could opt to look at similar records for other geographical areas, or other expenditures in Los Angeles. You could even jump up and/or down either hierarchy to request educational expenditures in general, or expenditures for school earthquake retrofits, or you could request any of those topics for the county, state, national, or international level.

Complete Data. All data would be present—no missing tables, no citations to other sources. We'd enjoy one-stop shopping.

Artificial Intelligence. Of course, the ideal database will point out suspect methodology and lead you to statistics that support or refute a particular point of view. But let's not be too greedy for now.

In the real world, such a system doesn't exist, though you'll find pieces of it. In the absence of this gift, we as searchers must devise ways to get at the data we want, even though it doesn't come in neat packages. Read on for some methods.

THE BEST SOURCES IN THE REAL WORLD

Any source that consists primarily or wholly of statistics is from heaven! With such tools, you don't have to tell the system that you want statistics, since that's all you can get. In this category you'll find:

- Almanacs
- Numeric databases
- Statistical compendia

Other reference sources may be statistics-rich, but they do not consist exclusively of numbers. Examples of this kind of animal include:

- Encyclopedias
- Fact books
- Databases composed of facts, such as Pierian Press's A Matter of Fact
- Handbooks
- Yearbooks
- Rankings

Just because sources are called *almanacs* or *statistical publications* does not mean they are not available at Web sites of associations, companies, and the like. In fact, you'll often find wonderful numeric data at fairly small Web sites.

SECOND-TIER SOURCES

To say that full text and abstracts are second-tier is to sell them short. In real life, there are many times you'll be thankful that such sources exist, because they'll be rich with useful data, and there won't be any numeric databases. However, they *are* a step down from statistics-only databases in ease of use, and they require different searching techniques.

The absolute best full-text databases are newspapers, major business magazines like *Forbes*, *Business Week*, and *Fortune*, and trade journals.

Citation-only databases are for desperation time, with the possible exception of CIS, which is an index with one- or two-sentence abstracts of the publications of the U.S. Congress, and ASI (American Statistics Index), in which complete text is beginning to appear (thank goodness!).

CHOOSING A SOURCE

Practically speaking, you're not going to compare every option before going off to search. You're going to ask yourself "What databases or Web sites do I have access to—right now—that are likely to answer my question?" Don't worry that you absolutely *have* to search one system or another to answer this or that question. Work with what you've got.

If you have subscriptions to fancy database services and know how to use them, great. If not, there's still a lot of free or low-cost, pay-as-you-go material on the Web which can help you. Don't let the necessity of a subscription throw you, though. Some services require them, but are reasonably priced, and fast as lightning to set up. Once you have an account on one of those services, such as Electric Library or the Wall Street Journal Interactive Edition, you'll use them again and again. And if you're going to do a lot of statistical research in a particular area, it might be worth it to get a subscription to a service that's so good that it will save you time and hair-pulling.

Tips for Choosing a Source

1. For **non-industry-specific material**, if you don't know where to look or who might have conducted a particular type of study, search general full-text sources such as newspapers, especially the most well-known, such as the *New York Times* and *Los Angeles Times*, and major business magazines like *Forbes*, *Fortune*, and *Business Week*. Many times these publications report on studies with interesting and/or significant findings of interest to large numbers of people. The information you find this way may be sufficient, but if not, you can contact the source directly. This tip applies to inquiries regarding health, economic indicators, polls and attitudes, how people spend their time, and so on.

2. For **industry-specific material**, search databases that cover trade journals. For example, for computer industry statistics, look at the Wall Street Journal Interactive Edition's Publications Library (the Computers and Communications category), or select a LEXIS-NEXIS library that covers computers. In this way, you'll be searching the sources most likely to contain your numbers, but you won't be limiting yourself to one publication at a time.

3. For a broad range of information on population, labor, the economy, transportation, agriculture, housing, and other general subjects, go to the **U.S. Census Bureau's Web site** (http://www.census.gov) and use the subject index or search engine to locate data on your subject (the former is better). Or consult the *Statistical Abstract of the U.S.* online at http://www.census.gov/stat_abstract.

4. Search **American Demographics** (Electric Library; LEXIS-NEXIS BUSFIN, MARKET, and NEWS Libraries; ProQuest Direct; Wall Street Journal Interactive Edition Publications Library; http://www.demographics.com) for information on how people spend their time and what they're thinking.

5. For **social, economic, environment, public policy, health, and political information**, search the A Matter of Fact database and/or one of the general almanacs,

such as World Almanac (Electric Library; FirstSearch) or Information Please Almanac (Cognito!, Encarta Online Library). For basic country information, search the CIA's World Factbook.

6. When searching the Web, **get a toehold and check links** carefully. Many of the resources in this book were uncovered by following links.

7. **Do not use a Web search engine for locating the facts themselves**. Because most Web search engines don't look at databases internal to a site (at1.com is an exception, but it only searches the internal databases of its partners, not all sites on the Web), that data is invisible to them. Rather, use Web search engines to find sites likely to cover your topic. Use a search engine that lets you restrict your search to the title of the site, and one that lets you search phrases. Alta Vista is still my first choice.

8. If you're going to do a lot of **market research**, you should have a subscription to at least one of the following:
- Dow Jones/News Retrieval
- DIALOG
- IAC InSite
- IAC InSite Pro
- LEXIS-NEXIS
- Profound
- Wall Street Journal Interactive Edition

These services include lots of full text, and they carry the largest numbers of major newspapers, general business magazines, and trade journals.

Finding a Good Web Site

Don't reinvent the wheel! One of the best ways of identifying good Web sites is to rely on someone else to have found the best ones for you. Try one or more of the following:

- Government sources. Search FEDSTATS, the U.S. government's metasite leading to federally generated statistics (http://www.fedstats. gov).

- Rating services. Turn to one or more Web site rating ser-

FIGURE 4-1

The FEDSTATS Web site directs you to statistics from more than 70 U.S. government agencies.

vices, such as Magellan (http://www.mckinley.com), which arrange sites by subject and also allow you to search by keyword. You may have to read some annotations, but that's a small price to pay for someone's having evaluated sites for you. *(Note: Don't pass by anything that says* Reference.*)*

- Also try these sites that rate and review venues:
    Excite (http://www.excite.com)
    Lycos (http://www.pointcom.com)
    Money$earch (http://www.moneysearch.com)
    NetFinder (http://www.aol.com/netfind/)
    NetGuide (http://www.netguide.com)
    WebCrawler (http://www.webcrawler.com)
    Wired Source (http://www.wired.com/cybrarian)

- Categorized lists. Other helpful lists include:
    The BUBL Information Service (http://bubl.ac.uk)
    Infoseek (http://guide-p.infoseek.com)
    Librarians' Index to the Internet (http://sunsite.berkeley.edu/InternetIndex/)
    World Wide Web Virtual Library (http://vlib.stanford.edu/Overview.html)
    Yahoo! (http://www.yahoo.com)

FIGURE 4-2

- Mine the excellent Scout Report (archives are at http://www.scout.cs.wisc.edu/scout/report/archive/) and Net-Happenings (http://scout.cs.wisc.edu/scout/net-hap/). Both are searchable. These two publications are the pre-eminent "town criers" of the Net, featuring the best resources across the entire spectrum of subjects. Rumor has it that the Scout Report will soon provide subject access based on Library of Congress subject headings.

Librarians' Index to the Internet is a good place to find a meaty Web site on your topic.

NOTE: While there are other services that gather, rate and / or review sites, those cited here are the best for locating resources rich in statistics.

- Follow links. If you can get a toehold at a site relevant to your topic, chances are you can follow a chain from its list of links/resources to some really terrific sites.

- Metasites. Sometimes universities, especially their libraries, sponsor rich metasites that point you toward helpful resources. For example, see the University of Michigan's Documents Center, Statistical Resources on the Web, at http://www.lib.umich.edu/libhome/Documents.center/stats.html. While not exhaustive, this site may exhaust *you* as you explore its many possibilities, including agriculture, health, demographics, military politics, energy, international sources, and more.

FIGURE 4-3

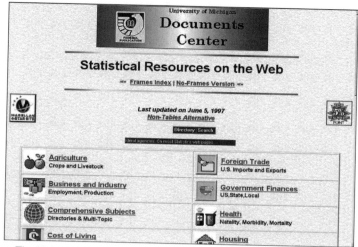

The University of Michigan Documents Center provides a spectacular metasite leading to all kinds of statistics.

- Government agencies and international statistics. The U.S. Census Bureau links to other U.S. government statistical agencies and also to those of other countries. While the latter list is not complete, if you jump to one of the country sites, you'll find more links to other country statistical agencies.

DEVELOPING AN EFFECTIVE STRATEGY

Doors leading to statistics

To find mites as elusive as statistics, one needs clues and entry points, such as:

The text itself. Statistics are often part of a narrative. It's important to learn to anticipate and recognize the signs that statistics are present in a particular passage.

Titles. Titles tell us what the article, chapter, Web page, book, report, or other matter is about. If we can get to a place that treats the subject in general, we may find statistics there.

Sponsoring organization. Chapter 3 highlighted the types of organizations that produce and publish statistics. If we can anticipate who has produced the statistic and go to them or their publications, we may find what we need.

Indexing and codes. How do you know what an article or passage is about? You can't always tell from the title. Sometimes you have to read the whole piece to get a good idea of its subject or subjects. To save you that trouble and to aid in searching by computer, where reading full text is often expensive, publishers add value by *describing* the material they publish. *Descriptors* can be keywords, phrases, or numeric codes that stand for a concept or category. Indexing and codes are two of the premium tools at the searcher's disposal; their importance and value cannot be overstressed. Because titles may not be descriptive of content, sometimes index terms and codes are the *only* indication of what the text is about.

Captions. Captions allow us to zero in on the area where the statistics reside. A caption may describe a table or a picture, such as a graph or chart. While most online systems look at captions when they search the full text, it can be helpful to isolate captions, particularly on a system that offers text and graphics separately (tables often take the form of a graphic).

Type of source. We know that some sources are better than others for finding statistics. Almanacs are statistical compendia and are likely to be useful; but we wouldn't bother with a dictionary.

Databases. Some databases are general; others are specific. By choosing the right kind of database for the question, we maximize the chances of finding statistics on our topic. The catch: We need to know the resources in order to make the best choice.

Links. Links are related to all of the above because they lead us somewhere the producer has deemed worthwhile and germane. Links may comprise a subject, a type of material (press releases, publications, data), an organization, a caption, etc. Of course, the producer's goal and ours may differ. Nevertheless, links are valuable signposts, describing material that is available if we follow the path.

WHAT DOES THE DATA LOOK LIKE?

In order to be able to search effectively, you have to know what the data looks like and which parts are searchable. You'll find statistics in the following places and types of formats:

Full text, with statistics within the text. Sometimes you'll find statistics in titles, but not often enough to be able to rely on their presence there. If you search the complete text, though, you may find some gems (see Figure 4-4).

Abstracts, with statistics within the text. Sometimes abstracts summarize articles, and they may give a high-level overview of studies.

Tables, standalone. You'll find standalone tables in almanacs and at Web sites.

FIGURE 4-4
Four Examples of Statistics Found Within Full Text

Six in ten Americans with postgraduate degrees visited art museums in 1992, compared with 16 percent of high school graduates. And 31 percent of suburban adults visited art museums in 1992, compared with 29 percent of central-city and 21 percent of nonmetropolitan residents....(*American Demographics*, November 1994)

Comments: Note that percent *is consistently spelled as one word. Sometimes you'll find both the one- and two-word forms in the same paragraph or document, so you should always search on both, if you get to the point where you can't find any other way to indicate that you want statistical information. The discrepancy between spelling out some numbers and not others is common but irrelevant, since searching on specific numbers in full text is usually a futile tactic (too unpredictable), and most systems won't let you search on strings of fewer than three characters anyway.*

The National Medical Expenditures Survey, last conducted by the Agency for Health Care Policy and Research in 1987, found that almost 6 million people received formal home-care services. (*American Demographics*, March 1994)

Comments: Note the use of the word million. *You have to be careful with this word because it will often bring you financial data. Nor can you count on the word being spelled out. This excerpt could just as easily have said "...found that almost 6,000,000 people...." You can't memorize the style books of every publication!*

There have been 101 record releases (including compact disk and cassettes) of Beethoven's Fifth Symphony, which makes it the world's most recorded symphony (*Christian Science Monitor* v.77, no.252: 21 November 1985).

Comments: There are no predictable quantitative words to grab onto in this excerpt. The only way to get to this is by searching on the subject. However, I found it by searching in the A Matter of Fact *database rather than in the* Christian Science Monitor *itself. Since the database producers have plucked the best statistical facts for use in their product, such a strategy is likely to yield excellent results. Had I searched in the newspaper, chances of success would have been lower because the database is so full of non-statistics-related verbiage.*

$118.00 of new supplies were ordered for every $100.00 worth of supplies shipped.

Comments: Forget searching on the dollar sign to indicate that you're looking for financial information; most systems won't accept it. This kind of phrasing makes it very difficult to get at the data. One hopes that a title or index term would provide a hook. Searching on the terms supplies, ordered, *and* shipped *is likely to be frustrating. And you can't search on a word like* ratio *or* relationship, *because those are concepts that aren't specifically spelled out.*

FIGURE 4-5
An Example of Statistics Presented in a Table

Honey: Price by Color Class, United States, 1995-96						
Color Class	Coop and Private		Retail		All	
	1995 1/	1996	1995 1/	1996	1995 1/	1996
Cents per Pound						
Water White, Extra White, White	68.7	89.7	98.9	119.4	69.8	90.7
Extra Light Amber	64.9	84.1	97.9	116.0	67.5	88.5
Light Amber, Amber, Dark Amber	62.7	82.9	101.1	117.1	66.8	86.7
All Other Honey Area Specialties	55.6	83.7	130.1	201.5	68.3	97.8
All Honey	66.4	86.9	100.0	119.4	68.5	89.4

1/ Revised, includes honey produced in 1995 that was sold in 1996.

Released February 20, 1997, by the National Agricultural Statistics Service (NASS), Agricultural Statistics Board, U.S. Department of Agriculture.

Comment: The way to this kind of table is usually through its title, or via the subject of the article or publication within which it appears. Sometimes the specific information sought is part of the table proper (such as "light amber" in this case). In that case, you'll need to browse through tables with likely sounding titles, unless you're using TableBase, where all the text is searchable.

FIGURE 4-6
An Example of a Fielded Record

```
DIALOG(R)File 503:Nielsen Mkt Statistics/Canada
(c) 1997 A.C. Nielsen Co. All rts. reserv.

00046085
File Segment:  PRODUCT
Product Group: CANNED & BOTTLED GROCERY PRODUCTS
Product Name:  SPAGHETTI SAUCE
          Canadian $ in (000s)
Current Year's Sales: 132,503
Prior Year's Sales:   122,435
Share Percentage:       10.3%
Share Change:            0.6%
Data For Two Years Ending December 7, 1996
Source: AC Nielsen, New Market Track, 52 weeks ending December
```

Comments: Each of the following is a discrete field in this record:
        File Segment
        Product Group
        Product Name
        Share Percentage
        Share Change

Sales, Share Percentage and Share Change are all numeric fields. By targeting them, you can search for products, companies, and brands that meet specific numeric criteria. Highly structured information like that found in this record is the easiest to search—a numbers seeker's dream.

FIGURE 4-7
An Example of a Downloadable Database (Raw Data)

```
Source:   Scottish Economic History Database
http://www.ex.ac.uk/~ajgibson/scotdata/yields/melv2.html

INPUT 1 2 N

 Crop Returns for Pease & Wheat at Melville, Fife; 1737 - 1757

 From: Scottish Record Office; GD 26/5/559
        Account Book of the Melville Estate; 1731 - 1751

 This file contains;

 1 - Pease sown (bolls)
 2 - Pease produced (bolls)
 3 - Pease increase (multiplier)
 4 - Wheat sown (bolls)
 5 - Wheat produced (bolls)
 6 - Wheat increase (multiplier)

     See also  for returns for oats and bear.

FORMAT
1 2 1 2 3 0 0 0 (I4,1X,F5.2)
1 2 1 2 3 0 0 0 (I4,7X,F7.4)
1 2 1 2 3 0 0 0 (I4,15X,F4.2)
1 2 1 2 3 0 0 0 (I4,20X,F4.2)
1 2 1 2 3 0 0 0 (I4,25X,F6.3)
1 2 1 2 3 0 0 0 (I4,32X,F4.2)
STOP
```

Crop Year	Sown Bolls	Pease Produced Bolls	Incr.	Sown Bolls	Wheat Produced Bolls	Incr.
DATA						
1737						
1739						
1741						
1742				2.25	17.375	7.72
1743						
1744				2.0	4.0	2.0
1745				1.25	5.25	4.2
1746	4.25	14.25	3.35			
1747	14.5	46.75	3.22			
1748						
1749	17.0	39.5625	2.33			
1750	16.0	62.50	3.91			
1751	17.0	50.5	2.97			
1752	9.0	9.0	1.0			
1753	8.2	30.0	3.64			
1754	5.5	10.0	1.82			
1755	16.0	34.5	2.16	1.00	4.5	4.5
1756	17.0	54.5	3.21			
1757	14.0	28.5	2.04			
9999						

Comments: This arcane-looking information is both description of the data and data itself. The information under FORMAT is explained elsewhere at the site. Suffice it to say that each number represents a code explaining a characteristic of the data. The parentheses contain FORTRAN statements identifying the location of the column(s) used. The information under DATA is just that.

These types of data sets are meant to be downloaded and manipulated by statistical programs. This one was originally designed to be processed by a FORTRAN program.

Sometimes data is downloadable in spreadsheet format, comma-delimited format, and so on, often at the user's discretion.

Tables within text. Tables have usually been omitted from commercial databases that carry articles, but increasingly they're being included, usually as separate graphics or as part of a full-page image (see Figure 4-5 for a sample table).

Database records, usually fielded. The types of numerical information you'll find in fields are usually financial data, number of employees, material properties, and the like, but some database records comprise fielded *tables*, such as those in Population Demographics (file 581 on DIALOG) (see Figure 4-6 for a sample fielded record).

Datasets in machine-readable form. This is raw data that requires documentation and auxiliary software to process. To use this kind of data, check the readme files or other documentation at the site or for the database. Some sites will generate formatted data on-the-fly. Occasionally, organizations offering raw data require you to sign an agreement (or to do so virtually by submitting some information about yourself and clicking on a button) stipulating that you'll use the data carefully and according to their terms. Registering does not usually entail a fee (see Figures 4-7 and 4-8).

<table>
<tr>
<td align="center">

FIGURE 4-8
An Example of a Link to Statistical
Databases Through FTP

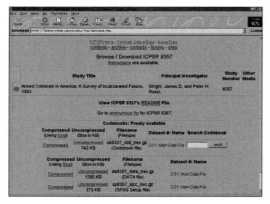

</td>
<td align="center">

FIGURE 4-9
An Example of Statistics
Presented in Pictorial Form

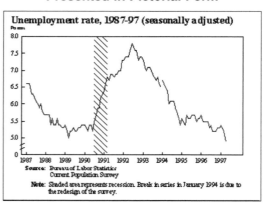

</td>
</tr>
</table>

Graphs and charts. Sometimes statistics are presented in pictorial form (see Figure 4-9).

Handbook data. This type of format may include sentences and/or fields (see Figure 4-10).

FIGURE 4-10
An Example of Handbook Data

Source: STN Database Summary Sheet, File COPPERDATA . Courtesy Copper Development Association.

```
Database:  CopperData/Standards Handbook Data     AN:   900-166
Alloy/Unified Numbering System Number:   C78200
Material Type:  metal
Material Class:  copper alloy
Material Subclass:  nickel silver
Product Type:  Wrought
CAS Registry Number:  57920-08-8
```

Composition

Element	Nominal %	Minimum %	Maximum %
Copper	65	63	67
Iron		0.35	
Manganese		0.5	
Nickel	8	7	9
Lead	2	1.5	2.5
Zinc (1)	25		

```
(1) Zinc content is the remainder of other elements

Common Forms and Tempers:  Rolled Strip - H01; H02; H03; H04; H06; OS015;
                              OS035

Suppliers:   (F) = Fabricator; (S) = Service Center
             Strip - MRM INDUSTRIES(F); WATERBURY ROLLING MILLS, INC.(F)

Typical Uses:  Other - Watch plates; Key blanks; Watch parts
```

Physical Properties

```
Melting Point
  Liquidus:                      1830 deg F
  Solidus:                       1780 deg F
Density:                         0.314 lb/in**3 at 68 deg F
Specific Gravity:                8.69
Linear Expansion Coefficient:    1.03E-05 deg F**-1 at 68 - 212 deg F
Specific Heat:                   0.09 Btu/lb*deg F at 68 deg F
Thermal Conductivity:            28 Btu*ft/ft**2*h*F at 68 deg F
Electric Conductivity:           10.9 %IACS at 68 deg F
Electric Resistivity:            103 ohm*cirmil/ft at 68 deg F

Common Fabrication Processes:  blanking; drilling; milling
```

Fabrication Practices/Properties

```
Annealing
 Temperature:            930 - 1150 deg F
Solderability:           excellent
Brazeability:            good
Weldability:
 Oxyacetylene            not recommended
 Resistance, Seam        not recommended
 Coated Metal Arc        not recommended
 Gas Shielded Arc        not recommended
 Resistance, Spot        not recommended
 Resistance, Butt        fair
```

continued on next page

FIGURE 4-10
An Example of Handbook Data (continued)

```
                  Mechanical Properties

Tensile Modulus of Elasticity:   17000 ksi
Modulus of Rigidity:   6400 ksi
```

Product Form	Material Thickness	Temper	Tensile Ultimate Strength	Tensile Yield Strength, 0.5% Ext.	Elong. in 2 in.
	in		ksi	ksi	%
Flat Products	0.040	H01	62	42	24
Flat Products	0.040	H02	69	58	12
Flat Products	0.040	H03	78	63	5
Flat Products	0.040	H04	85	73	4
Flat Products	0.040	H06	91	76	3
Flat Products	0.040	0S015	59	27	32
Flat Products	0.040	0S035	53	23	40

Product Form	Material Thickness in	Temper	RHN B	RHN 30T	RHN F	Shear Strength ksi
Flat Products	0.040	H01	65	63		44
Flat Products	0.040	H02	78	69		47
Flat Products	0.040	H03	84	72		51
Flat Products	0.040	H04	87	74		54
Flat Products	0.040	H06	90	75		58
Flat Products	0.040	0S015			85	43
Flat Products	0.040	0S035			78	40

Comments: You could search for a particular material, or a material meeting certain characteristics—for example, a property equals or falls within such-and-such a range.

Citations. A citation—the title, author, journal or other source, date, and publisher—is hard to use to find statistics because the information is so minimal. Sometimes, however, a citation will lead you to the real data.

YOUR SECRET SEARCHING WEAPONS

Words and phrases

To find this elusive data in a sea of text, some of your best tools are numbers-indicating words and phrases. The following terms may appear in the text, as subject terms, in titles, in links, or as part of the caption:

Type of information or place in which the information is found

- Annual report(s)
- Archive
- Bulletin(s)
- Data (The word *data* is sometimes used interchangeably with *statistics*. You may see the term *data collection(s)* or *data series*.)

- Databases
- Facts, factsheets
- FAQ (frequently-asked questions)
- Industry overview
- Library
- News
- Papers
- Poll
- Press releases
- Publications
- Reports
- Research
- Series
- Statistics
- Study
- Summaries
- Survey
- Time series
- Trend(s)

Units/measures

- Percent or per cent. Beware! Sometimes the percent sign (%) is used, and it is not searchable in most online systems.
- Rate/rated/rating(s)
- Hundred
- Thousand
- Million
- Billion
- The unit you're measuring, such as *copies* for books, *sales*, *dollars*, etc.
- Odds
- Chance(s)
- Probability

You probably won't want to use *hundred*, *thousand*, *million*, and *billion* very often because subject terms are better, but these terms might help if you need to narrow results from an overwhelming number, many of which contain non numeric information. Also note that you may not be able to predict which of these units applies, and that numbers rather than words might be used. However, such terms, or at least their abbreviations, can be helpful in searching numeric databases (see Tips for Searching Specific Systems: Searching DIALOG for Statistics on page 68).

Format

These terms may also be used to narrow results to items containing tables and/or graphs, which may be more likely than plain text to include numeric information.

- Figure
- Table
- Chart
- Graph
- Infobox
- Caption

Trends

Use these words, in various tenses, to help isolate text with numeric content.

- Increase(d)
- Decrease(d)
- Grow/grew
- Decline(d)
- Rise(n)
- Fall(en)

Comparisons

- As much as
- As many, as in "twice as many"
- As likely, as in "twice as likely"
- More likely
- Less likely
- Largest
- Smallest
- Most
- Least
- Fastest-growing
- Top, as in "The Top 100 Companies"

Other

- Found/finds/reports that, as in "A study has found that...."
- According to, as in "According to a study...."
- Is estimated at
- Says, as in "A study released by XYZ says...."

Tips for using words and phrases

- Do not attempt to search for specific numbers unless you're confident that they will appear. When you can't predict what the number is, you'll drive yourself and the system crazy trying to anticipate all possible values.

- When trying to find the right link at a Web site, look for names of particular reports, such as "State of the..." or "Such-and-such Report." Often these documents cover particular time periods, so watch for dates. Sometimes you will have to use the search engine at the site, browse lists of publications or indices, or look through the online journal/paper collection.

- If the text on your screen is particularly dense, use your browser's Find feature to search for keywords.

Captions and Tables

Certain words in captions, and the existence of tables in a document may indicate the presence of numeric data. Use LEXIS-NEXIS' TABLEINFO segment, which gives you the column and row titles for a table in the Market Research Library.

You can take advantage of the SF (Special Feature) field in DIALOG, which indicates the presence of a table, chart, or graph. Records with an indicator `SF=table` are likely to include statistics, though the table(s) may not be online.

Fields Containing Numeric Data

Because numeric fields usually allow you to search for a number even when you don't know what it is, they can be especially effective tools. Range searching, i.e., "Find me something that falls between x and y," lets you gather a group of items that fit your criteria.

Numeric fields are helpful even when you don't search on a range, because they isolate the numbers you're looking for.

Index Terms

Terms assigned by human beings to describe the content of articles and other material can be extremely helpful. Some terms (singular or plural) which may help you are:

- Statistics
- Market share
- Index(es)/indices

- Market research
- Numeric
- Financial data
- Sales
- Forecasts
- Demographics
- Market size
- Expenditures
- Costs
- Industry overview
- Prices
- Age(s)

Sometimes the word *trends* can be helpful, though it may indicate description rather than quantification.

Codes

Like index terms, market share, sales, prices, specific industries, class and other codes for statistics are assigned by human beings. UMI provides the class code 9140 for articles treating statistical data, and another, 1110, for economic conditions and forecasts. The IAC databases have the most complete list of codes I've seen. See Searching IAC Files on page 79 for a sample.

Specific Sources or Sections

Focusing in on particular sources, or relevant sections of particular sources, is a good way to eliminate extraneous material. You may want to identify a journal and confine the search just to its contents (as opposed to an entire database), or limit your search to the financial or business section of a newspaper.

Tips for Searching Full Text

When you're searching a full-text source, most of the time you'll be looking for needles in haystacks rather than articles about a topic. For that reason, limiting your search to titles and/or lead paragraphs probably won't help. You want that *one* sentence or table that's buried somewhere in the article.

However, at times searching titles is just what you want. Consider whether the sources you're thinking of trying might have published a feature article on your topic. If you can find an article on a hot topic or a trend by searching for words in the title, like *outsourcing*, that may be all you need. If not, your numbers may be buried in other material and you should look for words in the text.

When looking for statistics, you have to be particularly careful about the way words are used because statistics comprise information about an industry or profession rather than the subject itself. For example, to find statistics about travel and tourism, you can't go to any old Web site or source that treats travel because the information will probably focus on accommodations, transportation, and sightseeing. To find what you want, you need information about the tourism *industry*, not tourism itself. The same is true for law, where you'll usually find laws and judicial opinions, and history, where you'll generally find lots of narration and description.

TIPS FOR SEARCHING SPECIFIC SYSTEMS

Online Database Systems

The online systems treated in this book include systems designed for general consumers, for corporate and professional users, for information professionals and library users, and the Internet. Following are the important names you will see (there is some market overlap among the systems):

Consumer systems
- Brainwave (N2K)
- Cognito! (IAC)
- Electric Library (Infonautics)
- Encarta Online Library (IAC)

Corporate and professional systems
- Brainwave (N2K)
- Dow Jones News/Retrieval
- IAC InSite (IAC)
- IAC InSite Pro (IAC)
- Profound
- STN Easy (STN)
- Wall Street Journal Interactive Edition Publications Library (Dow Jones)

Information professional and library automation systems
- Autographics
- Brodart
- COMPanion Corp.
- DataStar (Knight-Ridder Information, Inc.)
- DIALOG (Knight-Ridder Information, Inc.)
- Dow Jones News/Retrieval
- Endeavor Information

- EPIC (OCLC)
- FirstSearch (OCLC)
- Gateway Library Management Systems
- IAC InSite Pro (IAC)
- Innovative Interfaces
- LEXIS-NEXIS (Reed Elsevier)
- NISC
- Questel•Orbit
- SilverPlatter
- STN
- Vista II
- Winnebago Software

The Internet

- The World Wide Web (WWW)
- Gopher sites
- FTP sites

Usually you will get to gopher and FTP sites through Web links. I personally do almost no more gopher and FTP searching, since the Web has become so popular and frequently will link you to gopher and FTP sites, but good sources of data remain available through these protocols.

Searching DIALOG for Statistics

While there is no one magic bullet for numeric searching on DIALOG, there are a few tricks that work more or less across the entire system, with groups of databases, or with individual databases. These tricks include:

- Identifying records with tabular information, because statistics are often found in tables

- Using limiters to specify that you want certain types of information, including records present in full-text format

- Searching on specific fields that include numeric information

Tables. Tables may appear in many of the directory, company information, and reference/handbook databases, as well as newspapers and general articles. However, tables can be problematic because they are often graphical rather than textual (in other words, non-ASCII) and because a number of other factors enter into whether or not they're included in the online version of an item. Length, nature of the information, copyright, graphics vs. text—all these parameters are considered by producers. Some producers will reformat graphical tables into ASCII; others will not. Some will include one table from an article but not another. And with the exceptions of some trademark images, patent drawings, and chemical structures, DIALOG is graphicless. For the statistics researcher, that means that some of the most fertile sources of statistics can only be obtained offline. However, the power of the system can be used to *identify* articles on a subject that also include tables. The secret is the special feature called "table." To use this technique, format your command as (for example) `select market(w)share and sf=table.`

This statement is not a true caption search; it will *not* necessarily get you tables that include the phrase `market share`. Rather it will retrieve any item that mentions `market share` in the text and that *also* includes tables. Such records may be more likely to contain figures, but you won't know without looking at them whether the table covers the information you want. In addition, you won't know if the table is included in the online version or not without actually retrieving the full text. (One exception to this rule is Business & Industry (File 9), where `sf=table` means not only that the article contains a table, but also that the table is online with the article.) DIALOG states that most producers will fax a copy of the article for free when tables are omitted. However, that practice may or may not help you when you're in a hurry.

Not every database supports the `sf=table` feature. To find out for certain, go into the database and `expand sf=` to see what special features are available. Nor can you necessarily count on tabular data being numeric, as it often is.

You may also use `nf=caption` on about 25 databases, but beware—captions often refer to photographs and drawings. However, on occasion, they may refer to tables and/or graphs. Because the caption field is searched as part of the full text, you will still pick up table/graph captions with a basic search. (*NOTE: TableBase (file 93) finesses the problem by providing only tables, so you don't need to invoke this feature when searching it.*)

Limiters. Many databases let you use limiters to restrict your search to particular kinds of information. I was aware of this feature in general before starting this book, but I didn't know how extensive the limits option really is. To use a limit, type your search term followed by a slash followed by the limit, as in `select cheese/data`. That statement should get you statistical information about cheese. Here are some of the field names of limits you can use in various databases:

- Budget
- Budget data
- Business segment analysis present
- Financial(s)
- Financial abstract available

- Financial statements only
- Fulltext
- Market data articles
- No budget data available (use with NOT)
- No sales data available (use with NOT)
- Notable (this is "no table," not the word that means worthy of attention; use with NOT)
- Number
- Price
- Price information present
- Pricing
- Records contain financial information
- Records containing tables
- Records with financials
- Records with tabular data
- Records without tabular data (use with NOT)
- Sales
- Statistical
- Statistical information
- Statistics
- Table not present (use with NOT)
- Table present
- Table records
- Tables
- Tabular
- Tabular records only
- Typical industry price included

These field names, obtained by EXPANDing on the limit field (`li= `) while in file 415 (DIALOG Bluesheets), are not necessarily the same as the term you use in practice. For the exact terminology, refer to the LIMITING box on the applicable Bluesheet. I cannot stress this point enough. (Guess who learned the hard way.) If you use the wrong terminology, your search won't work!

For example, to limit articles on cheese to market data articles in file 54, Foodline International Food Market Data, type `select cheese/data`. Do *not* type `select cheese/market data articles`.

Fields. When limiters aren't available for a database, fields will let you restrict your search to items in which certain kinds of data are present. Some of the fields available in various databases include:

- Annual sales
- Asset performance (%) (asset growth 1 year)
- Average household income
- Average price/earnings ratio
- Balance sheet
- Base sales
- Birth statistics
- Black American grad students
- Boiling point (Celsius)
- Budget
- Buying power index
- Capital expenditure
- Census
- Change in equity-net

To find out which fields are available in a particular database, check the Bluesheet for the file, or go into the file itself and EXPAND on n f = for the correct wording, which varies wildly ("nf" means *named field*). To see what's available across the entire system, I went into file 415 (Bluesheets) and typed e n f =. There are hundreds! I don't recommend doing this unless you're really curious, but if you are, try it. It's like going on a treasure hunt.

Tips for searching numeric fields in DIALOG

Nonnumeric fields. Don't try to perform range searching or sorting on nonnumeric fields, even if they might contain numbers. (In some cases, square footage, sales growth, and other numbers are not indexed as numeric fields. The Bluesheet for each file will tell you if the field is numeric or not; look in the indexing column.) DIALOG indexes numeric fields so that they will sort in proper numeric order; alphanumeric fields do not sort in numeric order—they sort by position from left to right. For example, 20007 will precede 201 because the 0 in the third position of 20007 is lower than the 1 in the third position of 201.

Display-only fields. Before you start, check the documentation to make sure the field you want is searchable. Some fields may be displayable but not searchable.

Specifying ranges. You may specify a range within which the numbers must fall. For example, `select sa= 100,000,000:500,000,000` means select records for which sales fall between 100 million and 500 million.

Be sure you know the format of the numbers in the database before you specify a range. For example, many business databases round numbers down to the two left-most digits and "bin" them, that is, stick them into a bucket that starts below the actual value. Thus 103,000,000 becomes 100,000,000 and goes into the 100,000,000 to 109,999,999 bucket. (The next bucket starts at 110,000,000). In other words, in these databases, numbers do not mean exactly what they say. A field value of 100,000,000 can actually mean anything between that number and 109,999,999!

Alternative ways of searching for numbers

Abbreviations. You may search by dropping off zeroes and using an abbreviation for thousands, millions, etc.—100K, 100M, 100B, 100T. The system recognizes the data in either form. You may also include commas and dollar signs without disturbing the system's ability to recognize the number: $100,000,000.

Percentages. You can search for percentages in numeric fields (not in full text) in one of two ways, either of which will yield the same results: decimal (as in .01) or percentage (as in 1%).

Exponents. Some scientific databases allow you to use either exponential notation or standard numeral notation. For example, the following are equivalent: 5E-2 and .05, as are 5E+2, 5E2, and 500.

In the first case, the exponent is negative, meaning 5 to the power of minus 2 (a two-place number to the right of the decimal). In the second, the exponent is positive, meaning 5 to the second power (two zeroes after the number). The plus sign is optional when working with positive values.

Post-processing formats on DIALOG

DIALOG allows you to format numeric data for importation into databases and spreadsheets via the REPORT command. The following formats are available:

- Fixed (or System Data) Format (FIXED). Fixed-length records and fields.
- Comma Delimited Format (DELIM). Commas separate each column.
- Data Interchange Format (DIF). For spreadsheets.
- Symbolic Logic Format (SYLK). For transfer to and from Microsoft programs.

Following is a direct quote from DIALOG's HELP (type `HELP POST`):

In each case the post-processing formats distinguishes text from numbers and strips numeric terms of dollar signs, percents, and commas before passing on the data. It will also convert a negative number in parentheses to a negative number with a leading minus sign. For example, ($1,234.56) would be converted to -1234.56. All four formats are transmitted in ASCII form.

The format of the command is:

- REPORT S2/CO,TA,NI,IX/1-10 FIXED (produces a Fixed format)
- REPORT S2/CO,TA,NI,IX/1-10 DELIM (produces a Comma Delimited format)
- REPORT S2/CO,TA,NI,IX/1-10 DIF (produces a Data Interchange format)
- REPORT S2/CO,TA,NI,IX/1-10 SYLK (produces a Symbolic Logic format)

For a list of files in which the REPORT command is valid, type HELP REPORT. A list valid as of the time of writing is included in Appendix B.

Searching UMI files on DIALOG

There are three techniques for identifying material with significant statistical content on UMI's databases on DIALOG. Unfortunately, you can't use all three on all databases.

- Class codes allow you to zero in on articles that feature statistics.
- The descriptor *statistics* will help you on files for which class codes are not assigned.
- The Special Feature field (SF) lets you check for the presence of tables and graphs.

Use class code 9140 (statistics) and 1110 (economic conditions and forecasts) in the following files:

- ABI/INFORM (file 15)
- Banking Information Source (file 268)
- Business Dateline (file 635)

Use the single descriptor *statistic* followed by a question mark (for truncation) in the previous three files (combine with the class code), *and* in the following files. The descriptor should be formatted as statistic?/df:

- Accounting and Tax (file 485)
- Criminal Justice Periodical Index (file 62)
- Newspaper Abstracts (file 483) (no weather or stocks)
- Periodical Abstracts (file 484)

Use sf=graph or sf=table or sf=charts to prospect for nontextual statistical material. The tables, graphs, and charts may not appear in the database, however, which will leave you casting around for other alternatives.

Examples:

In ABI/INFORM, search on libraries and cc=9140. When I did this, I got 38 hits. This means that there are 38 articles with significant statistical content possibly relating to libraries. (There is no way to insure that the statistics relate to libraries, even if the title includes the word libraries and there are codes and/or subject terms for libraries. Both concepts—libraries and statistical material—could appear in the article, separately or together.) However, we don't know if we'll be able to see the statistics online, and we don't necessarily know that the statistics are about libraries, only that statistics and libraries appear in the same article.

Searching DataStar for Statistics

DataStar is not nearly so finely indexed or fielded as DIALOG. However, in addition to the usual descriptors and free-text terms, a few databases feature numeric fields and limits, and you can use arithmetic operators with them. Some of these fields are:

- Balance sheet
- Financial information
- Quarterly figures
- Ratios
- Sales/revenue
- Total assets

Limits include:

- Accounts receivable
- Capital employed
- Income before tax
- Net income
- Number of employees
- Pretax profit margin

Check the Datasheet for each file to ascertain which limits may be used and how to format your statement. Note that TableBase (file BTBL) is all tables; use product, industry, and other subject-specific codes, but you don't have to tell the system that you want numeric data.

Searching ProQuest Direct

Searching UMI files on ProQuest Direct can be more satisfying than on DIALOG, since more tables are present, but it may still lead to a two-step process. Whether or not tables, charts, and graphs are included with the text depends on UMI's agreements with individual publishers, which makes for a holey system.

You have several options, not mutually exclusive:

Search the full text using words of your own choosing. Advantage: flexibility. Disadvantage: Possible to miss mentions using alternative terminology, and may retrieve items with excised tables.

Search the full text using codes and descriptors. To identify articles with significant statistical content, use class code 9140 and/or the descriptor *statistics*. Advantage: Better control over searching than with free text. Disadvantage: Possible to miss casual mentions, and may retrieve items with excised tables.

Perform a caption search. Any table or figure that has been assigned a caption, and there may be some that have not, is accessible by typing CAP(your search terms). (You will not go straight to the graphic; rather, you will get a results list including articles that match your criteria.) Captions *only* apply to graphics—not to ASCII text. Advantage: Impossible to retrieve articles with missing graphics. Disadvantage: When conducted without accompanying full text search, can miss mentions in full text. Caption searching should be performed as a complement to a code rather than instead of a code or free text search.

If you go the complete text route, you can tell at a glance whether or not graphics are available once you have a results list. If the full page image and/or text+graphics formats are available (the icons for those options will be highlighted), all tables and graphs will be present with the article. If only the full text is available (the icons for graphics formats will be dimmed), many tables and all graphs and diagrams will be excluded.

Just because graphs and tables are absent does not necessarily mean that the statistics you seek are missing since they may be contained in the full text, but there is substantial risk that they have been omitted. In that case, you have several options: acquire a hardcopy of the article; seek the statistics elsewhere; or download the full text with the understanding that the statistics might be missing.

Looking for the same article on another system will *not* solve the problem, since the graphics will probably be lacking there too.

Searching STN for Numeric Data

Choosing a database and field(s). The NUMERIGUIDE file is a reference for searching numeric data fields in STN files. It contains data about the properties in STN's numeric files, including: terminology, with broader, narrower, and related terms; definition of the property; files covering the property; and default units for the property in each file and the code to use.

It's important to use NUMERIGUIDE to identify the proper database and field code to use. It is also critical to EXPAND to see exactly what the right terminology for a substance is, or to use the CAS Registry file to get the Chemical Abstracts registry number for the substance.

Converting units. Units of measure are defined separately by each database producer. One file might use degrees Celsius, another degrees Fahrenheit. However, to ease the pain caused by having to work with disparate measures, STN offers a units-conversion function that allows you to work in a system other than that used in a particular file. If a file uses the meter/kilogram/second system, and you want properties in feet/pounds/seconds, for example, you can issue a command to convert for you either temporarily or permanently.

To change all units for the whole session or permanently, issue the SET UNIT ALL command in combination with the code for the name of the appropriate unit. To change units permanently, SET UNIT ALL=code-for-name-of-unit PERM. You may also change units for one SEARCH, EXPAND, or DISPLAY command by typing the name of the unit at the end of the command, as in search 32 deg F/mp. This means "Search for items with values of 32 degrees Fahrenheit in the melting point field."

This way, the system will find compounds with a melting point of 32 degrees Fahrenheit, even if the melting point is expressed as 0 degrees C. See Figure 4-11 for a chart showing STN's unit systems.

FIGURE 4-11
STN Unit Systems

STN uses the following unit systems, plus most unit specifications found in the literature.

Unit	SI	MKS	CGS	FPS	ENG	STN
Length	meter	meter	centimeter	foot	foot	meter
Mass	kilogram	kilogram	gram	pound	pound	kilogram
Time	second	second	second	second	second	second
Temperature	Kelvin	deg C	deg C	deg F	deg F	Kelvin
Electric Current	ampere	ampere	ampere	ampere	ampere	ampere
Energy	joule	joule	calorie	btu	btu	joule

For more information about the various systems of measure, type HELP SUNITS.

FIGURE 4-12

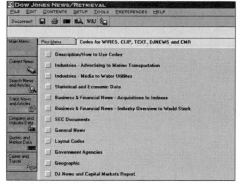

Dow Jones News/Retrieval's Guide lists helpful codes that will target your search. Click on the square next to the desired category to view the codes.

Searching Dow Jones News/Retrieval and the Wall Street Journal Interactive Edition Publications Library

Dow Jones News/Retrieval offers a myriad of codes to help you pinpoint subjects and particular kinds of data. These codes are more effective than free-text searching, though you can always use the latter. For complete documentation, go into //GUIDE.

Here's a sampling:

Financial Market Statistical Codes

- Building permits   BLP
- Construction spending   CSS

- Consumer price index   CPI
- Consumer savings rates   CSR
- Consumer sentiment index   UVM
- Dow Jones averages   DJA
- Gross national (domestic) product   GNP
- Housing completions   HCL
- Key interest rates   KIR
- Money rates   MNR
- Oil prices (cash market)   OIL
- Tracking the economy   TTE

Financial market statistical codes may be used in selected publications in the TEXT area (*Wall Street Journal*, Dow Jones News Service, *Barron's*, and International News), in WIRES and CLIP (current awareness tracking), and in DJNEWS. To use the codes in TEXT, enter the code followed by .ST. Or, you may use the code followed by the suffix =ST. For example, for key interest rates, type:

KIR.ST. or KIR=ST

Note that, in the Wall Street Journal Interactive Edition Publications Library, you *must* use =ST or the prefix S/ since the dot ST code does not work!

To use the codes in WIRES and CLIP, type the prefix S/ and the code S/KIR.
For DJNEWS, type the prefix .I/ and the code .I/KIR.

Economic Data Codes

- Housing affordability index   HAI
- Leading indicators   LIN
- Personal income   PIN
- Retail sales   RSL

Use these codes exactly as you would financial market statistical codes, except that, in DJNEWS, use the prefix .S/ instead of .I/. You cannot use =ST, even in the Wall Street Journal Interactive Edition.

Business and Financial News Codes

- Bond market statistics   BON
- Canadian economic
  & monetary indicators   CEM
- Dow Jones bond averages   DJB

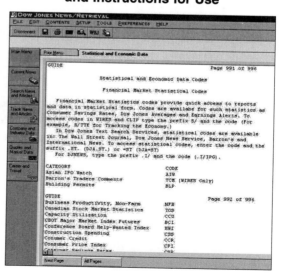

FIGURE 4-13
Some Dow Jones News/Retrieval's Statistical and Economic Data Codes and Instructions for Use

- Economic and monetary indicators   EMI
- Economic news, trends, analysis   ECO
- Foreign exchange table   FXT
- Gold prices and commentary   GPC
- Financial market indices   NDX
- Industry overview (includes outlook)   IOV
- Interest rate news, quotes on financial instruments   FIN
- International credit market news   ICM
- International economic and monetary indicators   IEI
- International economic predictions
  (non-U.S. economic indicators)   IEJ
- Selected market statistics   MKT
- Market share   MSH
- Mortgages and mortgage rates   MOR
- Mutual fund statistics   FND
- Petroleum market, including prices   PET
- Price changes by companies, industries   PRC
- Research and development, including reported
  figures and projections for companies and industries   RND
- Stock markets and statistical reports   STK

These codes are valid in the *Wall Street Journal* (including the Wall Street Journal Interactive Edition Publications Library), *Barron's*, Press Release Wires, International News, WIRES, and CLIP.

To use them in the first four, add the suffix .NS., as in BON.NS. To use them in CLIP or WIRES, type the prefix N/, as in N/BON.

Journal codes

Following are some of the best codes for locating numerical information in the *Wall Street Journal* (including the Wall Street Journal Interactive Edition Publications Library), the *Asian Wall Street Journal*, the *Wall Street Journal Europe*, and CLIP:

- Best selling books   SEL
- Currency markets   CUR
- Economy   ECN
- Foreign exchange   FEX
- Fund track/mutual funds   MFU
- Inside market items   IMK

- Major market items   MIM
- People patterns (demographics)   PPP
- Real estate   RLS

There are many additional useful codes covering particular industries, types of markets, and so on.

To use the codes in TEXT, add the suffix `.JN.` after a code, as in `SEL.JN.` To use the codes in CLIP, use the prefix `J/` followed by a code, as in `J/SEL`.

Post-processing formats with Dow Jones News/Retrieval

The Tradeline database offers historical quotes on stocks, bonds, mutual funds, government securities, indices, foreign exchange rates, and options. You may format data not only as text, but also as a spreadsheet (PRN format). For historical price information (as opposed to dividend histories), you may also use the Metastock charting software format. Tradeline is found in the Quotes and Market Data category in News/Retrieval's graphical software.

To format data from Tradeline, select Data Download, then follow the prompts. You will be transferred to terminal mode even if you are using Dow Jones's graphical interface.

Searching IAC Files

IAC files like PROMT, Predicasts Overview of Markets & Technology, have special Event Codes that help target types of data. A code is assigned when an article offers substantial information about that topic. Many codes are broken down further than listed here or carry additional scope notes. Those most pertinent to statistics follow, though others may retrieve articles containing numeric data (see Figure 4-16).

FIGURE 4-14
Dow Jones News/Retrieval's
Quotes and Market Data Menu

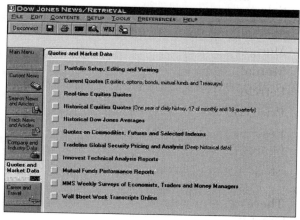

FIGURE 4-15

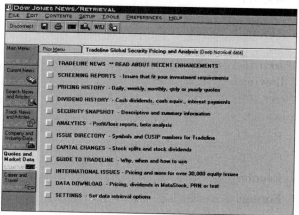

To reformat pricing and dividend data, select Data Download, the next-to-last menu item.

FIGURE 4-16
IAC's Event Codes

01	Forecasts, trends, outlook
38	Royalty income
4	Facilities, expenditures and resource use
40	Expenditures and obligations
42	Pollutants produced and recycled
43	Capital expenditures
443	New capacity, plant construction
444	Expanded capacity, plant expansion
445	Capacity
45	Research and development outlays
51	Population information (labor force, people licensed, etc.)
52	Personal income information
53	Labor force information
6	Market data and trends
60	Materials supply, inventories
604	Market share
62	Production data
63	Shipments data
64	Foreign trade
643	Imports
644	Exports
65	Sales and consumption data
66	Plant and equipment sales
67	Research and development distribution
68	Labor distribution by employer
69	Goods and services distribution
7	Unit costs and prices
70	Unit costs and prices
71	Unit costs
74	Commodity and service prices
743	Consumer prices
744	Wholesale prices
75	Securities prices
76	Interest rates
77	Exchange rates
8	Financial information
80	Capital funds and cash flow
81	Securities issued
82	Receipt of funds
83	Sales, profits, and dividends
84	Financial reports
86	Stockholder data
87	Financial assets
88	Use of funds
89	Liabilities, NEC
90	Government expenditures
91	Government revenues
92	Taxes

You will also find numerical and nonnumerical data relating to product specifications, as follows (all are given here, even if not numeric, to help you understand the scope of the code):

34 Mechanical properties

Chemical properties

Electrical properties

Structural properties

Functional properties

Energy per unit

Process health hazards

Price-performance data

Misc. properties

To use the codes on DIALOG, format as in the following example: s EC=604.

Note that a few new three-digit codes were added in early 1997. If you're doing retrospective searching, search also at the two-digit level to pick up all information on your topic. Combine the code with free-text searching. For example, to retrieve everything on market share before January 1997, type s EC=60 and market(w)share.

The code will cause you to retrieve records having to do with market information in general *and* market share specifically. The free text terms will limit your results to articles having *only* to do with market share. If you search with free text alone, you may pick up articles mentioning market share in passing, but not necessarily offering figures relating to market share.

IAC also offers product and geographical codes to help focus a search. You can find partial lists of product codes and complete lists of event and geographic codes at the IAC Web site at http://corporate.iacnet.com/enhance/first.htm.

FIGURE 4-17

IAC's Revised Event Codes and Event Name List

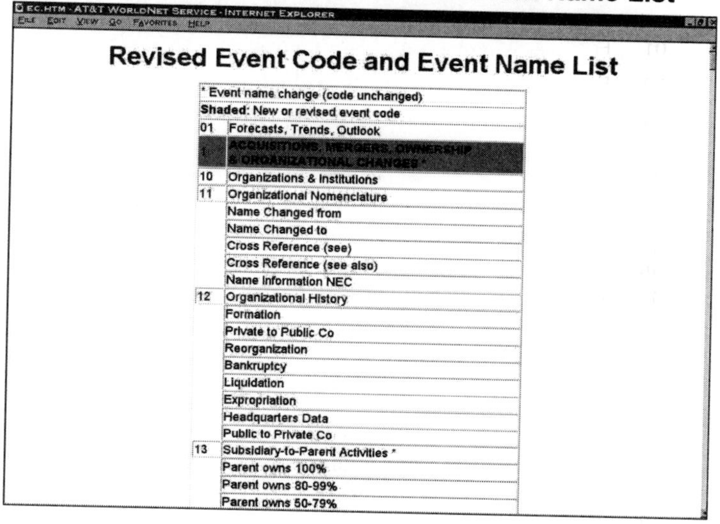
EC.HTM - AT&T WORLDNET SERVICE - INTERNET EXPLORER

FILE EDIT VIEW GO FAVORITES HELP

Revised Event Code and Event Name List

* Event name change (code unchanged)	
Shaded: New or revised event code	
01	Forecasts, Trends, Outlook
1	ACQUISITIONS, MERGERS, OWNERSHIP & ORGANIZATIONAL CHANGES *
10	Organizations & Institutions
11	Organizational Nomenclature
	Name Changed from
	Name Changed to
	Cross Reference (see)
	Cross Reference (see also)
	Name Information NEC
12	Organizational History
	Formation
	Private to Public Co
	Reorganization
	Bankruptcy
	Liquidation
	Expropriation
	Headquarters Data
	Public to Private Co
13	Subsidiary-to-Parent Activities *
	Parent owns 100%
	Parent owns 80-99%
	Parent owns 50-79%

Searching LEXIS-NEXIS for Numeric and Statistical Data

In LEXIS-NEXIS, your options beyond the general are fairly limited. Most tables are omitted from the full text, partly because the system only supports a width of 78 characters. However, in the Market Research Library, you can use the TABLEINFO segment to identify items with tables containing relevant captions or row/column titles. Caption and table information will also turn up in a full text search, but if you use TABLEINFO, you can be sure that the tables are present.

To save money in market research files, you may wish to search tables of contents, which are free. Doing so scans the full text, even though your results appear as tables of contents only. Only when you link to the actual text from the table of contents will you be charged.

LEXIS-NEXIS offers numeric fields that vary by file. For specific information on the way a particular file formats numeric fields, when in the file, type `.gu` to go into the guide for that file.

Numeric fields may be searched with arithmetic operators like greater than, less than, equal to, greater than or equal to, and less than or equal to. You cannot use these operators on text fields. To assure that only records with numeric data present in a particular field are retrieved, specify that the field must be greater than zero—unless the field could contain a negative number. (A profit/loss field could hold a negative number; a budget field could not.) The system is also smart enough to recognize numbers with or without the commas, so you can type 1000 or 1,000 and get the same results. *That is only true for numeric fields*, however. With text fields or full text, *you* must tell the system all the ways the number could be formatted.

You cannot use the abbreviations K, M, B, and T to stand for thousand, million, billion, or trillion, with numeric fields. However, you should include these abbreviations as options when searching full text and/or text fields.

Do not include dollar signs when searching numeric fields, but you can do so with full-text or text fields.

Some databases drop the last three zeros of a number, as when table headings say "In thousands." The documentation for the database may not tell you this ahead of time, so express the number with and without the zeroes to make sure you don't miss anything. Fortunately, you won't run into this situation very often.

The percent sign (%) is searchable in full-text and text fields. Be sure to also request *per cent* or *percent* to cover all bases.

TIP: Than *is a stop word.*

Using Attachments in LEXIS-NEXIS

LEXIS-NEXIS is making increasing use of attachments, such as images and spreadsheets, to provide important information. American Statistics Index, for example, includes tables formatted as images. LEXIS-NEXIS' Research Software graphical interface is automatically set up to allow you to view the images online. (If you are not using a graphical interface, you will need to download the image and view it offline using image viewing software.) You can recognize which documents carry attachments by the presence of special icons in the left frame of the Research Software.

Starting with Research Software 7.0, additional attachment file types (not just images) are pre-associated with the programs that read them (Excel, WordPerfect, and Word). You can also designate your own associations by going into the File menu, Settings option, and choosing Attachments. If you encounter an attachment that Research Software doesn't recognize, you will be prompted to associate its format with an application then and there.

Once the attachment is saved on your hard disk, use the associated program, such as Excel or Adobe Acrobat, to read and/or manipulate it.

The above tips should help you find statistics in various online systems. Remember, though, that finding statistics depends on three factors: selecting the right place to look, choosing an effective strategy, and evaluating the data. The succeeding chapters, which cover finding statistics in specific subject areas and provide concrete case studies, will help you determine where and how to look when you have a specific question.

Finding Demographics and Population Statistics

D emographics measure characteristics of human populations. Basic demographics are called *vital statistics*; they include measures of births, deaths, infant mortality, marriages, divorces, and life-expectancy. Vital statistics may also include "cohabitation," number of people never-married, causes of death, accidents, living arrangements of children and the elderly, child care arrangements, and average weights and heights for particular ages. Some producers broaden the term vital statistics to include not just birth, death, marriage, and living arrangements, but all kinds of basic information about populations, including health-related statistics, crime rates, ethnic identification, religious affiliation, and so on.

The domains of demographics, polling and opinion research, and market research overlap, since all deal with attitudes, beliefs, and practices. In this book, you will find demographic-type sources in the chapters on market information (Chapter 6) and public opinion (Chapter 11) as well as this one.

Demographics are often tallied by geographic or geopolitical area, such as country, region, state or province, city or metropolitan area, etc. Or they may be counted and reported by other factors. One Web site, The Right Site (http://www.easidemographics.com), even allows you to ask for a report by TV market.

While current data is critical for assessing today's situation, demographic *time series*—historical statistics that show changes in particular characteristics over time—help identify trends. By comparing numbers over time, you can tell whether and when birth rates have increased or slowed, how well literacy programs may be working, and how populations are moving geographically. Data from time series let us recognize the baby boom and the urbanization of the U.S.; they also bring home the horrors of Europe's decimation by the Black Plague. One caveat about time series: As mentioned in Chapter 2, differences in data collection methods and definitions over time can skew figures. Always read the fine print to see when and how assumptions changed during compilation.

Past and current data is used not only to paint a picture of where we've been, but also to construct forecasts (sometimes called outlook or predictions). As you might expect, such numbers are educated guesses and are often wrong, but absent a crystal ball, they're all we've got for seeing the future.

Demographics are used for innumerable purposes, e.g.:

- **Resource planning and deployment.** If officials know that a particular town is growing quickly, for example, they can budget and plan for increased fire and police protection, sanitation services, water and power delivery capacities, school facilities, and so on.

- **Marketing.** People with goods and services to sell want to target their marketing efforts at those most likely to purchase, so they want to know who needs what, who favors what, and how to reach them. This information can be gathered by knowing what people read, where they live, what places they frequent, and what groups they belong to—not necessarily at the individual level, but in general.

- **Distribution of aid.** Areas likely to be most in need of food or medical supply distribution can be recognized and served.

- **Identifying where public education is needed.** Teenage pregnancies and poor eating habits are two areas that might be targeted by using demographics.

- **Formulating and influencing policy.** Policy makers need reliable data to deal with issues ranging from Social Security (how many people will be drawing on it, paying into the fund, and when) to gun control (how many guns are used to commit crimes). The Federal Reserve Board tracks economic indicators and uses them to decide whether to raise or lower interest rates.

- **Making decisions.** Individuals, companies, governments, schools, groups, and organizations all need to know what's going on around them in order to make intelligent decisions. For example, if you're relocating, you'll want to know the characteristics of the places you're considering. Companies need to track wages and prices within their industry; governments need to know current and future population sizes and characteristics in order to budget for Medicare and Social Security benefits.

- **Apportioning government representation.** The U.S. Census is constitutionally mandated. Its original purpose: to apportion the legislature.

HOW DEMOGRAPHIC DATA IS GATHERED

Demographic data is gathered through the use of censuses (everyone is counted), surveys (samples), and extrapolation (projections and forecasts based on current and past data and the incorporation of information which may affect outcomes).

The major U.S. population census, the Census of Population and Housing, is taken every ten years. Various supplementary counts are made in between, including the monthly Current Population Survey, which is based on interviews of householders and focuses on employment and unemployment; Current Employment Statistics, collected from business payrolls every month (businesses return forms to state agencies by mail, and the agencies then report to the U.S. Bureau of Labor Statistics); the Census of Manufactures, which is taken every five years (there is also an Annual Survey of Manufactures); the Census of Retail Trade; et al. Data from these periodic censuses is used to augment the basic census, covering additional subjects as well as filling in data for non-census years. Sometimes administrative records from sources outside the Census Bureau are used for counting as well.

The decennial U.S. census is now conducted partly on a sample basis. Basic questions, such as age, marital status, race, sex, and family relationships, are asked of everyone. However, other questions, such as commute time and income, are asked of only a sample of the population.

TYPES OF DATA

These types of statistics are collected for demographics:

- Population numbers and distribution
- Racial, ethnic, religious, age, sex, and other similar distributions
- How people spend their time
- Income and wealth distribution
- Poverty
- Spending, purchasing, and saving habits
- Education levels
- Numbers of people in particular occupations or businesses
- Immigration, emigration, and migration
- Eating habits
- Transportation habits
- Religious beliefs and practices
- Housing patterns
- Birth and death rates
- Literacy
- Number of adherents to particular religions

KEY PRODUCERS

Government agencies are major producers of demographic statistics. Chief among these are the U.S. Census Bureau, the Bureau of Labor Statistics, the National Center for Health Statistics, and various non-U.S. statistical agencies. The same agencies that conduct general censuses may also involve themselves in specific ones, such as the U.S. Census of Manufactures. Other key producers are:

- State and local agencies
- The United Nations, especially its Population Division
- Universities (both public and private), such as the Inter-university Consortium for Political and Social Research
- Private companies, such as American Demographics and market research firms
- Religious and church organizations
- Yearbook of American and Canadian Churches

TYPES OF SOURCES

You will find demographic statistics collected and reported in:

- Almanacs
- Encyclopedias
- Government publications
- Specialized journals
- Market research reports
- Databases derived from publicly- or privately-produced data
- Statistical compendia

BEST PLACES TO LOOK

The best demographic information comes in table form, as you might expect. However, there exist a few excellent full-text sources as well, particularly in the market-oriented category, where journal publishers get into the act. Here are the best sources of demographic data, together with a list of the online services or Web sites where you can find them. Use the sources in this directory as a starting point when you need to find demographic data.

General

1990 Census Lookup (searchable)
  http://venus.census.gov/cdrom/lookup

ASI (American Statistics Index) (for *identifying* statistical publications produced by the U.S. government)
  DIALOG (file 102)
  Scheduled to be on LEXIS-NEXIS in 1998, including selected full text

Current Population Survey
  http://www.bls.census.gov/cps/cpsmain.htm

Almanac of American Politics
  LEXIS-NEXIS (file AMPOL in multiple libraries)

American Demographics magazine
  Dow Jones News/Retrieval
  Electric Library
  LEXIS-NEXIS (BUSFIN, MARKET, and NEWS Libraries)
  ProQuest Direct
  Wall Street Journal Interactive Edition Publications Library
  http://www.demographics.com

County Business Patterns
  http://www.census.gov/epcd/cbp/view/cbpview.html

FAOSTAT Forestry Statistics Database (country populations)
  http://www.fao.org/waicent/forestry.htm

Information Please Almanac
  Cognito!
  Encarta Online Library

Internal Revenue Service Tax Stats
  http://www.irs.ustreas.gov/prod/tax_stats/index.html

Kaleidoscope: Current World Data (overview of economy, people, media, population, armed forces, health care, transportation, communications, vital statistics for U.S. states, Canadian provinces, and countries around the world)
  LEXIS-NEXIS (file KCWD in ASIAPC, BUSFIN, EUROPE, MDEAFR, NSAMER, and WORLD Libraries)

LEXIS-NEXIS GEODEM Library (geodemographics)

Monthly Labor Review
  Dow Jones News/Retrieval
  Electric Library
  ProQuest Direct
  Wall Street Journal Interactive Edition Publications Library

Occupational Outlook Quarterly
  Dow Jones News/Retrieval
  Electric Library
  ProQuest Direct
  Wall Street Journal Interactive Edition Publications Library

Population Demographics (U.S.—current and projected)
  BrainWave
  DIALOG (file 581)

Public Health Reports
    Dow Jones News/Retrieval
    ProQuest Direct
    Wall Street Journal Interactive Edition Publications Library

Social Security Administration (profiles of Social Security recipients; earnings and employment of workers eligible for Social Security)
    http://www.ssa.gov/statistics/

Statistical Abstract of the U.S.
    http://www.census.gov/stat_abstract

United Nations Population Division (world population from year 0 projected to 2150)
    gopher://gopher.undp.org/00/ungophers/popin/wdtrends/histor

University of Michigan's Population Gopher (U.S., by state; also shows percent resident and percent overseas)
    gopher://una.hh.lib.umich.edu/00/census/summaries/statepop/

University of Virginia's Social Sciences Data Center (County and City Data Books)
    http://www.lib.virginia.edu/socsci/ccdb/

U.S. Immigration and Naturalization Service
    http://www.ins.usdoj.gov/

USA Counties 1996 (Oregon State University)
    http://govinfo.kerr.orst.edu/usaco-stateis.html

World Almanac
    Electric Library
    FirstSearch

World Almanac of U.S. Politics
    Electric Library

World Factbook (CIA profiles of various countries; includes population figures and demographics)
    Electric Library
    LEXIS-NEXIS (file WOFACT in multiple libraries)
    http://odci.gov/cia/publications/pubs.html

.xls (results in spreadsheet format)
    http://www.xls.com

Market-oriented

American Marketplace
    Dow Jones News/Retrieval
    Wall Street Journal Interactive Edition Publications Library

The Boomer Report (baby boomer demographics, purchasing habits, attitudes, activities)
    LEXIS-NEXIS (file BOOMER in BUSFIN, MARKET, and NEWS Libraries)

Minority Markets Alert
    LEXIS-NEXIS (file MMALRT in BUSFIN, MARKET, and NEWS Libraries)
    Dow Jones News/Retrieval
    Wall Street Journal Interactive Edition Publications Library

The Numbers News (demographic trends in the U.S. population)
    LEXIS-NEXIS (file TNN in BUSFIN, MARKET, and NEWS Libraries)

Official Guide to the American Marketplace (population, households, income and spending, education, labor, health, and attitudes)
    LEXIS-NEXIS (file AMMKTP in MARKET Library)

Research Alert (consumer trends)
    Dow Jones News/Retrieval
    LEXIS-NEXIS (file RSALRT in MARKET and NEWS Libraries)
    Wall Street Journal Interactive Edition Publications Library

Researchline Database
    Profound

Sales & Marketing Management (media markets, metro areas, etc.)
    DIALOG (files 15, 47, 148)
    Dow Jones News/Retrieval
    Electric Library
    LEXIS-NEXIS BIS file in BUSFIN Library
    ProQuest Direct
    Wall Street Journal Interactive Edition Publications Library

TableBase
    DataStar (file BTBL)
    DIALOG (file 93)
    http://www.tablebase.com

Youth Markets Alert (trends among young consumers)
    LEXIS-NEXIS (file YMALRT in MARKET and NEWS Libraries)
    Wall Street Journal Interactive Edition Publications Library

Religion
Britannica Online (for numbers of religious adherents, search the index using the term *religion* or the name of the religion or church or denomination, and browse the results looking for tables and/or maps; check countries or regions under The People or Religion; check specific religions, churches, or denominations for in-text figures, or search the articles (not the index) using terms like *percent*, *numbers*, *adherents*, etc.)
    http://www.eb.com

The National Council of Churches of Christ publishes the *Yearbook of American and Canadian Churches*. While the book as a whole is not online, you can find a critical chart (U.S. Religious Bodies with more than 60,000 Members) at http://www.dnaco.net/~kbedell/ybstats2.htm. Some of the information in the book also finds its way into the *Statistical Abstract of the U.S.* (see Religious Populations of the World)

Information Please Almanac
  Cognito!
  Encarta Online Library

Magazine Database
  DIALOG (file 47)
  DataStar (file MAGS)

A Matter of Fact (multidisciplinary)

Walden Country Reports (religious demographics in various countries)
  Electric Library
  FirstSearch
  LEXIS-NEXIS (file COUREP in multiple libraries)
  World Almanac

World Factbook (CIA profiles of various countries, includes religions)
  Electric Library
  LEXIS-NEXIS (file WOFACT in multiple libraries)
  http://www.odci.gov/cia/publications/pubs.html

CASE STUDIES

Case Study 5-1: City Population
Purpose: This case study illustrates how to use Census Bureau information to find the population of a major U.S. city between censuses.

Question: What is the population of Los Angeles?

Likely sources: U.S. Census Bureau; State of California; City/County of Los Angeles; Statistical Abstract of the U.S.; County and City Data Book

Access points used: Sponsoring organization; title of survey; subject terms

Systems: Web sites

This looked like a census question, so I started at the U.S. Census Bureau. I knew that the decennial census was last taken in 1990, but that information was too old to be of use to me. However, I also knew that the Census Bureau conducts interim surveys. I went first to the Census Bureau WWW site (http://www.census.gov) to see if I could find one of those interim surveys (see figure 5-1).

FIGURE 5-1
The U.S. Census Bureau's Home Page

On the welcome page, I selected Search. Then I had the choice of searching by Word, by Place, or by Map. Since I was dealing with a major city, Place seemed like the best option.

FIGURE 5-2

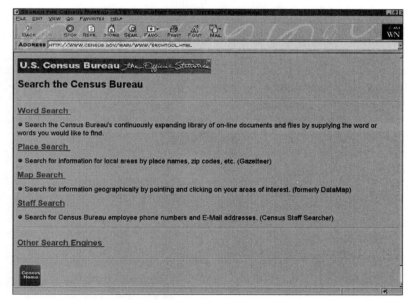

The Census Bureau offers you a choice of searching by Word, Place, or Map.

I selected Place and was confronted with boxes for Place Name, an optional State, and a Zip Code. One zip code wasn't enough, so I entered `Los Angeles` and `CA` in the Place Name and State boxes (see Figure 5-3).

FIGURE 5-3
The Place Search Option at the Census Bureau Site

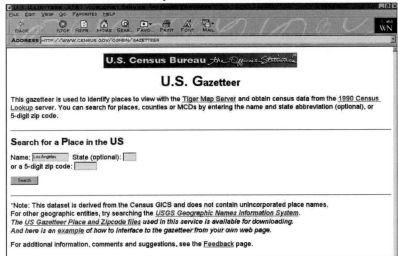

While this strategy brought me to a screen that covered Los Angeles, the data was from the 1990 Census. Too old. I was hoping that a query would bring up more recent data.

Unfortunately, I didn't remember the exact name of the interim report—maybe it was Current Population Survey.

I checked the directory of sources listed earlier in this chapter and found an address for Current Population Survey at http://www.bls.census.gov/cps/cpsmain.htm. When I read the description of the survey, I realized it wasn't going to work. It measures characteristics of the labor force. I was looking for the whole population.

I went back to the welcome page to see what else was available. When I returned, I noticed that I could browse by subject, so I chose that option. I found a listing called Population:—Estimates—Projections. This was probably what I wanted, since I knew any count between censuses is an estimate.

From Population:—Estimates—Projections, I selected City/Place Population Estimates, then 1990-94 Estimates of Cities with Populations over 100,000. And there it was, ranked number

FIGURE 5-4
An Excerpt from the Census Bureau's Subject Index

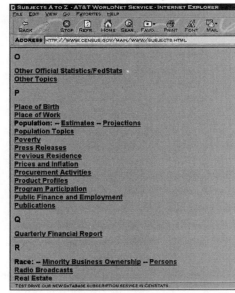

Population:—Estimates—Projections looks like a good choice.

two in size in the country: Los Angeles' population as of 7/1/94 was estimated to be 3,448,613. I was content to go with this number, even though it was a little old.

FIGURE 5-5

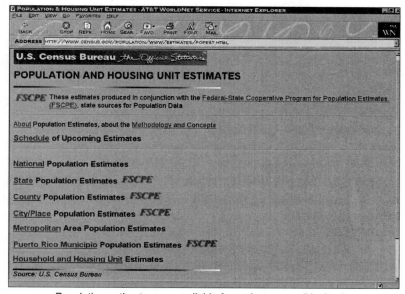

Population estimates are available for various geopolitical units.

FIGURE 5-6

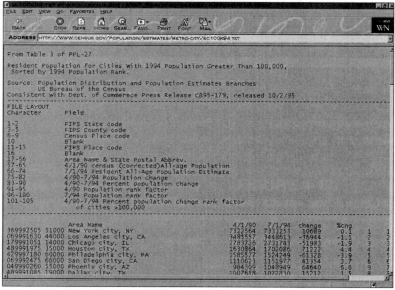

Here's our answer: The population of Los Angeles in an off-census year. Gorgeous it isn't, but the information is there.

NOTE: Because I live there, I know that Los Angeles is far larger than 3 million peo-ple. This definition is not for the metropolitan area, but for the city itself, i.e., only those areas directly under the Los Angeles city government's jurisdiction.

Lessons learned:

√ Being familiar with organizations likely to offer the data you need is important.

√ Between-census population surveys are an important source of relatively current demographic data.

√ Titles of surveys can be misleading—Current Population Survey does not cover cur-rent population as a whole. You have to read the documentation.

√ There are various ways of defining cities: zip codes, name, Metropolitan Statistical Area (MSA).

√ You have to decide when to keep looking for more current information and when to settle for older information. When you stop and what you accept depends on your deadline, budget, and purpose.

√ Use your own personal knowledge to question results that seem unlikely; you may be able to find a reason for surprising statistics.

Case Study 5-2: Religious Adherents

Purpose: This case study shows how to find information that seems obvious but can be well-hidden. During the writing of this book, I discovered that finding numbers of adherents to specific reli-gions online was quite difficult.

FIGURE 5-7

Type World Almanac in the Publications box.

Question: How many Catholics are there in the United States?

Likely sources: World Almanac

Access points used: Fields; titles

System: Electric Library

I wanted to be able to restrict the search to the World Almanac, so I chose More Options so that I could search fields. In the Publication box, I typed World Almanac. In the search box, I type catholics and united states and got 0 hits.

I broadened the search and typed `religions united states`. Again I got 0 hits. Next I tried `catholics u.s.`

Bingo! This time I got 2 hits. Here they are:

```
a) Religious information: Census of Religious Groups in the U.S.
b) Religious information: Major Christian Denominations
```

The information in the first answer was arranged strangely—not quite in alphabetical order, and even though the term *catholic* was in bold type, it was hard to find. To ease the eyestrain, I used the Find command on my browser's Edit menu to find "catholic" on the screen. Finally, at the end of the list I located: Roman Catholic Church (19,863)...59,220,723

The number in parentheses is the number of congregations in the U.S. It is followed by the number of adherents.

FIGURE 5-8
Census of Religious Groups in the U.S., from The World Almanac

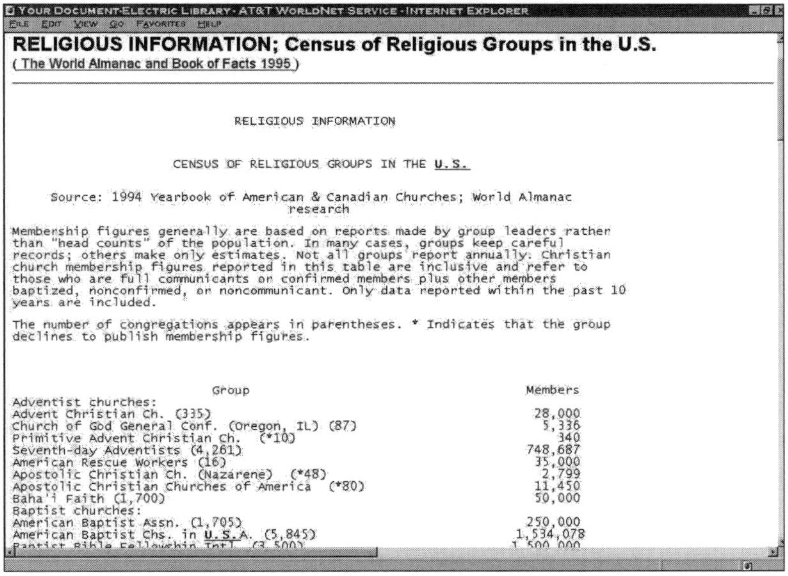
YOUR DOCUMENT-ELECTRIC LIBRARY- AT&T WORLDNET SERVICE - INTERNET EXPLORER

FILE EDIT VIEW GO FAVORITES HELP

RELIGIOUS INFORMATION; Census of Religious Groups in the U.S.

(The World Almanac and Book of Facts 1995)

RELIGIOUS INFORMATION

CENSUS OF RELIGIOUS GROUPS IN THE U.S.

Source: 1994 Yearbook of American & Canadian Churches; World Almanac research

Membership figures generally are based on reports made by group leaders rather than "head counts" of the population. In many cases, groups keep careful records; others make only estimates. Not all groups report annually. Christian church membership figures reported in this table are inclusive and refer to those who are full communicants or confirmed members plus other members baptized, nonconfirmed, or noncommunicant. Only data reported within the past 10 years are included.

The number of congregations appears in parentheses. * Indicates that the group declines to publish membership figures.

Group	Members
Adventist churches:	
Advent Christian Ch. (335)	28,000
Church of God General Conf. (Oregon, IL) (87)	5,336
Primitive Advent Christian Ch. (*10)	340
Seventh-day Adventists (4,261)	748,687
American Rescue Workers (16)	35,000
Apostolic Christian Ch. (Nazarene) (*48)	2,799
Apostolic Christian Churches of America (*80)	11,450
Baha'i Faith (1,700)	50,000
Baptist churches:	
American Baptist Assn. (1,705)	250,000
American Baptist Chs. in U.S.A. (5,845)	1,534,078
Baptist Bible Fellowship Intl. (3,500)	1,500,000

The second hit (b) turned out to be a summary of how the denominations differ in belief and practice, rather than a statistical compilation. But, after some experimentation, I found an acceptable answer with (a).

Lessons learned:

√ You have to experiment with terminology to find what you want. (In this database, `United States` didn't work, but `U.S.` did.)

√ Almanacs can include nonstatistical information (such as the practices of various religious denominations).

√ The Find command on a Web browser is a helpful tool for pinpointing relevant terms in a sea of text.

Finding Industry, Market, and General Business Statistics

Market data is as valuable as oil, and sometimes as slippery. Business people, inventors, scientists, financial wizards, and advertising professionals seek it. Careers are built around it. Businesses and industries live and die by it.

Numbers help tell the story. For example, you can:

- Predict likely expenses by following supplies and costs of raw materials;

- Lessen risk by studying product successes and failures (Does anyone remember Jolt Cola or the NeXT operating system?);

- Find your competitive edge by knowing your rivals and their operations inside out, and by understanding customer attitudes.

Industry trends show not only where we've been, but also where we're likely to go. For example, shrewd referral and placement services saw the temporary worker and outsourcing revolutions coming before they hit full force. Consequently, they were geared up to place workers as they poured out of downsized companies. How did they do it? They watched the numbers.

HOW INDUSTRY, MARKET, AND GENERAL BUSINESS DATA ARE GATHERED

Industry, market, and business data comes from the following sources:

- National statistical offices
- International statistical offices
- Government surveys
- Government publications
- Government administrative records
- Research and industry reports (consultants, scholars, private companies)
- Analyst (brokerages and financial firms) and bank reports
- News releases

- Trade journals
- Trade associations

TYPES OF DATA

Market Data

Current, historical, and forecast data all go into the pot of the market researcher, who may also stir in:

Measures of market size and characteristics

- Market shares
- Market sizes
- Product segments
- Demand
- Sales (in dollars or other units of currency, per item, or in units of measure, such as tons, gallons, bushels, and so on.) Sales can be used to rank the players and calculate market shares. Sales figures are essential for tracking which kinds of products are selling, where, and to whom.
- Market growth or decline
- Types of producers (conglomerates, small specialty companies, etc.)
- Mergers and acquisitions

Financials

- Profits and losses
- Returns
- Prices
- Dollar amount of average, low, and high transactions
- Advertising prices and expenditures
- Financing, including government funding
- Labor costs, worker salaries and benefits costs, payrolls
- Imports/exports, tariffs

Innovation and promotion

- New products (introductions)
- Advertising angles (such as companies that promote environmental benefits), channels
- Promotions
- Packaging
- Distribution channels

Customers

- Brand recognition
- Demographics of consumers and other buyers; purchasing patterns; customer loyalty
- Product successes and failures

Internal operations

- Locations (domestic, foreign, by state or other geographic division)
- Numbers and types of employees
- Equipment use
- Capital and other expenditures (for example, for pollution control, transportation, insurance, and research and development)
- Raw materials and ingredients used
- Use of space and other resources

Other

- Trends in regulation
- Demographics and earnings and/or perks of CEOs, CFOs, and other company leaders and business owners

Industry Data

In addition to data on markets, researchers may add a cup or three of information about the entire industry, using additional ingredients such as:

- Production
- Productivity
- Insurance risk
- Leading industries per geographic area, nation, or world

Business Data

Finally, general business information seasons the brew, adding measures such as:

- Business failures
- Numbers of home-based businesses
- Numbers of telecommuters
- Numbers of consultants
- Businesses owned by women, minorities, and the foreign-born

KEY PRODUCERS

Industry, market and general business statistics are made available by a variety of producers, including:

- Market research firms, such as AC Nielsen, Simmons Market Research Bureau, Forrester Research, Find/SVP, Frost & Sullivan

- Trade and business journals and newspapers, such as *Business Week*, *Advertising Age*, *Beverage Industry*, and *The Wall Street Journal*
- Trade associations, such as the American Society of Travel Agents and National Small Business United
- U.S. Bureau of Economic Analysis
- U.S. Bureau of the Census

TYPES OF SOURCES

You will find industry, market, and general business statistics collected and reported in:

- Almanacs
- Analysts' reports
- Annual reports
- Association reports
- Government censuses and surveys, e.g.,
  Annual Survey of Manufactures
  Bureau of Economic Analysis' Survey of Current Business
  Census Bureau's Survey of Retail Trade
  Census of Manufactures
  Current Industrial Reports
  Service Annual Survey
  Survey of Wholesale Trade
- Investment reports
- Market research reports
- Newspapers
- Press releases (at company Web sites, and from PR Newswire, Businesswire, Wall Street Transcript)
- Regional business papers and journals
- SEC filings (10-K, 10-Q)
- Trade and business journal articles, including industry overviews

BEST PLACES TO LOOK

Of special note for business, market and industry statistics are several libraries on the LEXIS-NEXIS service. Be sure to check out the following:

- LEXIS-NEXIS BUSFIN Library (business and finance)
- LEXIS-NEXIS MARKET Library (markets and industry)
- LEXIS-NEXIS Market Research Library (MKTRES) (includes about 25 separate files plus table of contents files)
- LEXIS-NEXIS INVEST Library (analyst reports on U.S. and non-U.S. companies, industries, regions, investing, securities, economics)

Following is a directory of resources that are excellent for business, industry, and market statistics. Note the central place of trade and business journals and market research reports throughout. The Census Bureau and other government agencies get in on the act too, even where specific industries are concerned. This directory is arranged with general business and industry sources (and their locations) first and is followed by general market research sources and locations; the directory concludes with sources and locations for specific industries.

General
ABI/INFORM
  BrainWave
  DIALOG (file 15)
  DataStar (file INFO)
  Orbit (file INFO)
  STN (file ABI/INFORM)

ASAPII Publications
  LEXIS-NEXIS (file ASAPII in BUSFIN and NEWS Libraries)

Asia-Pacific Business Journals
  DIALOG (file 748)

The Bloomberg Library
  LEXIS-NEXIS (multiple files in BLMBRG Library)

Brokerline Database (industry reports from brokerage houses)
  Profound

Business & Industry Database
  BrainWave
  DIALOG (file 9)
  DataStar (file BIDB)

Business Dateline (U.S. regional business conditions)
  DIALOG (file 635)
  LEXIS-NEXIS (file BUSDTL in BUSFIN, ENTERT, MARKET, NEWS, NSAMER, and PEOPLE Libraries

Business Rankings Annual
  http://galenet.gale.com

Business Week
  DIALOG (file 624)
  Dow Jones News/Retrieval
  Electric Library
  LEXIS-NEXIS (file BUSWK; multiple libraries)

Wall Street Journal Interactive Edition Publications Library
http://www.businessweek.com

COMLINE Daily News of Japan (computer, telecommunications, medical, biotechnology, chemical, auto, aerospace, and electronics industries; also industrial automation)
STN (file JPNEWS)

Current Industrial Reports
http://www.census.gov/pub/cir/www/index.html

FEDSTATS (federal government agency statistics locator)
http://www.fedstats.gov

The Financial Post (Canadian)
DIALOG (files 148, 635, 727, 771, 772, 799)
LEXIS-NEXIS (NEWS and WORLD Libraries)

Financial Times Full Text
DIALOG (file 622)

Financial World
DIALOG (files 15, 47, 148, 485, 771, 772)
Dow Jones News/Retrieval
Wall Street Journal Interactive Edition Publications Library

Forbes
DIALOG (files 12, 15, 16, 47, 88, 148, 211, 268, 484, 485, 675, 772, 799)
Dow Jones News/Retrieval
LEXIS-NEXIS (assorted libraries)
ProQuest Direct
Wall Street Journal Interactive Edition Publications Library
http://www.forbes.com

Fortune
DIALOG (files 15, 47, 88, 148, 485, 675, 746)
Dow Jones News/Retrieval
Electric Library
LEXIS-NEXIS (BUSFIN, CMPGN, EXEC, and LEGIS Libraries)
ProQuest Direct
Wall Street Journal Interactive Edition Publications Library
http://www.fortune.com

Gale Business Resources (covers the following sources: *Ward's Business Directory of U.S. Private and Public Companies; Business Rankings Annual; Market Share Reporter;* and more)
http://galenet.gale.com

German and European Market Statistics
DataStar (file FAKT)

IAC Business A.R.T.S.
    DIALOG (file 88)
    DataStar (file ACAD)

IAC Industry Express
    BrainWave
    DIALOG (file 12)
    IAC InSite
    IAC InSite Pro

IAC Marketing & Advertising Reference Service
    BrainWave
    DIALOG (file 570)
    DataStar (file PTMA)

IAC Newsletter Database
    BrainWave
    DIALOG (file 636)
    DataStar (file PTBN)

IAC PROMT (Predicasts Overview of Markets and Technology)
    BrainWave
    DIALOG (file 16)
    DataStar (files PTSP, PT91, PT86)
    LEXIS-NEXIS (file PROMT in the MARKET Library)
    Questel (file PROMT)
    STN (file PROMT)

IAC Trade & Industry Database
    BrainWave
    DIALOG (file 148)
    DataStar (files INDY and ID91)

Inc.
    Electric Library
    Dow Jones News/Retrieval
    LEXIS-NEXIS (file INC in BUSFIN, MARKET, NEWS, and PEOPLE Libraries)
    ProQuest Direct
    Wall Street Journal Interactive Edition Publications Library

Industry Scan (scans all databases for information on a specific industry)
    Profound

MEDIAWEEK (formerly Marketing and Media Decisions, deals with new products)
    DIALOG (file 148)
    LEXIS-NEXIS (MARKET and NEWS Libraries)
    ProQuest Direct

New Product News (new product introductions by category)
    LEXIS-NEXIS (file NPRODN in MARKET and NEWS Libraries)

New York Times
    DIALOG (files 471 and 472)
    Dow Jones News/Retrieval
    LEXIS-NEXIS (BUSFIN, AUST, and NEWS Libraries) (most complete backfile)
    Wall Street Journal Interactive Edition Publications Library

Newsline Database
    Profound

Occupational Hazards
    DIALOG (files 15, 148, 149)
    Dow Jones News/Retrieval
    LEXIS-NEXIS (BUSFIN and NEWS Libraries)
    Wall Street Journal Interactive Edition Publications Library

Standard & Poor's Daily News Reports (in addition to financial information, this file contains auto industry and airline industry statistics and business failures—use event names and event codes)
    DIALOG (file 132)

TableBase
    DataStar (file BTBL)
    DIALOG (file 93)
    http://www.tablebase.com

Time Publications (includes *Fortune, Money, Time,* and *Time International,* among others)
    DIALOG (file 746)
    http://www.pathfinder.com

Wall Street Journal Interactive Edition Publications Library (industry reviews and forecasts)
    Key Business & News, Marketing, and Media & Entertainment Publications
        categories; in Advanced Search, choose Major Business Publications and/or
        Major News Publications and/or one or more newspapers

Ziff Newsletters (market information newsletters)
    LEXIS-NEXIS file ZAM1 in MARKET and NEWS Libraries)

Market research
BCC Market Research (mostly U.S.; tables are contained within text (TX) field)
    BrainWave
    DIALOG (file 764)

Business Communications Company
LEXIS-NEXIS (files BCCRPT and BCCTOC in MKTRES Library)

Business Trends Analysis
LEXIS-NEXIS (files BTARPT and BTATOC in MKTRES Library)

Collector Trends Analysis (licensing markets and themes)
LEXIS-NEXIS (files CTARPT and CTATOC in MKTRES Library)

Corporate Intelligence on UK and European Retailing
DataStar (file CIRE)

Datamonitor Market Research (tables are contained within text (TX) field)
BrainWave
DIALOG (file 761)
DataStar (file DMON)
LEXIS-NEXIS (file DATRPT in MKTRES Library)

Euromonitor Market Reports (consumer goods and services; international, with emphasis on Europe)
DataStar (file MOMR)

Euromonitor Market Research
Brainwave
DIALOG (file 762)

Euromonitor Market Direction (consumer goods and services; selected European countries and the U.S.; search the full text)
DataStar (file MONI)
(Various forms of Euromonitor reports and journals are found in the LEXIS-NEXIS MKTRES Library.)

FIND/SVP Market Research Reports
BrainWave
DIALOG (file 766) (tables are contained within text (TX) field)
LEXIS-NEXIS (files FNDRPT, FINTOC, FNDALL, and FNDTOC in MKTRES Library)

Freedonia Market Research (Primarily U.S.; search the full text)
BrainWave
DIALOG (file 763)
DataStar (file TFGI).
LEXIS-NEXIS (files FRERPT and FRETOC in MKTRES Library)

Frost & Sullivan Market Intelligence
Brainwave
DIALOG (file 765)

Frost & Sullivan Market Research (international; search the full text)
DataStar (file FSMR)
LEXIS-NEXIS (files FNSRPT and FNSTOC in MKTRES Library)

ICC International Business Research (tables are contained within text (TX) field)
DIALOG (file 563)

ICC Key Note Market Analysis (UK and Western Europe)
DataStar (file ICKN)

ICC Stockbroker Research (heavy emphasis on UK; also Western Europe, Japan, Australia)
DataStar (file ICBR)
LEXIS-NEXIS (file ICCSBR in ASIAPC, COMPNY, EUROPE, MDEAFR, NSAMER, and WORLD Libraries)

IMSworld Drug Market—Countries
DIALOG (files 448 and 948)

IMS World Drug Markets (search the full text)
DataStar (file IPWE)

Industry Trends and Analysis (search the Tables and Figures (FN) field)
DIALOG (file 192)

International Market Research Information
DataStar (file IMRI)

Investext
DIALOG (file 545)
Dow Jones News/Retrieval
STN (file INVESTEX)

Investext Broker Reports (international; for tables, search the text field (TX) or the special feature field (SF=table))
DataStar (files INVE and IV92)
LEXIS-NEXIS (file INVTXT in COMPNY Library)

Investext Geographic Reports (analyzes region(s))
LEXIS-NEXIS (file GEO in COMPNY Library)

Investext Industry Reports (forecasts, current, and historical information for 52 industries)
LEXIS-NEXIS (file IND in COMPNY Library)

Jupiter Market Research (consumer online and interactive technologies)
DIALOG (file 769)

Market & Business Development (UK; mostly utilities, construction, engineering, healthcare)
DataStar (file MBDE)

Market Briefings
    Profound

Market Share Reporter
    LEXIS-NEXIS (file MKTSHR in MARKET Library)

Market Structure and Trends in Italy
    DataStar (file MAST)

MarketLine International Market Research Reports
    DataStar (file MKTL)
    LEXIS-NEXIS (files MKLRPT and MKLTOC in the MKTRES Library)

MSI Reports (primarily UK, but also Europe)
    DataStar (file MSIR)

Nielsen Market Track, SCANTRACK Market Planner
    LEXIS-NEXIS (file NILMTK in MKTRES Library)

Nielsen Market Statistics Canada (consumer product data)
    DIALOG (file 503)

Nielsen Marketing Research
    LEXIS-NEXIS (file NILSEN in MKTRES Library)

Onesource.com
    http://www.onesource.com

Packaged Facts
    LEXIS-NEXIS (files PKFRPT and PKFTOC in MKTRES Library)

Researchline Database
    Profound

Specialists in Business Information
    LEXIS-NEXIS (files SBIRPT and SBITOC in MKTRES Library)

.xls (results in spreadsheet format)
    http://www.xls.com

Specific Industries
This section of the industry, market, and business statistics source directory lists sources for specific industries, including:

- Advertising
- Appliance
- Chemical and plastics
- Construction
- Corporate giving
- Cosmetics

- Defense
- Electronics
- Ethnic- and women-owned (or run) businesses
- Food and beverage
- Furniture
- Garment
- Healthcare and pharmaceuticals
- Hospitality and travel
- Lumber, pulp, and paper
- Metals
- Packaging
- Retail

Advertising

Advertising Age (marketing data on national advertisers, expenditures in newspapers, top 100 U.S. markets)
    DIALOG (files 16, 570, and 799)
    Dow Jones News/Retrieval
    LEXIS-NEXIS (BIS file in BUSFIN Library)
    Wall Street Journal Interactive Edition Publications Library

ADWEEK
    LEXIS-NEXIS (file ADWEEK in ENTERT, MARKET, NEWS, and
        PEOPLE Libraries)

Adweek's Marketing Week
    DIALOG (files 16, 148, and 570)

Asian Mass Communication and Information Centre
    http://irdu.nus.sg/amic/

Brandweek
    DIALOG (files 16, 148, 570)
    LEXIS-NEXIS (file BRNDWK in MARKET, NEWS, and PEOPLE Libraries)

Cahners Research (readership of business journals, advertising effectiveness, Internet advertising)
    http://www.cahners.com/research/research.htm

Marketing and Advertising Reference Service (market size and market share, consumer products and service industries; advertising and agencies, media)
    LEXIS-NEXIS (file MARS in MARKET Library)

Reuters Media World
    http://www.mediaworld.com/

Appliance industry

Appliance Magazine
  DIALOG (file 148)
  Dow Jones News/Retrieval
  LEXIS-NEXIS (ASAPII file in NEWS Library)
  Wall Street Journal Interactive Edition Publications Library

Appliance Manufacturer
  DIALOG (file 148)
  Dow Jones News/Retrieval
  LEXIS-NEXIS (ABI file in BUSFIN Library)
  Wall Street Journal Interactive Edition Publications Library

Chemical and plastics industry

Chemical and Engineering News
  Dow Jones News/Retrieval
  LEXIS-NEXIS (PROMT file in MARKET Library and ABI file in BUSFIN
      Library, abstracts only)
  STN (file CEN)
  STN Easy (file CEN)
  Wall Street Journal Interactive Edition Publications Library

Chemical Business NewsBase
  BrainWave
  DIALOG (file 319)
  DataStar (file CBNB)
  STN (file CBNB)

Chemical Economics Handbook (chemical industry supply and demand)
  DIALOG (files 359 and 959)
  Orbit (files CEH80, CEH132, and CEHINDEX)

Chemical Engineering (equipment and machinery costs, wholesale chemical prices,
construction costs, and other business indicators)
  Dow Jones News/Retrieval
  LEXIS-NEXIS (file CHEMEN in MARKET, NEWS, and PEOPLE Libraries)
  Wall Street Journal Interactive Edition Publications Library

Chemical Industry Notes
  BrainWave
  DIALOG (file 19)
  DataStar (file CIND)
  Orbit (file CIN)
  STN (file CIN)
  STN Easy (file CIN)

Chemical Week
DIALOG (files 15, 16, 148)
Dow Jones News/Retrieval
Electric Library
LEXIS-NEXIS (file CHEMWK in MARKET, NEWS, and PEOPLE Libraries)
ProQuest Direct
Wall Street Journal Interactive Edition Publications Library

Chemplant Plus (chemical manufacturing and production plants)
DIALOG (file 318)

Chemstats (chemical industry—trade and production)
DIALOG (file 328)

European Chemical News (prices, market trends, Europe only)
DataStar (file CNEW)
Dow Jones News/Retrieval
Wall Street Journal Interactive Edition Publications Library

HCIN (Worldwide chemical industry, including prices, sales, and production)
STN (file HCIN)

ICIS Online (prices of chemicals and feedstocks worldwide, freight rates, refinery operations, trade data, market trends)
http://www.icislor.com

International Petrochemical Report (prices for petrochemicals; also shipping rates)
LEXIS-NEXIS (file PETCHM in ENERGY, MARKET, MDEAFR, NEWS, PEOPLE, and WORLD Libraries)

Modern Plastics
DIALOG (file 624)
Dow Jones News/Retrieval
LEXIS-NEXIS (file MODPLA in MARKET and NEWS Libraries)
Wall Street Journal Interactive Edition Publications Library

PLASNEWS Daily News (feedstock prices and other market-related statistics of the plastics industry)
STN (file PLASNEWS)

Plastics World
DIALOG (file 148)
Dow Jones News/Retrieval
LEXIS-NEXIS (ASAPII and PLSWLD files in NEWS Library)
Wall Street Journal Interactive Edition Publications Library

Specialty Chemicals Update Program (market share, profitability, market size, growth rates of specialty chemical industry segments, such as cosmetics)
Orbit (file SCUP)

Construction industry

Construction Equipment
    DIALOG (file 148)
    Dow Jones News/Retrieval
    LEXIS-NEXIS (file ASAPII in NEWS Library)
    Wall Street Journal Interactive Edition Publications Library

ENR (formerly Engineering News-Record) (construction industry statistics, including wages and prices)
    DIALOG file 624
    Dow Jones News/Retrieval
    LEXIS-NEXIS (file ENR in MARKET, NEWS, and PEOPLE Libraries)
    Wall Street Journal Interactive Edition Publications Library

Pit & Quarry
    Dow Jones News/Retrieval
    LEXIS-NEXIS (PROMT file in MARKET Library, abstracts only)
    Wall Street Journal Interactive Edition Publications Library

Wall Street Journal Interactive Edition Publications Library (Construction and Real Estate Publications category)

Corporate giving

Across the Board
    DIALOG (files 15 and 148)
    Dow Jones News/Retrieval
    LEXIS-NEXIS (ASAPII file in NEWS Library)
    ProQuest Direct
    Wall Street Journal Interactive Edition Publications Library

Business Month
    DIALOG (files 47 and 148)
    Dow Jones News/Retrieval
    Wall Street Journal Interactive Edition Publications Library

Cosmetics industry

American Druggist
    Wall Street Journal Interactive Edition Publications Library

Drug and Cosmetic Industry
    DIALOG (files 16 and 148)
    Dow Jones News/Retrieval
    LEXIS-NEXIS (BUSFIN, MARKET, and NEWS Libraries)
    Wall Street Journal Interactive Edition Publications Library

Defense industry

Aviation Week & Space Technology
  DIALOG (file 624)
  Dow Jones News/Retrieval
  LEXIS-NEXIS (MILTRY, NEWS, PUBCON, and TRANS Libraries)
  Wall Street Journal Interactive Edition Publications Library

Defense News (U.S. and international defense industry statistics)
  Dow Jones News/Retrieval
  LEXIS-NEXIS (file DEFNEW in MILTRY and NEWS Libraries)
  Wall Street Journal Interactive Edition Publications Library

DMS/FI Market Intelligence Reports (government spending, future requirements, civil and military aviation, weapons and military equipment)
  DIALOG (file 589)

Far Eastern Economic Review (Japanese defense contractors)
  DIALOG (file 15)
  Dow Jones News/Retrieval
  Wall Street Journal Interactive Edition Publications Library

Jane's Defence Publications (budgets, markets, corporate performance)
  LEXIS-NEXIS (file JANDEF in NEWS, MARKET, and WORLD Libraries)

Jane's Defence Weekly
  Dow Jones News/Retrieval
  Wall Street Journal Interactive Edition Publications Library

Jane's Defence & Aerospace News/Analysis (defense industries and budgets both U.S. and non-U.S.)
  BrainWave
  DIALOG (file 587)

Electronics industry

Consumer Electronics
  Dow Jones News/Retrieval
  LEXIS-NEXIS (file CNSMEL in MARKET and NEWS Libraries)
  Wall Street Journal Interactive Edition Publications Library

Electronic Business
  DIALOG (files 148 and 675)

Electronic Engineering Times
  DIALOG (file 16)
  Dow Jones News/Retrieval
  LEXIS-NEXIS (file EETMS in CMPCOM Library; PROMT file in MARKET Library)
  Wall Street Journal Interactive Edition Publications Library

Electronics
    DIALOG (files 47, 88, 148, 675)
    Dow Jones News/Retrieval
    LEXIS-NEXIS (file ELECTR in CMPCOM, MARKET, and NEWS Libraries)
    ProQuest Direct
    Wall Street Journal Interactive Edition Publications Library

Merchandising
    DIALOG (file 148)

Ethnic- and women-owned (or-run) businesses

Black Enterprise
    DIALOG (files 15, 47,88 148)
    Dow Jones News/Retrieval
    LEXIS-NEXIS (file BLKENT in BUSFIN, MARKET, and NEWS Libraries)
    ProQuest Direct
    Wall Street Journal Interactive Edition Publications Library

The Ethnic NewsWatch (ethnic and minority news sources)
    LEXIS-NEXIS (file ENW in ENTERT, MARKET, NEWS, NEXIS, NSAMER, and
    WORLD Libraries)

Hispanic Business
    Dow Jones News/Retrieval
    LEXIS-NEXIS (MARS file in MARKET Library, abstracts only)
    Wall Street Journal Interactive Edition Publications Library

Food and beverage industry

Beverage Industry
    DIALOG (files 16, 148, 570)
    Dow Jones News/Retrieval
    LEXIS-NEXIS (MARKET and NEWS Libraries)
    Wall Street Journal Interactive Edition Publications Library

Beverage World
    DIALOG (files 15 and 148)
    Dow Jones News/Retrieval
    LEXIS-NEXIS (file BEVWLD in MARKET, NEWS, and PEOPLE Libraries)
    ProQuest Direct
    Wall Street Journal Interactive Edition Publications Library

Foodline: International Food Market Data (advertising expenditures, market volumes
and shares, production and trade, sales and consumption)
    BrainWave
    DataStar (file FOIM)

DIALOG (file 54)
Dow Jones News/Retrieval
Wall Street Journal Interactive Edition Publications Library

Nation's Restaurant News
Dow Jones News/Retrieval
FirstSearch
IAC InSite
IAC InSite Pro
LEXIS-NEXIS (file NTNRES in MARKET and NEWS Libraries)
ProQuest Direct
Wall Street Journal Interactive Edition Publications Library

Quick Frozen Foods (transportation)
DIALOG (file 148)

Quick Frozen Foods International
Dow Jones News/Retrieval
Wall Street Journal Interactive Edition Publications Library

Restaurants & Institutions
DIALOG (file 148)
Dow Jones News/Retrieval
LEXIS-NEXIS (RESTIN file in NEWS Library)
ProQuest Direct
Wall Street Journal Interactive Edition Publications Library

Snack Food
DIALOG (files 16 and 570)
Dow Jones News/Retrieval
LEXIS-NEXIS (file PROMT in MARKET Library)
Wall Street Journal Interactive Edition Publications Library

Wall Street Journal Interactive Edition Publications Library (Food & Beverage Publications category)

Furniture industry
Furniture Today
Dow Jones News/Retrieval
LEXIS-NEXIS (file PROMT in MARKET Library, abstracts only)
Wall Street Journal Interactive Edition Publications Library

Garment industry
Apparel Industry Magazine
DIALOG (files 15, 148, 149, 485)
Dow Jones News/Retrieval

ProQuest Direct
Wall Street Journal Interactive Edition Publications Library

Footwear News
DIALOG (file 148)
Dow Jones News/Retrieval
LEXIS-NEXIS (MARKET and NEWS Libraries)
Wall Street Journal Interactive Edition Publications Library

Office of Textiles and Apparel, U.S. Department of Commerce (trade statistics)
http://otexa.ita.doc.gov

Women's Wear Daily (WWD)
DIALOG (file 9)
Dow Jones News/Retrieval
LEXIS-NEXIS (files ASAPII and WWEAR in NEWS Library)
Wall Street Journal Interactive Edition Publications Library

Healthcare and pharmaceuticals industries

Chemical & Engineering News
Dow Jones News/Retrieval
LEXIS-NEXIS (ABI file in BUSFIN Library; PROMT file in MARKET Library, abstracts only)
Wall Street Journal Interactive Edition Publications Library

Drug Topics
DIALOG (files 15 and 148)
Dow Jones News/Retrieval
LEXIS-NEXIS (BUSFIN and NEWS Libraries)
Wall Street Journal Interactive Edition Publications Library

F-D-C Reports
BrainWave
DataStar (file FDCR)
DIALOG (file 187)
Dow Jones News/Retrieval
Wall Street Journal Interactive Edition Publications Library

IAC Pharmabiomed Business Journals
DataStar (file PTPB)

Medical Marketing & Media
DIALOG (files 15 and 148)
Dow Jones News/Retrieval
ProQuest Direct
Wall Street Journal Interactive Edition Publications Library

Modern Healthcare
   DIALOG (file 16)
   Dow Jones News/Retrieval
   Wall Street Journal Interactive Edition Publications Library

Pharmaceutical and Healthcare Industry News Database (PHIND) (some market data is found in records designated by PLUS at the end of the name of the journal; these records represent items not included in the printed versions of the newsletters and are called collectively Online Plus)
   DIALOG (files 129 and 130)
   DataStar (files PHIN, PHIC, PHID)

PhRMA (Pharmaceutical Research Companies) (pharmaceutical industry facts and figures)
   http://www.phrma.org/

Hospitality and travel industries
International Trade Administration Tourism Industries (arrivals/departures, impact on state economies, receipts and payments, historical arrivals and departures, air travelers, outlook for travel to and from the U.S.)
   http://tinet.ita.doc.gov/free

Lodging Hospitality
   DIALOG (files 15 and 148)
   Dow Jones News/Retrieval
   Wall Street Journal Interactive Edition Publications Library

Lumber, pulp, and paper industries
Forest Industries
   DIALOG (files 15 and 148)

Pulp & Paper
   DIALOG (files 15 and 148)
   Dow Jones News/Retrieval
   LEXIS-NEXIS (PULP file in NEWS Library)
   ProQuest Direct
   Wall Street Journal Interactive Edition Publications Library

Metals industry
Iron Age
   DIALOG (file 148)

Metal Industry Indicators (U.S. Geological Survey)
   http://minerals.er.usgs.gov/minerals/pubs/mii/

Metals Week
  Dow Jones News/Retrieval
  LEXIS-NEXIS (file METLWK in MARKET and NEWS Libraries)
  Wall Street Journal Interactive Edition Publications Library

Mineral Resource Surveys Program (U.S. Geological Survey, includes commodity summaries, mineral industry surveys, domestic and international area reports)
  http://minerals.er.usgs.gov/minerals/

Mining Annual Review
  LEXIS-NEXIS (file MINREV in multiple libraries)

Mining Journal (includes fuels as well as metals)
  Dow Jones News/Retrieval
  LEXIS-NEXIS (file MINJNL in multiple libraries
  Wall Street Journal Interactive Edition Publications Library

Packaging industry
PIRA (Packaging, Paper, Printing and Publishing, and Nonwovens Abstracts)
(abstracts only; includes market statistics worldwide)
  BrainWave
  DIALOG (file 248)
  DataStar (file PIRA)

Retail industry
Chain Store Age—General Merchandise Edition
  DIALOG (files 148, 149, 553)
  Dow Jones News/Retrieval
  LEXIS-NEXIS (file CHNSTR in MARKET and NEWS Libraries)
  ProQuest Direct
  Wall Street Journal Interactive Edition Publications Library

Chain Store Age—General Merchandise Trends
  DIALOG (files 148, 149, 553)

Chain Store Age Executive with Shopping Center Age
  Dow Jones News/Retrieval
  IAC Business InSite
  IAC InSite Pro
  Wall Street Journal Interactive Edition Publications Library

Chain Store Age Supermarkets
  DIALOG (files 148, 149, 553)

Convenience Store News
  DIALOG (file 9)

Dow Jones News/Retrieval
Wall Street Journal Interactive Edition Publications Library

Discount Merchandiser
DIALOG (file 15)
Dow Jones News/Retrieval
ProQuest Direct
Wall Street Journal Interactive Edition Publications Library

Discount Store News
DIALOG (files 15, 16, 148, 570)
Dow Jones News/Retrieval
LEXIS-NEXIS (file DISSTR in MARKET and NEWS Libraries)
ProQuest Direct
Wall Street Journal Interactive Edition Publications Library

Drug Store News
DIALOG (files 16, 148, 570)
Dow Jones News/Retrieval
LEXIS-NEXIS (file DRGSTR in MARKET and NEWS Libraries)
Wall Street Journal Interactive Edition Publications Library

Drug Topics
DIALOG (files 15 and 148)
Dow Jones News/Retrieval
ProQuest Direct
Wall Street Journal Interactive Edition Publications Library

Progressive Grocer
DIALOG (files 15 and 148)
Dow Jones News/Retrieval
ProQuest Direct
Wall Street Journal Interactive Edition Publications Library

Retail and Wholesale Trade (U.S. Census Bureau)
http://www.census.gov/econ/www/retmenu.html

Stores
DIALOG (file 15)
Dow Jones News/Retrieval
Wall Street Journal Interactive Edition Publications Library

Supermarket Business
DIALOG (file 648)
Dow Jones News/Retrieval
Wall Street Journal Interactive Edition Publications Library

Supermarket News
> DIALOG (files 16 and 148)
> Dow Jones News/Retrieval
> LEXIS-NEXIS (MARKET and NEWS Libraries)
> Wall Street Journal Interactive Edition Publications Library

Wall Street Journal Interactive Edition Publications Library (Retail and Consumer Goods Publications category)

SPECIAL SEARCH TIPS

- When in doubt, consult Business Week, Forbes, and/or Fortune, the numbers hunter's desert island top three. Watch especially for lists and rankings, like "The Global 1000" (Business Week), "International 500" (both Forbes and Fortune), and the like.

- Use subject descriptors like "industry overview" or "trends" as search terms. IAC's InSite databases allow you to specify Industry Overview as an article type.

CASE STUDIES
Case Study 6-1: The Skates and Skateboard Industry

Purpose: This case study shows how to find market data for a class of product. The study illustrates the effectiveness of codes.

Question: What is the consumption and usage of skates and skateboards?

Likely sources: Trade journals; market research reports

Access points used: Full text; codes

Systems: ProQuest Direct; DataStar

Using ProQuest Direct (PQD)

I started by selecting the Search by Word option. Since PQD lets you search by class code, I used that to narrow the search to items with significant statistical content (class code 9140). In the search box, I typed cc(9140) and skates and got 45 hits.

Hit number 12 was: "The Wheel World" in *Sporting*

FIGURE 6-1
Using the Class Code
for Statistics on ProQuest Direct

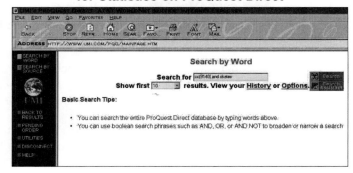

Goods Business, July 1996. It said that "...American Sports Data estimates that 22.5 million Americans donned a pair of in-line **skates** at least once last year, a 20 percent increase over the year before. Previous growth levels of 49 percent (1994) and 51 percent (1992) may never again be achieved, but the industry is hoping...."

There was also an article called "Fair Play" from *Discount Merchandiser*, July 1996. It met the search criteria, but the statistics were prices rather than market size. The search word `skates` appeared in the text.

FIGURE 6-2
Search Results for a Skates Market Question

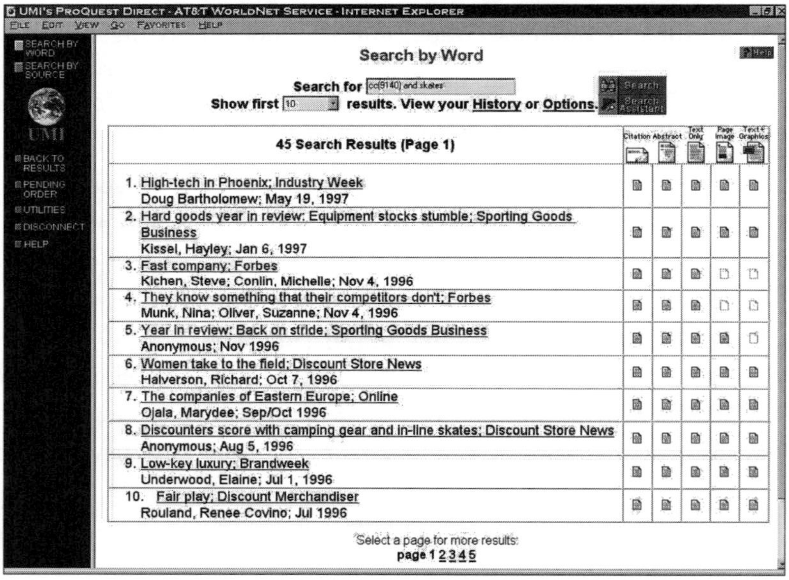

I could have combined the code for statistical data with an SIC code or official descriptor for skates to eliminate some false drops. However, by looking at the articles I found, I could see two things:

- The SIC codes that were used are very general, such as 8600 Manufacturing Industries and 8390 Retail Stores, includes Groceries. In the case of skates and skating, the codes may not have helped, and I might have accidentally excluded the right code for skates and missed relevant items.

- To deduce a proper term, I could find an article that was relatively on target and see how it was indexed. The best article already found used *inline skating* as an index term. *Skating* alone would have worked, too. I used *skates*, which appeared in the text.

When I redid the search as `cc=9140 and sub(skating)`, I got only 6 hits, but in fact, I picked up an excellent article from American Demographics titled "In-line Skaters Gain on Walkers," and I retained the article "The Wheel World" seen earlier.

Lessons learned:

√ Using codes can be a useful way of limiting results to material likely to be relevant; however it is not a guarantee. In the case of the second item examined, statistical material was present, but the statistics were about prices rather than numbers of skates sold.

√ You may have to do a fair amount of browsing to get to the items you want. Depending on the cost structure of the system, such browsing may or may not penalize you.

√ There's a fine line between starting a search too narrow and too broad; use the results from the first pass to guide you. (Only on a system that charges by the search will you be penalized by starting too narrow.)

Using the DataStar System and PROMT File

I used the excellent tools provided in PROMT: product and event codes. The codes I wanted were pc=394955 (skates & skateboards) and ec=65 (sales & consumption). I went into file PTSP (PROMT) and entered three search statements, with the following results:

PTSP 1_: p394955
   RESULT 279

PTSP 2_: e65
   RESULT 250454

PTSP 3_: 1 and 2
   RESULT 38

The first five hits, examined in free format, looked pretty good. In fact, I didn't have to do anything other than look through these items a little bit to find good, recent material, such as an article from *Plastics News*, September 16, 1996. This piece told me that "Plastics may be on the verge of making further inroads in the skateboard market, according to the executive director of the International Association of Skateboard Cos. IASC's 45 members had 1995 sales of about $400 million...."

I also found that, according to *SportStyle* in July 1996, "...roller hockey surpassed both ice hockey and inline skating as the fastest growing sport in 1995, with 43 percent growth to 3.2 million participants." The same issue told me that "The NSGA counted 23.9 million inline skaters in 1995, a 23 percent increase over the previous year, and participation numbers are likely to double before the energy level flattens."

I hit the jackpot with this search. A number of articles had good statistics. There was even a table from the May 1994 *SportStyle*, showing in-line skate sales for 1992-93 by company.

Lessons learned:

√ Using a database that specializes in market information can be a very effective strategy.

√ Codes are a useful way of searching for relevant statistical material; in some cases, they're so effective that using keywords isn't necessary.

√ Free browsing formats can help you scan results and save money by reducing searching.

Case Study 6-2: Book Returns

Purpose: This case study shows how to search the full text of major business magazines to find industry-specific information.

Question: What percentage of books was returned unsold from stores to publishers in 1996? (*Note:* "returns" is the official industry term to describe this activity.)

Likely sources: General business journals

Access points used: Full text; narrowing the search to a specific subset of journals

System: Dow Jones News/Retrieval, graphical user interface

I started by selecting Search News and Articles from the main menu.

I clicked the Select Source tab, then Remove All to clear the sources used in the previous search. Then I selected specific sources to use in this search.

FIGURE 6-3
Dow Jones News/Retrieval's Web Site

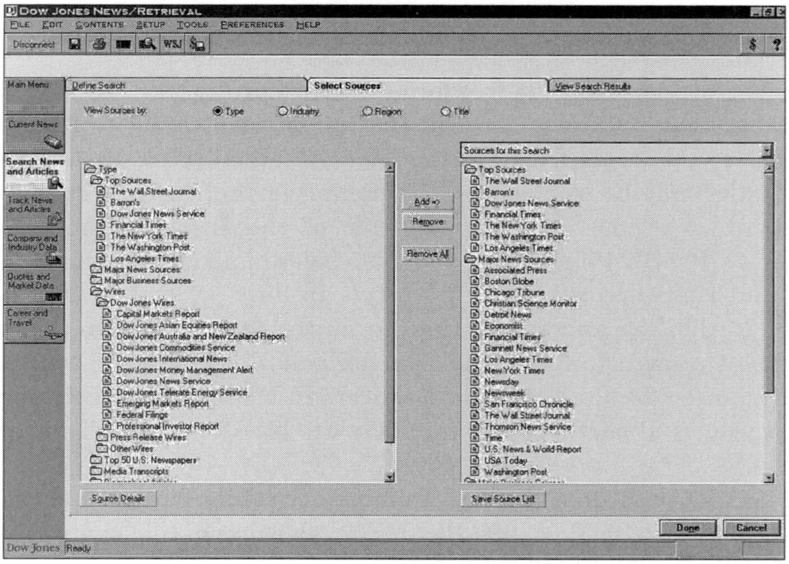

Select Remove All to Clear the Box on the Right, which Lists
Sources Used in the Previous Search.

I highlighted Major Business Sources and removed *Financial Times, Far Eastern Economic Review*, and *Economist* to focus on American sources. I was left with

Barron's, Business Week, Forbes, Fortune, Investors Business Daily, and *Wall Street Journal*. Save the sources.

FIGURE 6-4
Major Business Sources Category on
Dow Jones News/Retrieval's Graphical Interface

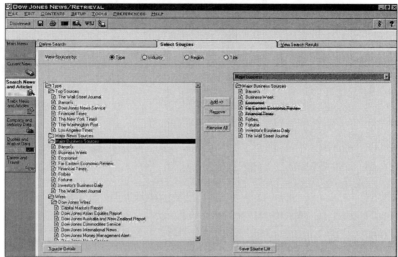

Highlight Major Business Sources, then remove Economist, Far Eastern Economic Review, and Financial Times to eliminate non-U.S. material

Now to choose dates and fields. I clicked the Define Search tab and, in the Look for Words, Keywords or Phrases box, I selected Full Article. I also specified that items should have appeared in the Current year (1997 at the time of this writing). I typed `publishing near3 (book or industry) and returns` and got six hits.

The third one was perfect. "Superstores, Megabooks—and Humongous Headaches...." from *Business Week*, April 14, 1997. It says, "Publishers say returns of new hardcover books last year ran between 35% and 50%, compared with 15% to 25% ten years ago."

FIGURE 6-5
Search Results for a Book Returns Question
on Dow Jones News/Retrieval

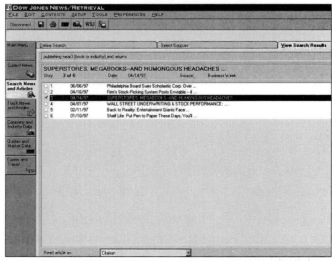

Our strategy yields six hits. To read the text, check the box to the left of the item, select a format, and click on the item.

Lessons learned:

√ Selecting a general category of sources and then considering the applicability of specific titles can shortcut an otherwise lengthy process of specifying sources title by title.

√ General business sources can be fertile grounds for industry-specific statistics, especially if the topic is hot. (Returns were such a major phenomenon in the publishing industry in 1996 that general journals ran articles on the subject).

Finding Financial and Economic Statistics

E conomic indicators are based on national income and product account figures; monthly surveys focusing on employment/unemployment and prices of consumer goods; surveys of purchasing agents and their views on inventories, orders, and prices; and similar data. Some of this data is "adjusted" to compensate for seasonal variations before the indicator is calculated. Indicators are supposed to be representative of an economy as a whole, and may be of three types: leading, coincident, or lagging. *Leading* indicators predict a turning point; *coincident* indicators indicate the current state of affairs, and *lagging* indicators show up after a trend is already occurring and verify that it is, in fact, doing so.

The U.S. Consumer Price Index (CPI) and similar indicators are calculated from survey data by the Bureau of Labor Statistics and other agencies. Did you know that the Consumer Price Index measures goods and services purchased by *wage earners and clerical workers only*? It is *not* a general cost of living index. Surprise!

Prices, interest rates, yields, and trading volumes derive from stock and commodity exchange bulletins, documents, and lists, as well as banks and other financial institutions.

Company financial statistics come from interim and annual reports, public filings, regulatory reports, proxy reports, prospectuses, credit reports, and news releases.

Other sources of financial and economic data include:

- Newspapers, wires, journals
- Interviews (phone, mail, in-person)
- Bank and analyst reports
- Banks and mortgage bankers
- Credit institutions
- Insurance companies
- Mutual fund managers
- Municipalities and states (property taxes and real estate statistics)
- U.S. Bureau of the Census

TYPES OF DATA

The following types of institutions, transactions, and phenomena contribute to financial and economic statistics:

Banking and currency

- Bank, credit union, savings & loan assets, liabilities, deposits
- Currencies
- Banker salaries and demographics
- ATM and other computer use in banking
- Electronic funds transfers
- Credit cards
- Loans
- Credit
- Precious metals

Company financials

- Balance sheets
- Income statements
- Cash flow
- Capacities
- Numbers of employees
- Earnings information
- Ownership

Economic indicators

- Interest rates and yields
- Discount rate
- Prime lending rate
- Employment and unemployment
- Consumer price index
- Producer price index
- Stock market indices
- Inflation
- Consumer spending
- Gross national and domestic products

Insurance

- Insurance premiums
- Insurance claims
- Demographics of claimants, insureds
- Insurance agent earnings and demographics

Investment

- Securities and investment vehicle prices
- Earnings per share, price/earnings ratios
- Dividends
- Technical stock market measures
- Stock market indexes
- Mutual funds
- Investment rate
- Stock broker earnings, demographics
- Management fees

Real estate

- Real estate values, sales
- Loan interest rates
- Real estate trusts
- Property taxes
- Real estate agents and brokers

Personal finance

- Family expenditures; ratio of house and other payments to total income
- Savings rate

Trade

- Imports
- Exports

KEY PRODUCERS

Database systems like LEXIS-NEXIS, Dow Jones News/Retrieval (and its Wall Street Journal Interactive Edition Publications Library), and DIALOG excel at providing financial and economic information. It is not possible to include every source here, so be sure to consult each vendor's documentation if you don't find what you need in this book.

U.S. Government agencies

The "White House Briefing Room"

Company Web sites

Newspapers, such as:
  Wall Street Journal
  USA Today
  New York Times
  Los Angeles Times
  Washington Post
  Financial Times (London)

The Business Dateline database, which collects articles from regional business newspapers and magazines

Major business magazines, especially Business Week, Forbes, Fortune, and the Economist

Financial-information companies, such as:
  Dun & Bradstreet
  Disclosure, Inc.
  IAC
  Moody's
  McGraw-Hill/Standard & Poor's
  Reuters

International Trade Administration

STAT-USA (formerly Office of Business Analysis, part of the Economics and Statistics Administration in the U.S. Department of Commerce)

U.S. Federal Reserve and its banks

U.S. Bureau of Labor Statistics

U.S. Department of Commerce, Bureau of Economic Analysis

Major brokerage houses

New York Stock Exchange

TYPES OF SOURCES

You can find financial and economic statistics reported in:

- Newspaper and magazine articles
- Securities and Exchange Commission filings (10K, 10Q, etc.)
- Annual reports
- Press releases
- Databases that include company financials

- Web sites
- Statistical compendia

BEST PLACES TO LOOK

Following is a directory of resources that are excellent for financial and economic statistics. This chapter is particularly heavy on sources provided by the traditional online vendors, who are still number one when it comes to aggregating financial information. However, government plays a central role in producing economic indicators and measures of world, national, and regional economies; despite decreasing funding for such activities, government agencies are still the best game in town for assessing the macroeconomic picture.

This directory first lists a few large financial and economic collections and specialized services provided by professional online services. The bulk of the directory is arranged with general financial and economic sources (and their locations) first, followed by categories of more specific sources and locations for banking, company financials (listed geographically), currencies, economic indicators, finance, insurance, investing/securities, labor, metals, real estate, and trade.

Collections and Specialized Services

DIALOG MONEYCENTER (most recent three days—economic indicators, foreign exchange rates, securities, prices, etc.)

LEXIS-NEXIS BNKNG Library (banking)

LEXIS-NEXIS BUSFIN Library (business and finance)

LEXIS-NEXIS COMPNY Library (companies, includes SEC filings)

LEXIS-NEXIS EUROPE Library

LEXIS-NEXIS INSURE Library (insurance)

LEXIS-NEXIS INVEST Library (analyst reports on U.S. and non-U.S. companies, industries, regions, investing, securities, economics)

LEXIS-NEXIS NAARS Library (Accounting Information) (annual reports)

LEXIS-NEXIS QUOTE Library (real-time and historical stock and bond quotes)

LEXIS-NEXIS REALTY Library (real estate)

TradStat World Trade Statistics Service (DataStar) (custom-formatted import and export data for 24 countries, plus extrapolated data for any country in the world—by product and trading partner)

General

Asia-Pacific Business Journals
  DIALOG (file 748)

ASAP Publications (these sources are drawn from IAC's full-text collection and focus on banking, business, and finance)
LEXIS-NEXIS (files INDPUB, REGPUB, INVPUB in BANKS group, and file ASAPII in BUSFIN Library)

ASI (American Statistics Index) (for identifying statistical publications produced by the U.S. federal government)
DIALOG (file 102)
Scheduled to be on LEXIS-NEXIS in 1998, including selected full text

Bridge World Markets News (commodity and financial markets, banking, securities)
Brainwave
DIALOG (file 609)

Business Monitor (business and financial information worldwide)
DataStar (file BMON)
Dow Jones News/Retrieval
Wall Street Journal Interactive Edition Publications Library

Business Week
DIALOG (file 624)
Dow Jones News/Retrieval
Electric Library
LEXIS-NEXIS (file BUSWK in multiple libraries)
Wall Street Journal Interactive Edition Publications Library
http://www.businessweek.com

COMLINE Daily News of Japan (Japanese financial markets and industries)
LEXIS-NEXIS (file COMLNE in multiple libraries)
STN file (JPNEWS)

EIU Country Forecasts (five-year forecasts and historical)
SilverPlatter

EIU Country Reports (current and historical trade and economic data, industrial trends, economic outlook)
LEXIS-NEXIS (file COURPT in multiple libraries)

FactSearch
FirstSearch

Federal Reserve Statistical Releases (foreign exchange rates, interest rates, money supply, consumer credit, industrial production, flow of funds)
http://www.bog.frb.fed.us/releases/

Fedstats (federal government agency statistics locator)
http://www.fedstats.gov

The Financial Data Finder (Department of Finance, Ohio State University; a metasite well worth your attention)
    http://www.cob.ohio-state.edu/dept/fin/osudata.htm

Financial Times Full Text
    DIALOG (file 622)

Forbes
    DIALOG (files 12, 15, 16, 47, 88, 148, 211, 268, 484, 485, 675, 772, 799)
    Dow Jones News/Retrieval
    ProQuest Direct
    Wall Street Journal Interactive Edition Publications Library
    http://www.forbes.com

Fortune
    DIALOG (files 15, 47, 88, 148, 485, 675, 746)
    Dow Jones News/Retrieval
    Electric Library
    LEXIS-NEXIS (BUSFIN, CMPGN, EXEC, and LEGIS Libraries)
    ProQuest Direct
    Wall Street Journal Interactive Edition Publications Library
    http://www.fortune.com

Information Please Almanac
    Cognito!
    Encarta Online Library

Investext Topic Reports (research on collections of companies, securities, investments, macroeconomic issues)
    LEXIS-NEXIS (file TOPIC in COMPNY Library)

The Journal of Commerce (international trade, banking and finance, insurance, maritime industries)
    BrainWave
    DIALOG (file 637)
    Dow Jones News/Retrieval
    Wall Street Journal Interactive Edition Publications Library

Lafferty Banking, Insurance and Professional Services Intelligence
    DataStar (file LAFF)

A Matter of Fact
    FirstSearch (file FactSearch)
    SilverPlatter
    (plus others; see p. 4)

Money
    Dow Jones News/Retrieval
    LEXIS-NEXIS (file MONEY in BANKS, BUSFIN, MARKET, and NEWS Libraries)

ProQuest Direct
Wall Street Journal Interactive Edition Publications Library

Reuters
DIALOG (file 611)

Time Publications (includes *Fortune*, *Money*, *Time*, and *Time International*, among others)
DIALOG (file 746)
http://www.pathfinder.com

Wall Street Journal Interactive Edition Publications Library
Key Business & General News, Economics, and Financial Services Publications
categories; in Advanced Search, choose Major Business Publications and/or
Major News Publications and/or one or more newspapers

World Almanac
Electric Library
FirstSearch

Banking

American Banker
DIALOG (files 148, 625, 771, 772, and 799)
Dow Jones News/Retrieval
LEXIS-NEXIS (file AMBANK in multiple libraries)
Wall Street Journal Interactive Edition Publications Library

ASAPII Publications
LEXIS-NEXIS (file ASAPII in NEWS Library)

The Banker
DIALOG (file 553)
Dow Jones News/Retrieval
ProQuest Direct
Wall Street Journal Interactive Edition Publications Library

Banking Information Source
DIALOG (file 268)

Federal Deposit Insurance Corporation
http://www.fdic.gov/

Federal Reserve Bank of Cleveland (includes Beige Book of current economic conditions)
ProQuest Direct
http://www.clev.frb.org/research/index.htm

Federal Reserve Bulletin
DIALOG (files 88 and 148)

Dow Jones News/Retrieval
ProQuest Direct
Wall Street Journal Interactive Edition Publications Library

Thomson Bank Directory (financial information for U.S. banks)
LEXIS-NEXIS (file TBUS in COMPNY, BUSREF, and MARKET Libraries)

Thomson Savings Directory (financial information for U.S. savings and loans)
LEXIS-NEXIS (file TSVGS in BUSREF, COMPNY, and MARKET Libraries)

U.S. Banker (for stocks of banks and other financial institutions, covers market prices, price/earnings ratios, dividend rates, market to book value, comparison of U.S. Banker Index with Dow Jones Industrial Average)
Dow Jones News/Retrieval
LEXIS-NEXIS (file USBANK in BANKS, MARKET, and NEWS Libraries)
Wall Street Journal Interactive Edition Publications Library

Ziff Newsletters (banking newsletters)
LEXIS-NEXIS (file ZBN1 in BANKING, BANKS, MARKET, and NEWS Libraries)

Company financials—U.S.

American Business Directory (U.S. sales, by location and total; employees, by location and total; number of locations)
DIALOG (file 531)

Brokerline Database
Profound

CFARbase (banks, financial service companies, industrials, insurance)
LEXIS-NEXIS (multiple CFAR files in multiple libraries)

Company Briefings
Profound

Company Scan (scans all Profound databases for news, financials, broker and market analysis)
Profound

Companyline Database
Profound

Corporate Affiliations (sales, number of employees, net worth, assets, liabilities)
DIALOG (file 513)

D&B Dun's Financial Records Plus (U.S. assets, liabilities, sales, ratios, some comparison with rest of industry)
DIALOG (file 519)
Dow Jones News/Retrieval

D&B Dun's Market Identifiers (U.S. sales and employees—current and historic, sales growth, square footage, number of accounts, net worth)
 DIALOG (file 516)
 Dow Jones News/Retrieval

D&B Eastern Europe Marketing File (employees, sales, profit—reliability varies)
 DataStar (file DNEE)

D&B U.S. Dun's Market Identifiers
 DataStar (file DBUS)

DISCLOSURE Database (U.S. five-year summary, income statement, balance sheet, stock information, ownership)
 DataStar (file DSCL)
 DIALOG (file 100)
 Dow Jones News/Retrieval

DISCLOSURE/Spectrum Ownership (U.S. institutional ownership, ownership by insiders, ownership by 5% owners)
 DIALOG (file 540)

Dow Jones News/Retrieval (select Company and Industry Data, search by individual company, create list of companies that fit criteria, compare companies)

Dun & Bradstreet
 http://www.dbisna.com/dbis/dbishome.htm

Hoover's Online
 http://www.hoovers.com

IAC Company Intelligence (revenue, sales turnover, profit, dividends, earnings, share capital, shareholder funds, number of employees)
 DataStar (file INCO)
 DIALOG (file 479)

Internet Non-Profit Center
 http://www.nonprofits.org/

Investext Company Reports (publicly traded corporations)
 LEXIS-NEXIS (file CO in COMPNY Library)

Media General Plus (U.S. product price statistics, stock market value and volume, income statement, balance sheet, ratios—including comparison to industry)
 BrainWave
 DIALOG (file 546)
 Dow Jones News/Retrieval

Moody's
 http://www.moodys.com

Moody's Corporate News—U.S. (U.S. sales and earnings; financial data is in tables)
DIALOG (file 556)

Moody's Corporate Profiles (U.S. dividends, earnings, balance sheet, capitalization, historical stock statistics and ratios)
DIALOG (file 555)

Onesource.com
http://www.onesource.com

PR Newswire
BrainWave
DIALOG (file 613)
LEXIS-NEXIS (file PRNEWS in multiple libraries)
ProQuest Direct
http://www.prnewswire.com

SEC Online (companies on the New York and American Stock Exchanges plus some NASDAQ companies—annual reports, 10-Ks, 10-Qs, 20-Fs)
BrainWave
DIALOG (files 541-544)
Dow Jones News/Retrieval

Standard & Poor's Corporate Descriptions plus News (U.S. extensive financials, including capitalization)
BrainWave
DIALOG (file 133)
LEXIS-NEXIS (file SPDESC in COMPNY, ENTERT, and INSURE Libraries)

Standard & Poor's Daily News Reports (in addition to financial information, this file contains auto industry and airline industry statistics and business failures—use event names and event codes)
DIALOG (file 132)

TRW Business Credit Profiles (U.S.) (payment histories, sales ranges, tax and legal history, financials)
DIALOG (file 547)

xls (results in spreadsheet format)
http://www.xls.com

Zacks Corporate Earnings Estimates
Dow Jones News/Retrieval

Zacks Investment Research (company earnings forecasts)
LEXIS-NEXIS (file EARN in COMPNY Library)

Company financials—world (non-U.S.)

Asia-Pacific

D&B Asia-Pacific Dun's Market Identifiers (sales, profits, employees)
DataStar (file DNAP)

FBR Asian Company Profiles (revenue, income, assets, employees)
DIALOG (file 505)

Teikoku Databank: Japanese Companies (extensive financials)
BrainWave
DataStar (file TOKU)
DIALOG (file 502)

Teikoku Japanese Companies: Full Financial Data
DataStar (file TOFF)

Europe

D&B European Dun's Market Identifiers (sales in local and U.S. currencies, number of employees)
DIALOG (file 521)

D&B European Financial Records (balance sheet, historical financials in local currency and U.S. dollars, profit and loss, key ratios)
DataStar (file DEFR)
DIALOG (file 523)

D & B European Marketing File (number of employees, sales, profit)
DataStar (files DBZZ, DBOS, DBBL, DBDK, DGFR, DGWG, DGHE, DBEI, DBIT, DBLU, DBNL, DBPO, DBSP, DBCH, DBGB)

Dun's Europa (63,000 companies in Europe, Finland, and Turkey, including capital and number of employees)
Questel (file EUROPA)

Kompass Western Europe (company financials in 60-80% of the records)
BrainWave
DIALOG (file 590)

Europe—Austria

Creditreform: Austrian Companies (sales, capital, employees)
DataStar (file AVVC)

Kreditschutzverband: Austrian Companies (varies)
DataStar (file KSVA)

Europe—Benelux

Hoppenstedt: Benelux (for some companies only, sales, capital, number of employees)
DataStar (file BNLU)
Questel (file BENELUX)

Infotrade: Belgian Company Financial Data (current and historical financial data)
DataStar (file BECO)

Europe—Denmark

Danish Companies: Full Financial Data
DataStar (files DKFF and DKEF)

Europe—Eastern

The Official Register of Czech and Slovak Organisations (employees; in some cases, capital)
DataStar (file CZCO)

Europe—France

Firmimport/Firmexport: French Importers & Exporters (sales, value of imports and exports, employees)
DataStar (file FRIE)

French Companies: Full Financial Data (balance sheet, income statement, assets and liabilities, ratios)
DataStar (files FRFF and FREF)

SCRL French Company Financial Profiles. In French on Questel-Orbit. (balance sheets, profit and loss)
DataStar (file SCEF is in English)
Questel (file BILAN)

Europe—Germany

BDI German Industry (sales, capital, employees)
DataStar (file BDIE)

Creditreform: German Companies (sales, capital, employees)
DataStar (file DVVC)

German Business and Industry Directory (employees, stock)
DataStar (file ABCE)

German Buyers Guide (sales, employees)
DataStar (file E1X1)

German Company Financial Data (balance sheets, profit and loss, ratios)
  DataStar (files FINN and COIN)

Hoppenstedt Directory of German Companies (sales, employees, capital stock, share-holders' equity)
  BrainWave
  DataStar (file HOPE)
  DIALOG (file 529)
  Questel (file HOPGER)

Wer Gehoert zu Wem: Who Belongs to Whom (capital, ownership)
  DataStar (file WGZW)

ZVEI Electro/Electronics Buyers' Guide (Germany) (sales, capital, employees)
  DataStar (file ZVEE)

Europe—Italy

Italian Company Profiles: Financial (sales, profits, assets, liabilities, ratios, employees)
  DataStar (file ITFF)

Sistema Ditte Operanti con l'Estero/Italian Trading Companies (employees, sales, exports)
  DataStar (files SDOE and ITIE)

Europe—Switzerland

D&B Switzerland Full Financial Records (balance sheet, profit and loss, some historical information)
  DataStar (file SWFF)

D&B Switzerland Marketing File (sales, employees, some historical)
  DataStar (file SWCO)

Europe—UK

ICC British Company Annual Reports (profit and loss, balance sheet)
  DataStar (file ICAC)
  DIALOG (file 564)

ICC British Company Directory (capital)
  BrainWave
  DataStar (file ICDI)
  DIALOG (file 561)

ICC British Company Financial Datasheets (extensive financial data)
  BrainWave
  DataStar (file ICFF)
  DIALOG (file 562)

ICC Full-Text Quoted Annual Reports (British companies plus the top 500 European companies)
    LEXIS-NEXIS (file ICCCO in multiple libraries)

Infocheck British Company Financial Datasheets (profit and loss, balance sheet, ratios, comparison with rest of industry, share information)
    DataStar (file CHCK)

Irish Companies and Businesses (employees, profit and loss, balance sheet, ratios, capital, numbers of mortgages)
    DataStar (file IRFF)

JordanWatch: British Companies (ratios, basic financials including historical)
    DataStar (file JORD)

Key British Enterprises Financial Performance
    DataStar (file DKBE)

Kompass UK (assets, liabilities, shareholder funds, sales, profit, capital employed, return on turnover, return on capital)
    BrainWave
    DIALOG (file 591)

Middle East
D&B Israel Marketing File (sales, profit, employees)
    DataStar (file DNIS)

North America (non-U.S.)
Canadian Business Directory (employees, sales)
    DIALOG (file 533)

CanCorp Canadian Financials (balance sheet, income statement, financial ratios, cash flow, share information)
    DataStar (file CNCO)
    DIALOG (file 491)
    LEXIS-NEXIS (file CNCORP in COMPNY, NSAMER, and WORLD Libraries)

D&B Canadian Dun's Market Identifiers (sales in Canadian and U.S. dollars)
    DataStar (file DNCA)
    DIALOG (file 520)

World/Multiregional
Brokerline Database
    Profound
CFARbase (banks, financial service companies, industrials, insurance)
    LEXIS-NEXIS (multiple CFAR files in multiple libraries)

Company Briefings
  Profound

Company Scan (scans all Profound databases for news, financials, broker and market analysis)
  Profound

Companyline Database
  Profound

D&B International Dun's Market Identifiers (number of employees, sales in local currency and U.S. dollars)
  DIALOG (file 518)

Directory of Corporate Affiliations (sales, number of employees, net worth, assets, liabilities)
  DIALOG (file 513)

Extel Cards Database
  LEXIS-NEXIS (file EXTEL in ASIAPC, COMPNY, EUROPE, MDEAFR, NSAMER, and WORLD Libraries)

Extel International Cards (balance sheets for U.K. and international companies)
  DataStar (file EXTL)

Extel International Financial Cards (dividends, share capital data, borrowings, profit and loss, key ratios, cash flow, balance sheet, historical stock prices, detailed assets and capital commitments)
  BrainWave
  DIALOG (file 500)

IAC Company Intelligence (revenue, sales turnover, profit, dividends, earnings, share capital, shareholder funds, number of employees)
  DataStar (file INCO)
  DIALOG (file 479)

ICC International Business Research (company financials, competitive analysis, market and industry information)
  DIALOG (file 563)

ICC Stockbroker Research (heavy emphasis on UK; also Western Europe, Japan, Australia; share price histories, financial summaries, forecasts)
  DataStar (file ICBR)

IMS World Drug Market — Companies (sales and sales ratios)
  DataStar (file IPDI)
  DIALOG (file 443 and 943)

IMS World Pharmaceutical Company Profiles (financial review and forecasts in text form)
  DataStar (file IPCP)
  DIALOG (files 449 and 984)

Moody's Corporate News—International (financial data is in tables)
  DIALOG (file 557)

Worldscope (financial profiles, stock performance data, ratios for companies around the world)
  LEXIS-NEXIS (file WLDSCP in multiple libraries)

WorldWide Companies (balance sheets, statements of income and ratios of world's largest companies)
  LEXIS-NEXIS (file WWC in ASIAPC, COMPNY, EUROPE, MDEAFR, NSAMER, and WORLD Libraries)

Currencies
The Bloomberg Library
  LEXIS-NEXIS (multiple files in BLMBRG Library)

Foreign Exchange
  Profound

O & A 164 Currencies Converter (1990 to present)
  http://www.olsen.ch/cgi-bin/exmenu

Economic indicators
The Beige Book
  http://www.bog.frb.fed.us/fomc/bb/current/

BNA Daily Report for Executives
  LEXIS-NEXIS (file DREXEC in EXEC, LEGIS, LEGNEW, and NEWS Libraries)

EconBase: Time Series and Forecasts (economics, demographics, business conditions, etc.—U.S. and international)
  DIALOG (file 565)

Economic Indicators
  Dow Jones News/Retrieval
  IAC InSite (Consumer InSite)
  IAC InSite Pro
  Profound
  ProQuest Direct
  Wall Street Journal Interactive Edition Publications Library

Evans Economics Electronic News Service
  LEXIS-NEXIS (file ENS in BANKING Library)

Federal Reserve Bank of Cleveland
ProQuest Direct
http://www.clev.frb.org/research/index.htm

Industry Week (economic indicators)
LEXIS-NEXIS (file INDWK in BUSFIN, MARKET, NEWS, and WORLD Libraries)
ProQuest Direct
http://www.industryweek.com

Quest Economics Database (economic, money market, financial indicators from countries around the world)
DataStar (file QUES)
LEXIS-NEXIS (file QUESTD in multiples libraries)

Survey of Current Business (national, international transactions, and state data, including foreign investment in the U.S.)
Dow Jones News/Retrieval
ProQuest Direct
Wall Street Journal Interactive Edition Publications Library
http://www.bea.doc.gov/bea/beadata.html

.xls (results in spreadsheet format)
http://www.xls.com

Finance
The Bloomberg Library
LEXIS-NEXIS (multiple files in BLMBRG Library)

EIU: The Economist Intelligence Unit (international trade, investment, finance, economics, equity markets, taxes)
DIALOG (file 627)

Knight-Ridder/Tribune Business News (financial and credit markets, commodities, foreign exchange, stock exchange, financial instruments)
DIALOG (file 609)

Reuter Financial Service (national and international finance, business, trade, securities markets)
LEXIS-NEXIS (file REUFIN in multiple libraries)

Insurance
Best's Life-Health
DIALOG (files 15 and 148)
Dow Jones News/Retrieval
ProQuest Direct
Wall Street Journal Interactive Edition Publications Library

Best's Property-Casualty
  DIALOG (file 148)
  Dow Jones News/Retrieval
  ProQuest Direct
  Wall Street Journal Interactive Edition Publications Library

Business Insurance (includes losses from fires, explosions, natural disasters, and litigation)
  DIALOG (files 16 and 799)
  Dow Jones News/Retrieval
  LEXIS-NEXIS (file BUSINS in BUSFIN, INSURE, MARKET, NEWS, and
      PEOPLE Libraries)
  Wall Street Journal Interactive Edition Publications Library

Insurance Information Institute's Abstracts (abstracts only)
  LEXIS-NEXIS (file IIABS in INSURE Library)

Insurance Information Institute Reports
  LEXIS-NEXIS (file IIRPTS in INSURE Library)

Insurance Information Institute's Abstracts (includes rankings)
  LEXIS-NEXIS (file IIABS in COMPNY, INSURE, and NEWS Libraries)

Insurance Periodicals Index
  DIALOG (file 169)
  LEXIS-NEXIS (file IPI in INSURE Library)

National Underwriter Life & Health/Financial Services
  Dow Jones News/Retrieval
  LEXIS-NEXIS (file NULIFE in INSURE, MARKET, and NEWS Libraries)
  ProQuest Direct
  Wall Street Journal Interactive Edition Publications Library

National Underwriter Property & Casualty
  Dow Jones News/Retrieval
  LEXIS-NEXIS (file NUPROP in INSURE, MARKET, and NEWS Libraries)
  ProQuest Direct
  Wall Street Journal Interactive Edition Publications Library

Onesource.com
  http://www.onesource.com

Predicasts Insurance Information
  LEXIS-NEXIS (file PINS in INSURE Library)

Reuters Insurance Briefings
  http://www.reuters.com/

World Corporate Insurance Report
  Dow Jones News/Retrieval

LEXIS-NEXIS (file WCINSR in INSURE, MARKET, NEWS, UK, and
      WORLD Libraries)
Wall Street Journal Interactive Edition Publications Library

World Policy Guide
   Dow Jones News/Retrieval
   LEXIS-NEXIS (file WPG in INSURE, MARKET, NEWS, UK, and
      WORLD Libraries)
   Wall Street Journal Interactive Edition Publications Library

Ziff Newsletters
   LEXIS-NEXIS insurance information newsletters (file ZIS1 in INSURE,
      MARKET, and NEWS Libraries)

Investing/securities
American Banker
   DIALOG (files 9 and 12)
   Dow Jones News/Retrieval
   Wall Street Journal Interactive Edition Publications Library

American Banker/Bond Buyer Newsletters
   LEXIS-NEXIS (file ABBB in multiple libraries)

American Stock Exchange (Information Exchange and Market Summary)
   http://www.amex.com

Asiamoney
   DIALOG (file 15)
   LEXIS-NEXIS (ABI file in BUSFIN Library)
   ProQuest Direct

The Bloomberg Library
   LEXIS-NEXIS (multiple files in BLMBRG Library)

Bond Buyer Full Text
   DIALOG (file 626)
   Dow Jones News/Retrieval
   LEXIS-NEXIS (file BNDBYR in BANKS, BUSFIN, MARKET, and
      NEWS Libraries)
   Wall Street Journal Interactive Edition Publications Library

Corporate Ownership Watch (insider transactions of individuals and companies)
   Dow Jones News/Retrieval

Dow Jones News/Retrieval Quotes and Market Data (current and historical; stocks,
mutual funds, treasuries, options, bonds, commodities, futures; historical Dow Jones
averages; mutual fund performance reports; technical analysis reports)
   Dow Jones News/Retrieval

EDGAR (Securities and Exchange Commission Filings)
http://www.sec.gov/edgarhp.htm

Insider Trading Monitor
DIALOG (file 549)

Institutional Investor
DIALOG (files 15, 148, 485, 771, 772, 799)
Dow Jones News/Retrieval
LEXIS-NEXIS (file INVEST in BANKS, BUSFIN, COMPNY, MARKET, NEWS,
PEOPLE, and REALTY Libraries)
Wall Street Journal Interactive Edition Publications Library

Investor's Business Daily
Dow Jones News/Retrieval
LEXIS-NEXIS (file INVDLY in BANKS, BUSFIN, COMPNY, MARKET, and
NEWS Libraries)
Wall Street Journal Interactive Edition Publications Library

Moody's (defaults, credit, securities ratings)
http://www.moodys.com

New York Stock Exchange Historical Statistics Archive
http://www.nyse.com/public/market/2c/2cix.htm

Pensions and Investments
DIALOG (file 16)
Dow Jones News/Retrieval
LEXIS-NEXIS (BIS file in BUSFIN Library)
Wall Street Journal Interactive Edition Publications Library

Quotes (Historical) (historical quotes for bonds, stocks, indexes, metals prices, currency
exchange rates—U.S. and Canada)
LEXIS-NEXIS (files PRI and DIV in QUOTE Library)

Quotes (Real Time) (market indicators, prices of mutual funds, U.S. and Canadian
equities)
LEXIS-NEXIS (file RT in QUOTE Library)

Standard & Poor's Industry Surveys
Profound

Standard & Poor's Rating Services (company bond ratings)
http://www.ratings.standardpoor.com

Stock Quotes
Profound

Trusts and Estates
DIALOG (files 15, 148, 485)
Dow Jones News/Retrieval
Wall Street Journal Interactive Edition Publications Library

U.S News & World Report (mutual funds)
DIALOG (files 47, 88, 148)
Dow Jones News/Retrieval
Electric Library
LEXIS-NEXIS (file USNEWS in multiple libraries)
ProQuest Direct
Wall Street Journal Interactive Edition Publications Library

Vickers Securities Report (insider and institutional holdings data)
LEXIS-NEXIS (file VICSEC in COMPNY Library)

.xls (risk analysis statistics on globally-traded securities; top 20 shareholders or all institutional shareholders; both U.S. and non-U.S. companies; results in spread-sheet format)
http://www.xls.com

Labor

BNA Daily Labor Report
LEXIS-NEXIS (file DLABRT in EXEC, LEGIS, and NEWS Libraries)

BNA Pensions and Benefits Daily
LEXIS-NEXIS (file BNAPEN in EXEC, INSURE, LEGIS, MARKET, and NEWS Libraries)

Bureau of Labor Statistics
http://stats.bls.gov/

Employee Benefits Infosource (includes statistics by industry, region, and employer size, as well as in general)
BrainWave
DIALOG (file 22)

International Labour Organization (databases under construction)
http://www.ilo.org/public/english/190bibl/index.htm

Monthly Labor Review (also consumer prices, manufacturing, producer prices, international)
Dow Jones News/Retrieval
Electric Library
ProQuest Direct
Wall Street Journal Interactive Edition Publications Library

Occupational Outlook Handbook
   http://stats.bls.gov/ocohome.htm

Metals
Gold, Silver, & Platinum Prices
   http://www.bullion.org.za/prices.htm

Info-Mine
   http://www.info-mine.com/investment/

Metal Quotes
   Profound

Spot Gold and Silver Prices
   http://www.kitco.com/gold.live.html

Real Estate
Census of Finance, Insurance, and Real Estate
   http://www.census.gov/econ/www/se0100.html

Service Annual Survey
   http://www.census.gov/svsd/www/sas.html

Statistical Abstract of the United States—Construction and Housing
   http://www.census.gov/stat_abstract

Trade
BNA International Trade Daily
   LEXIS-NEXIS (file BNAITD in BUSFIN, NEWS, NSAMER, and WORLD Libraries)

National Trade Data Bank
   http://www.stat-usa.gov/BEN/databases.html
   http://www.tradeport.org

PIERS Exports (U.S. Ports) (cargo weights, numbers of units of cargo, by product)
   BrainWave
   DIALOG (file 571)

PIERS Imports (U.S. Ports) (cargo weights, numbers of units of cargo, by product)
   BrainWave
   DIALOG (file 573)

U.S. Commerce National Trade Data Bank Market Reports
   LEXIS-NEXIS (file MKTRPT in ITRADE Library)

U.S. Global Trade Outlook (U.S. Department of Commerce)
   LEXIS-NEXIS (file USGTO in BUSREF, MARKET, and NEWS Libraries)
   http://www.tradeport.org/ts/ntdb/usgto/

CASE STUDIES

Case Study 7-1: Non-U.S. Company Financials

Purpose: This case study shows how to use numeric fields to find companies meeting particular criteria. It also illustrates how you can use system features to generate your own statistics based on database content.

Question: Identify Japanese companies with sales of more than $50 billion.

Likely sources: Teikoku Databank: Japanese Companies

Access points used: Fields

System used: DIALOG (file 502)

In this database, the sales field (in dollars) is SA. There's also a sales in yen field: SL, which is designated on the Bluesheet as SL=Total Sales (Y). Both fields are numeric (see Indexing column on the DIALOG Bluesheet).

I entered `s sa>50B`. This statement says find all companies for which sales exceed $50 billion U.S.

There were 48 companies with sales greater than $50 billion. I could have used the abbreviation B to stand for billion. I could also have entered the term as $50,000,000,000; as 50,000,000,000; or as 50000000000. In a numeric field, I would *not* want to use the word billion, but I might if I were searching text.

At this point, I could have printed the data in one of several formats, even mailing labels. However, I wanted to see the distribution of these huge companies (how they rank in terms of sales)—and I was curious to see who's number one. To see the distribution, I used the RANK command to generate some statistics of my own. I typed `rank s1 sa` to sort and tally the 48 records according to sales volume, with the *most common*—not the largest—sales volumes appearing first in the list. The result is in Figure 7-1.

Notice the clustering. In this distribution, there are three modes (values around which the data tends to group):

- Mode 1: 58, 85, 120, and 300 billion
- Mode 2: 140 and 360 billion
- Mode 3: 130 and 210 billion

To find out which company is number one, I needed to sort the data. The statement `sort s1/all/sa,d` says to sort the results in set 1 by sales in descending order. The result of the sort appears as:

```
S2  48  Sort  S1/ALL/SA,D
```

I typed a brief format of the first one to see what it was and found THE SANWA BANK LTD.

In order to see what Sanwa Bank's sales actually were, I used a command to display just the sales field (see Figure 7-2).

FIGURE 7-1
DIALOG RANK Results

```
RANK: S1/1-48 Field: SA= File(s): 502
(Rank fields found in 48 records--34 unique terms) Page 1 of 5
```

RANK	No.Items	Term
1	4	130,000,000,000
2	4	210,000,000,000
3	3	140,000,000,000
4	3	360,000,000,000
5	2	58,000,000,000
6	2	85,000,000,000
7	2	120,000,000,000
8	2	300,000,000,000
9	1	51,000,000,000
10	1	52,000,000,000
11	1	53,000,000,000
12	1	54,000,000,000
13	1	55,000,000,000
14	1	56,000,000,000
15	1	59,000,000,000
16	1	60,000,000,000
17	1	61,000,000,000
18	1	66,000,000,000
19	1	73,000,000,000
20	1	74,000,000,000
21	1	75,000,000,000
22	1	78,000,000,000
23	1	82,000,000,000
24	1	91,000,000,000
25	1	110,000,000,000
26	1	160,000,000,000
27	1	180,000,000,000
28	1	220,000,000,000
29	1	260,000,000,000
30	1	270,000,000,000
31	1	280,000,000,000
32	1	330,000,000,000
33	1	340,000,000,000
34	1	370,000,000,000

```
-end of results-
```

FIGURE 7-2
Using DIALOG System Commands to Determine Highest Sales in a Sorted Set

```
S2 48 Sort S1/ALL/SA,D

? t 2/ti/1

THE SANWA BANK LTD.

? t 2/sa/1

2/SA/1
DIALOG(R)File 502:(c) 1997 Teikoku Databank. All rts. reserv.

03/1996
Conversion Rate : $1=Y105.9

Sales (000):
$ 376,077,798
```

Notice that this company was put into the "bin" denoting $370 billion (item number 34 in the list in Figure 7-1). As mentioned in Chapter 4, DIALOG rounds large numeric fields down to the leftmost significant digits (plus zeroes) and puts the record into a bin for the rounded value. For example, sales of $107 million would be rounded down to $100 million. By grouping records with similar values and thus simplifying the data, the system makes trends easy to spot. Sanwa Bank's sales, $376 billion plus, were rounded down to $370 billion for purposes of RANKing and SORTing, but when you type the record, you get the exact, unrounded sales figure.

Lessons learned:

√ When searching numeric fields on DIALOG, you can format the numbers in your search statement in various ways (with or without zeroes, with or without dollar signs, etc.)

√ When searching ranges on DIALOG, you can't be exact. The system sorts numeric fields into generalized bins for range searching. However, you can get exact figures by looking at the records themselves.

√ You can derive your own statistics by massaging data. Various systems have their own tools for doing so, or you can use your own ingenuity.

Case Study 7-2: Insurance Losses

Purpose: This case study shows how to find articles with significant statistical content by identifying those articles with tables using the SF=TABLE feature in DIALOG.

Question: How much money have U.S. insurance companies lost in earthquake claims since the 1994 Northridge, California quake?

Likely sources: Best's Review—Property-Casualty Insurance Edition

Access points used: SF=TABLE; Full Text

System used: DIALOG (file 148)

Best's Review is carried in full text in the IAC Trade & Industry Database. I could have searched the entire database, but limiting to the particular journal targets the search more tightly. Since I didn't know exactly how the journal title reads in this file, I EXPANDed to make sure to pick up all variations. I typed EXPAND JN=best's and got the display in Figure 7-3.

I selected items E5 through E7—the various ways Best's Review—Property-Casualty Insurance Edition is entered—to get set 1.

I used the special feature=table to target articles with tables by typing s s1 and sf=table and losses and earthquake?

There were 54 articles in Best's Review—Property-Casualty Insurance Edition that used my terms and had tables. I cut these down by limiting them to the time period

---

FIGURE 7-3
EXPANDing on the JN Field to Find the Right Journal Title

Ref	Items	Index-term
E1	257	JN=BENEFITS QUARTERLY
E2	14	JN=BERKELEY JOURNAL OF EMPLOYMENT AND LABOR LAW
E3	0	*JN=BEST'S
E4	5544	JN=BEST'S REVIEW - LIFE-HEALTH INSURANCE EDITION
E5	11	JN=BEST'S REVIEW - PROPERTY
E6	3066	JN=BEST'S REVIEW - PROPERTY-CASUALTY INSURANCE ED
E7	2	JN=BEST'S REVIEW PROPERTY-CASUALTY INSURANCE EDI
E8	15	JN=BETTER HOMES AND GARDENS
E9	3366	JN=BEVERAGE INDUSTRY
E10	4575	JN=BEVERAGE WORLD
E11	239	JN=BEVERAGE WORLD DATABANK
E12	1090	JN=BEVERAGE WORLD PERISCOPE EDITION

---

between 1994 and the present; there were 30. I looked at the first few in KWIC (KeyWord in Context) format to get a feel for their relevance.

Item number 10 was an article from April 1996, entitled "Insurers chip away at E&A liabilities." The lead paragraph included this sentence: "Still reeling from the $12.5 billion of Northridge earthquake losses in 1994, the industry was shaken again in 1995 by mounting environmental and asbestos incurred losses totalling $10 billion, according to A.M. Best Co.'s estimate."

Unfortunately, the tables included with the article focused on environmental and asbestos liabilities, the subject of the article—not on earthquake losses. And despite the rich statistics in the article, look at the indexing—there was no descriptor including the term *statistics*.

FIGURE 7-4.
Indexing for an Article Identified with SF=Table

```
SPECIAL FEATURES: illustration; table
INDUSTRY CODES/NAMES: INSR Insurance and Human Resources
DESCRIPTORS: Insurance-Reserves; Insurance industry-Finance; Pollution
liability insurance-Finance; Liability for environmental damages-Finance;
Asbestos-Economic aspects
```

Note that I only got a partial answer to this question. I found 1994 losses from the Northridge earthquake, rather than all losses since 1994. This may be because most of the money was paid out in 1994 (though having lived through this event, I'm doubtful that *all* claims were paid in 1994). I only checked one source, and not very thoroughly at that. There are many other ways I could have conducted this search. I could have used different or additional sources or used descriptors instead of free text terms; I could have omitted sf=table and cast a wider net; or I could have used more terms. If I needed to find the answer to this question in real life, I would pursue some of those strategies.

8

Lessons Learned:

√ It is important to check the way the name of a journal is worded in a database.

√ Using the `sf=table` feature is a good way to identify articles rich in statistics.

√ Using the `sf=table` feature with subject terms guarantees that there will be a table with the record, but not that the table or the main topic of the article matches the terms.

√ Searching in only one source may be good for eliminating noise, but a possible drawback is lack of comprehensiveness.

√ It is possible to find the statistics you seek in an article that is off-topic.

√ Indexing is not infallible.

Finding Health and Medical Statistics

This chapter is extremely heavy on Web-based resources provided by organizations whose primary mission does *not* revolve around aggregating and selling information. That's because government, international organizations, and associations, which increasingly feature strong Web presences, are primary sources of health-related statistics.

Sources that go into the compilation of health and medical data include:

- Clinical studies—clinical studies may be *prospective* (before something happens, to see if it does) or *retrospective* (after the fact, to determine potential causes)

- The medical literature (journals)

- Hospital discharge records (National Hospital Discharge Survey)

- Government records showing amounts spent on Medicare and Medicaid

- Insurance company records

- Censuses

- Death investigations by coroners and medical examiners

- Surveillance by public health departments and universities

- Reports received from clinics, hospitals, doctors and other healthcare practitioners by the Centers for Disease Control and other health-related agencies (how and whether this reporting is done depends to some extent on applicable laws)

- Sampling and surveys by the National Center for Health Statistics and other agencies

- Disease registries

- Interviews

While much of the data is gathered with names attached to it, it is summarized and depersonalized so that no one's privacy is compromised.

TYPES OF DATA

These types of statistics are important in the health and medical fields:

Health and medicine

- Disease incidences and prevalences
- Mortality and morbidity
- Cure rates
- Accidents and poisonings
- Health practices

Healthcare industry

- Healthcare costs
- Medicare and Medicaid spending
- Physician and hospital fees
- Hospital capacities and usage
- Demographics and earnings of healthcare practitioners
- Government spending on medical research
- Insurance costs and payouts
- Drugs, treatments, and medical devices dispensed
- Drug, medical devices, and treatment costs
- Drug, treatment, and medical devices expenditures
- Malpractice statistics

KEY PRODUCERS

Health and medical statistics come from a wide variety of sources, including:

- Associations organized around a particular disease or condition
- Centers for Disease Control
- Health Care Financing Administration
- National Cancer Institute
- National Center for Health Statistics
- Occupational Safety and Health Administration (OSHA)
- Pan American Health Organization
- University departments of biostatistics (conduct survey research) and schools of public health (epidemiological studies)
- U.S. Department of Health and Human Services
- World Health Organization

TYPES OF SOURCES

Health and medical statistics can be reported in:

- Trade and medical journal articles
- Statistical compendia
- Web sites
- Reports and studies
- Government publications
- Pamphlets
- Almanacs

BEST PLACES TO LOOK

The directory of best places to look for health and medical statistics is arranged with general sources and their locations first, followed by categories for healthcare expenditures and financing, the healthcare industry, and incidences and prevalences.

General

A Matter of Fact
SilverPlatter and others

CDC Wonder: Other Information Resources (extensive list)
http://wonder.cdc.gov/rchtml/Convert/data/other.html

TableBase
DataStar (file BTBL)
DIALOG (file 93)
http://www.tablebase.com

Healthcare expenditures and financing

Bureau of Labor Statistics Safety and Health Statistics (healthcare expenditures)
http://stats.bls.gov/oshhome.htm

Health Care Financing Administration (healthcare employment, expenditures, prices)
http://www.hcfa.gov/stats/stats.htm

Health Care Financing Review
ProQuest Direct

Health Insurance Statistics
http://www.census.gov/ftp/pub/hhes/www/hlthins.html

Information Please Almanac
Cognito!
Encarta Online Library

Social Statistics Briefing Room (healthcare expenditures, utilization)
http://www.whitehouse.gov/fsbr/ssbr.html

Statistical Abstract of the United States—Health and Nutrition (healthcare expenditures, prices, HMOs, health practices)
http://www.census.gov/stat_abstract

World Almanac
Electric Library
FirstSearch

Healthcare industry

Census of Manufactures (healthcare devices)
http://www.census.gov/econ/www/ma0100.html

HMO Ratings
http://www.usnews.com/usnews/nycu/hmohigh.htm

Inter-university Consortium for Political and Social Research—National Archive of Computerized Data on Aging (healthcare for older adults)
http://www.icpsr.umich.edu/NACDA/archive.html

Service Annual Survey (healthcare industry)
http://www.census.gov/svsd/www/sas.html

Incidences and Prevalences

American Cancer Society Facts & Figures
http://www.cancer.org/cancinfo.html

American Diabetes Association
http://www.diabetes.org/Publications/

American Liver Foundation—Liver Diseases in the U.S. Fact Sheet
http://sadieo.ucsf.edu/alf/alffinal/infolivdis_us.html

Arthritis Foundation
http://www.arthritis.org/facts/

Cardiovascular Disease (WHO)
http://www.who.ch/ncd/cvd/cvd_home.htm

The CDC Diabetes Home Page
http://www.cdc.gov/diabetes

CDC Wonder (mortality)
http://wonder.cdc.gov/

Communicable Disease Surveillance Centre
http://www.open.gov.uk/cdsc/

Demographic and Health Surveys
    http://www.macroint.com/dhs/

Diabetes Statistics
    http://www.niddk.nih.gov/DiabetesStatistics/DiabetesStatistics.html

Digestive Diseases—National Institute of Diabetes and Digestive and Kidney Diseases
(National Institutes of Health)
    http://www.niddk.nih.gov/

Expanded Programme on Immunization Information System
    http://www.who.org/whosis/epi/epi.htm

Global Health Situation and Projections
    http://www.who.org/whosis/globest/globest.htm

Haemoglobin Disorders
    http://www.who.ch/programmes/ncd/hgn/haemogl.htm

Health for All Database
    http://www.who.dk/country/country.htm

Health for All Global Indicators Database
    http://www.who.org/whosis/hfa/hfa.htm

Health Services Research Group Public Statistics (Australia)
    http://econ-www.newcastle.edu.au/hsrg/stats.html

HIV/AIDS Prevention (Division of HIV/AIDS Prevention—National Center for HIV,
STD, and TB Prevention)
    http://www.cdc.gov/nchstp/hiv_aids/dhap.htm

Incidence and Prevalence Database
    DataStar (file IAPV)
    DIALOG (file 465)

Information Please Almanac
    Cognito!
    Encarta Online Library

Kidney Diseases— National Institute of Diabetes and Digestive and Kidney Diseases
(National Institutes of Health)
    http://www.niddk.nih.gov/

Malaria Information
    http://www.who.org/whosis/malinfo/malinfo.htm

Morbidity and Mortality Weekly Report
    http://www.cdc.gov/epo/mmwr/mmwr.html

Morbidity and Mortality Weekly Report at the Virtual Hospital
http://www.vh.org/Providers/Publications/MMWR/

National Environmental Data Referral Service (in addition to earth sciences, covers health and demography worldwide; includes historical data; *much of the data itself is offline*)
http://www.esdim.noaa.gov/

OSHA Home Page (occupational illness and injury rates, nonfatal occupational illnesses and injuries)
http://www.osha.gov

Pan American Health Organization (health profiles of countries in the Americas)
http://www.paho.org

PLL Online (WHO)
http://www.who.ch/pll/

Public Health Reports
Dow Jones News/Retrieval
ProQuest Direct
Wall Street Journal Interactive Edition Publications Library

Social Statistics Briefing Room
http://www.whitehouse.gov/fsbr/ssbr.html

State Injury Mortality Data
http://wonder.cdc.gov/rchtml/Convert/data/injury.html

Statistical Abstract of the United States—Health and Nutrition
http://www.census.gov/stat_abstract

SEER (Surveillance, Epidemiology, and End Results)—National Cancer Institute
http://www-seer.ims.nci.nih.gov/

UNAIDS
http://www.unaids.org/index.html

United Nations Statistics Division
http://www.un.org/Depts/unsd/

Urologic Diseases—National Institute of Diabetes and Digestive and Kidney Diseases (National Institutes of Health)
http://www.niddk.nih.gov/

Weekly Epidemiological Record
http://www.who.ch/wer/wer_home.htm

WHOSIS (World Health Organization Statistical Information System)
http://www.who.org/whosis/

World Almanac
  Electric Library
  FirstSearch

World Health Organization Division of Control of Tropical Diseases
  http://www.who.ch/ctd/

World Survey of Rabies
  http://www.who.org/whosis/vph/vph.htm

CASE STUDIES

Case Study 8-1: Healthcare Spending

Purpose: This case study illustrates how to find healthcare spending information using a full-text source and a statistical compendium. It also demonstrates the occasional necessity of combining and massaging numbers from various sources.

Question: What percentage of the U.S. Gross Domestic Product (GDP) is spent on healthcare?

Likely sources: Health Care Financing Administration; Health Care Financing Review; The Bureau of Economic Analysis; Statistical Abstract of the U.S.

Access points used: Sponsoring organization; full text; links; titles of tables

Systems: Web site; ProQuest Direct

Because the answer to this question represents an important national statistic, it is likely to be found in the Statistical Abstract of the U.S. I checked there first, but I also investigated to see if some other sources would work.

Statistical Abstract (http://www.census.gov/stat_abstract)

From the table of contents, I selected the section Health and Nutrition. Doing so downloaded a PDF file into RAM and launched the Adobe Acrobat viewer. This particular section was 294K and took a couple of minutes to load.

There was no list of tables in the section, but it was easy to page

FIGURE 8-1
Statistical Abstract of the U.S.

To proceed, you must have installed Adobe Acrobat as a helper application.

through quickly to see what was there. I used the Thumbnails and Page function that can be activated from the View menu. This option allowed me to page through by selecting the thumbnail for the corresponding page. I could also have used the forward and back arrows.

One of the first tables showed total U.S. health expenditures for selected years, 1980 to 1994, broken down by Spent By and Spent For. Surprisingly, however, there was no table in this section showing healthcare expenditures as a percent of GDP. Total healthcare spending for 1994 was $949,419,000,000.

FIGURE 8-2

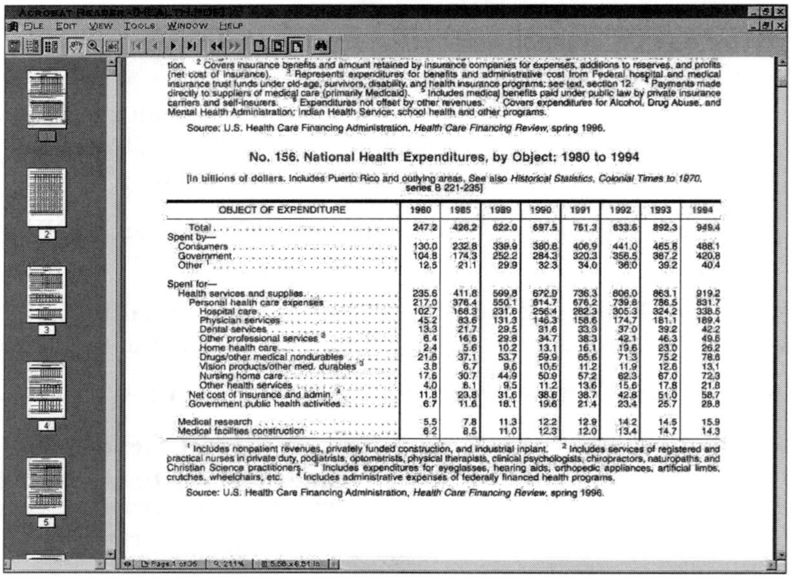

tion. [2] Covers insurance benefits and amount retained by insurance companies for expenses, additions to reserves, and profits (net cost of insurance). [3] Represents expenditures for benefits and administrative cost from Federal hospital and medical insurance trust funds under old-age, survivors, disability, and health insurance programs; see text, section 12. [4] Payments made directly to suppliers of medical care (primarily Medicaid). [5] Includes medical benefits paid under public law by private insurance carriers and self-insurers. [6] Expenditures not offset by other revenues. [7] Covers expenditures for Alcohol, Drug Abuse, and Mental Health Administration; Indian Health Service; school health and other programs.

Source: U.S. Health Care Financing Administration, *Health Care Financing Review*, spring 1996.

No. 156. National Health Expenditures, by Object: 1980 to 1994

[In billions of dollars. Includes Puerto Rico and outlying areas. See also *Historical Statistics, Colonial Times to 1970*, series B 221-235]

OBJECT OF EXPENDITURE	1980	1985	1989	1990	1991	1992	1993	1994
Total	247.2	426.2	622.0	697.5	761.3	833.6	892.3	949.4
Spent by—								
Consumers	130.0	232.8	339.9	380.8	406.9	441.0	465.8	488.1
Government	104.8	174.3	252.2	284.3	320.3	356.5	387.2	420.8
Other [1]	12.5	21.1	29.9	32.3	34.0	36.0	39.2	40.4
Spent for—								
Health services and supplies	235.6	411.8	599.8	672.9	736.3	806.0	863.1	919.2
Personal health care expenses	217.0	376.4	550.1	614.7	676.2	739.8	786.5	831.7
Hospital care	102.7	168.3	231.6	256.4	282.3	305.3	324.2	338.5
Physician services	45.2	83.6	131.3	146.3	158.6	174.7	181.1	189.4
Dental services	13.3	21.7	29.5	31.6	33.3	37.0	39.2	42.2
Other professional services [2]	6.4	16.6	29.8	34.7	38.3	42.1	46.3	49.6
Home health care	2.4	5.6	10.2	13.1	16.1	19.6	23.0	26.2
Drugs/other medical nondurables	21.6	37.1	53.7	59.9	65.6	71.3	75.2	78.6
Vision products/other med. durables [3]	3.8	6.7	9.6	10.5	11.2	11.9	12.6	13.1
Nursing home care	17.6	30.7	44.9	50.9	57.2	62.3	67.0	72.3
Other health services	4.0	6.1	9.5	11.2	13.6	15.6	17.8	21.8
Net cost of insurance and admin. [4]	11.8	23.8	31.6	38.6	38.7	42.8	51.0	58.7
Government public health activities	6.7	11.6	18.1	19.6	21.4	23.4	25.7	28.8
Medical research	5.5	7.8	11.3	12.2	12.9	14.2	14.5	15.9
Medical facilities construction	6.2	8.5	11.0	12.3	12.0	13.4	14.7	14.3

[1] Includes nonpatient revenues, privately funded construction, and industrial inplant. [2] Includes services of registered and practical nurses in private duty, podiatrists, optometrists, physical therapists, clinical psychologists, chiropractors, naturopaths, and Christian Science practitioners. [3] Includes expenditures for eyeglasses, hearing aids, orthopedic appliances, artificial limbs, crutches, wheelchairs, etc. [4] Includes administrative expenses of federally financed health programs.

Source: U.S. Health Care Financing Administration, *Health Care Financing Review*, spring 1996.

This table from the Statistical Abstract of the United States shows the amounts spent on healthcare in selected years. The thumbnails at the left help you navigate through the document.

In order to use this information, I needed to compare the amount with the figure for GDP for 1994.

To get the figure for GDP, I returned to the table of contents and selected Income, Expenditures, and Wealth. In this section, table 685 showed GDP for selected years from 1980 to 1995. In 1994, GDP was $6,931,400,000,000. The kicker was that this figure represented GDP in 1992 "chained dollars." According to the documentation, in 1996 the Bureau of Economic Analysis changed the way it calculated a number of measures, including GDP. If I used this amount, it might not have been figured in the same kind of dollars as the healthcare expenditure amount from the other table.

However, here's what happened when I did the math. To calculate the percentage, I divided 949,419,000,000 by 6,931,400,000,000 and came up with about 13.7%. Because of the change in calculation of GDP, however, I needed to confirm through another source.

ProQuest Direct

I decided to confirm by searching ProQuest Direct. I limited the search to *Health Care Financing Review* and looked for terms in the full text. I typed `GDP and (percent? or per cent) and health w/1 care and source (health care financing review)` and got 45 results.

FIGURE 8-3

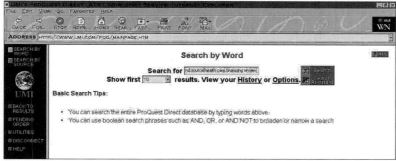

Only a portion of the search statement shows in the search box on ProQuest Direct, but the system recognizes all of it.

FIGURE 8-4
Search Results for a Healthcare Spending Question on ProQuest Direct

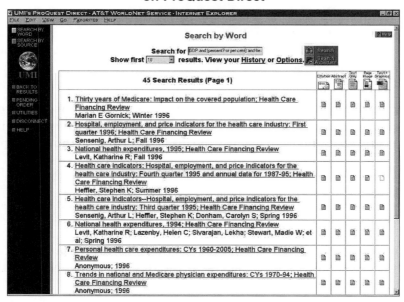

Result number three was titled "National Health Expenditures, 1995." I looked at it in full text, which cost $4.00. This article was excellent, and told me that "During the 1993-95 period, **healthcare** spending as a **percent** of gross domestic product

(**GDP**) exhibited virtually no change: It stabilized between 13.5 and 13.6 **percent** (Figure 1)."

Note that these percentages are very close to the 13.7% I calculated based on figures from two separate tables in the Statistical Abstract.

If I wanted to look at Figure 1, I could have spent a few extra dollars (a total of $10.75) to see the full-page image in PDF format, or in PQD's text+graphics format (a total of $12.75). When you buy the more expensive formats on PQD, you aren't charged for the less expensive format previously viewed, so you haven't incurred an extra cost by having looked at the full text first.

Lessons Learned:

√ Read closely and beware of changing definitions.

√ It is important to verify information that appears suspicious.

√ Searching a narrowly-focused publication with general terms can be a useful strategy. Had I been searching a newspaper rather than *Health Care Financing Review*, I might have wanted to add more specific terms, such as *spending* or *expenditure*. I might also have wanted to specify that the words appear as a phrase, e.g., *as a percentage of GDP*.

√ Statistics don't always come in the form you seek. Sometimes you have to calculate your own figures.

Case Study 8-2: Incidence of AIDS
Purpose: This case study illustrates how to use the Statistical Abstract of the U.S. to find incidence information for a particular disease. The study also illustrates how to spot anomalies in the data.

Question: Describe the growth in AIDS in the U.S. since the disease was first recognized. (Note: the term *incidence* refers to the *number* of cases; *prevalence* refers to the *rate* of cases, that is, it measures how frequently the disease is found within the population.)

Likely sources: Statistical Abstract of the U.S.

Access points used: Links; titles of tables

Systems: Web site

Using the same Web site for Statistical Abstracts as in the previous case study (http://www.census.gov/stat_abstract), I selected the Health & Nutrition category from the table of contents (Figure 8-1).

Again, I paged through the tables by using the Acrobat Thumbnail and Page feature from the View menu.

Figure 8-5 (Table 217) showed AIDS Cases Reported, by Patient Characteristic: 1981 to 1995 and gives yearly totals and a grand total of 496,896. A footnote explained that the total of 496,896 didn't match the sum of the yearly figures because it included states not shown separately in this table, and persons whose residence was unknown.

FIGURE 8-5

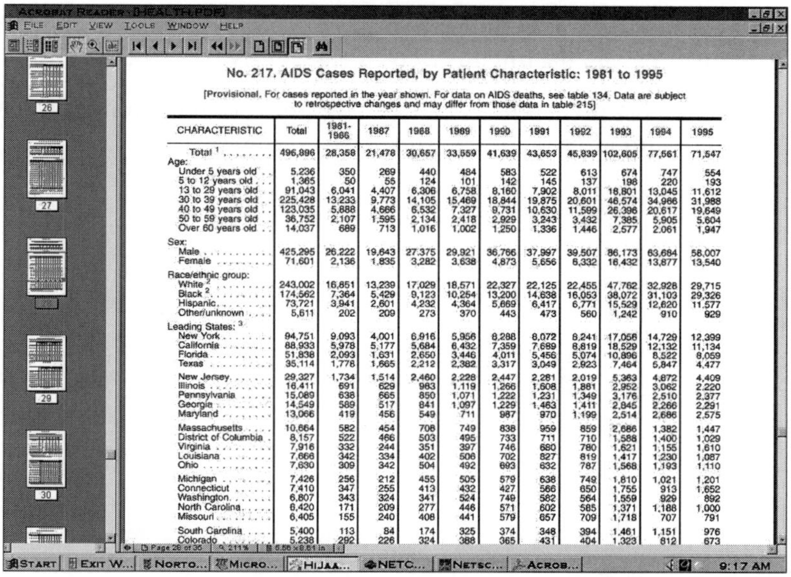

No. 217. AIDS Cases Reported, by Patient Characteristic: 1981 to 1995

[Provisional. For cases reported in the year shown. For data on AIDS deaths, see table 134. Data are subject to retrospective changes and may differ from those data in table 215]

CHARACTERISTIC	Total	1981-1986	1987	1988	1989	1990	1991	1992	1993	1994	1995
Total [1]	496,896	28,358	21,478	30,657	33,559	41,639	43,653	45,839	102,605	77,561	71,547
Age:											
Under 5 years old	5,236	350	269	440	484	583	522	613	674	747	554
5 to 12 years old	1,365	50	55	124	101	142	145	137	198	220	193
13 to 29 years old	91,043	6,041	4,407	6,306	6,758	8,160	7,902	8,011	18,801	13,045	11,612
30 to 39 years old	225,428	13,233	9,773	14,105	15,469	18,844	19,875	20,601	46,574	34,966	31,988
40 to 49 years old	123,035	5,888	4,666	6,532	7,327	9,731	10,630	11,599	26,396	20,617	19,649
50 to 59 years old	36,752	2,107	1,595	2,134	2,418	2,929	3,243	3,432	7,385	5,905	5,604
Over 60 years old	14,037	689	713	1,016	1,002	1,250	1,336	1,446	2,577	2,061	1,947
Sex:											
Male	425,295	26,222	19,643	27,375	29,921	36,766	37,997	39,507	86,173	63,684	58,007
Female	71,601	2,136	1,835	3,282	3,638	4,873	5,656	6,332	16,432	13,877	13,540
Race/ethnic group:											
White [2]	243,002	16,851	13,239	17,029	18,571	22,327	22,125	22,455	47,762	32,928	29,715
Black [2]	174,562	7,364	5,429	9,123	10,254	13,200	14,638	16,053	38,072	31,103	29,326
Hispanic	73,721	3,941	2,601	4,232	4,364	5,669	6,417	6,771	15,529	12,620	11,577
Other/unknown	5,611	202	209	273	370	443	473	560	1,242	910	929
Leading States: [3]											
New York	94,751	9,093	4,001	6,916	5,956	8,288	8,072	8,241	17,056	14,729	12,399
California	88,933	5,978	5,177	5,684	6,432	7,359	7,689	8,819	18,529	12,132	11,134
Florida	51,838	2,093	1,631	2,650	3,446	4,011	5,456	5,074	10,896	8,522	8,059
Texas	35,114	1,778	1,665	2,212	2,382	3,317	3,049	2,923	7,464	5,847	4,477
New Jersey	29,327	1,734	1,514	2,460	2,228	2,447	2,281	2,019	5,363	4,872	4,409
Illinois	16,411	691	629	983	1,119	1,266	1,608	1,881	2,952	3,062	2,220
Pennsylvania	15,089	638	665	850	1,071	1,222	1,231	1,349	3,176	2,510	2,377
Georgia	14,549	589	517	841	1,097	1,229	1,463	1,411	2,845	2,266	2,291
Maryland	13,066	419	456	549	711	987	970	1,199	2,514	2,686	2,575
Massachusetts	10,664	582	454	708	749	838	959	859	2,686	1,382	1,447
District of Columbia	8,157	522	466	503	495	733	711	710	1,588	1,400	1,029
Virginia	7,916	332	244	351	397	746	680	780	1,621	1,155	1,610
Louisiana	7,666	342	334	402	506	702	827	819	1,417	1,230	1,087
Ohio	7,630	309	342	504	492	693	632	787	1,568	1,193	1,110
Michigan	7,426	256	212	455	505	579	638	749	1,810	1,021	1,201
Connecticut	7,410	347	255	413	432	427	566	650	1,755	913	1,652
Washington	6,807	343	324	341	524	749	582	564	1,559	929	892
North Carolina	6,420	171	209	277	446	571	602	585	1,371	1,188	1,000
Missouri	6,405	155	240	408	441	579	657	709	1,718	707	791
South Carolina	5,400	113	84	174	325	374	348	394	1,461	1,151	976
Colorado	5,238	292	226	324	388	365	431	404	1,323	812	673

This table, No. 217, AIDS Cases Reported, by Patient Characteristic: 1981 to 1995, has the answer but shows a project-stopping anomaly for 1993.

But why the big jump in 1993? This anomaly raised a red flag. The documentation said, "Data are subject to retrospective changes and may differ from those data in Table 215." Did this statement mean that the figures were strange because they hadn't been verified?

Table 215 was Specified Reportable Diseases—Cases Reported: 1970 to 1994. In that table, there was also a huge jump in 1993. However, there was nothing to explain the jump. I suspected a change in reporting, or in the definition of the disease.

Examination of the particular categories in Table 217—the original table—didn't help. I was hoping that I might see that one particular group was responsible for the rise. Cases in *every* category soared in 1993—every state, male and female, all races, all ages except children and the elderly.

I needed to consult a source that explained the methodology. There are several possibilities listed in the Directory of Online Statistics Sources (http://www.berinsteinresearch.com) under "AIDS." One is the CDC's Division of HIV/AIDS Prevention—National Center for HIV, STD, and TB Prevention (http://www.cdc.gov/nchstp/hiv_aids/dhap.htm). Indeed, the answer was there. In a PDF file containing the 1993 figures, I found that the uniform surveillance case definition was modified in 1993 (as well as in 1985 and 1987). In 1993, it said, "The revisions incorporated a broader range of AIDS-indicator diseases and conditions and used HIV diagnostic tests to improve the sensitivity and specificity of the definition." Thus, the jump, which *was* due to a change in definition rather than a rise in actual cases.

Lessons learned:

√ Even when data is readily available, there may be questions and stumbling blocks which are not helped by the documentation in the source.

√ If a number looks fishy, investigate. It may be a reflection of changing methodology or definition rather than of real change in the situation.

Finding Scientific, Agricultural, and Environmental Statistics

O ne method of gathering scientific data is measurement by instruments, such as seismographs, which measure earthquakes. Another way of gathering scientific and environmental data is by observation. For example, the National Biological Service, part of the U.S. Department of the Interior, conducts a roadside survey to estimate population change for songbirds. Observations must be conducted and verified in a systematic way in order to be valid. While anecdotal evidence is acceptable for *description*, it is insufficient for quantitative purposes.

Toxic chemical data may be gathered from lists published by the U.S. Federal Register and the Code of Federal Regulations, U.S. government publications, technical reports, manufacturers' safety data sheets, and scientific journals and books. Such data may also come from manufacturers.

Material safety data sheets are compiled by safety and health professionals.

The National Science Foundation conducts surveys of scientists and engineers, research institutions, and private industry.

TYPES OF DATA
These types of data are collected for scientific and environmental statistics:

General
- Science expenditures
- Numbers and demographics of scientists

Agriculture
- Farm acres
- Acres in production
- Numbers of farms
- Demographics of farmers
- Crop yields
- Crop prices

- Crop production
- Erosion

Environment

- Levels of pollutants
- Ozone hole
- Expenditures for pollution avoidance and control, cleanup
- Numbers of species

Physical sciences

- Material, physical, and chemical properties
- Numbers and characteristics of celestial bodies, substances, materials
- Weather data

KEY PRODUCERS

Government agencies, research institutions, professional associations, and advocacy organizations are important producers of scientific statistics. Among these are:

- U.S. Department of Agriculture, Economic Research Service
- U.S. Department of Agriculture, National Agricultural Statistics Service
- Environmental advocacy organizations, such as the Natural Resources Defense Council
- Environmental Protection Agency
- U.S. Department of the Interior, Fish and Wildlife Service
- NASA
- Observatories
- American Chemical Society
- National Institute of Standards & Technology (NIST)
- National Oceanic and Atmospheric Administration and its sub-agencies, such as National Climatic Data Center (NCDC), National Weather Service, National Ocean Service, and National Oceanographic Data Center
- National Science Foundation

TYPES OF SOURCES

You will find scientific data collected and reported in these types of sources:

- Handbooks
- Databases

- Statistical compendia
- Industry journals and newsletters
- Web sites

BEST PLACES TO LOOK

If you skim through this section, you'll notice that chemical and materials sources are heavily sponsored by traditional online vendors, most specifically by STN International (and STN Easy), which offer the Chemical Abstracts Service databases, among others. Other scientific topics treated here, conversely, are well-covered by Web-based government agencies, observatories, and other noninformation vendor organizations.

A special scientific service is NISTFLUIDS, which covers properties of industrial fluids. This file consists of a calculation program to determine thermophysical and transport properties of various industrial fluids and is on STN as file NISTFLUIDS.

Following this list of general sources and their locations, the directory of best places to look for scientific data is arranged by the following categories:

- Agriculture
- Astronomy
- Chemistry and materials
- Environment
- Geology
- Oceanography
- Physics
- Weather and climate

General

A Matter of Fact (multidisciplinary, environment)
    FirstSearch (file FactSearch)
    SilverPlatter
    (and others; see p. 4)

ASI (American Statistics Index) (for *identifying* statistical publications produced by the U.S. government)
    DIALOG (file 102)
    (scheduled to be on LEXIS-NEXIS in 1998, including selected full text)

FactSearch
    FirstSearch

FEDSTATS (federal government agency statistics locator)
    http://www.fedstats.gov

GPS Time Series (global positioning satellites' positions, velocities, latitudes, longitudes, and heights)
http://sideshow.jpl.nasa.gov/mbh/series.html

Niel Brandt's Timelines and Scales of Measurement Page (various measurements and what they represent, e.g., 120 arcseconds is the resolution of the human eye; 30,000 meters is typical thickness of the earth's crust, etc.; also geological and cosmological timelines)
http://www.astro.psu.edu/users/niel/scales/scales.html

NIST WebBook (data compiled and distributed by the National Institute of Standards and Technology under the Standard Reference Data Program)
http://webbook.nist.gov/

National Environmental Data Referral Service (climate, oceanography, geophysics, snow and ice, marine fisheries, health; scope is worldwide; includes historical data— *much of the data is offline)*
http://www.esdim.noaa.gov/

SI Units
http://www.chemie.fu-berlin.de/chemistry/general/si.html

Agriculture

Agricultural Market Information Virtual Library (Michigan State University)
http://www.aec.msu.edu/agecon/fs2/market/contents.htm

Agricultural Marketing Service (commodity prices, demand, movement volume, quality)
http://www.usda.gov/ams/titlepag.htm

Census of Agriculture
http://www.census.gov/econ/www/ag0100.html

Crop Index
http://www.hort.purdue.edu/newcrop/indices/index_ab

Economic Research Service (U.S. Department of Agriculture)
http://www.econ.ag.gov/Prodsrvs/

FAOSTAT Forestry Statistics Database (agriculture, forestry, fisheries, pesticides— includes some time series)
http://www.fao.org/waicent/forestry.htm

Foreign Agricultural Service (U.S. Department of Agriculture) (trade data and foreign market research reports; see especially the food market overview, which covers countries around the world. This is a great site for commodity-specific information.)
http://www.fas.usda.gov/

Handbook of International Economic Statistics (CIA)
http://www.odci.gov/cia/publications/pubs.html

Mann Library (Cornell) Home Page: Gateway: Index by Subject: Agriculture (metasite covering agricultural property taxes, prices, trade, Farm Credit System and bank operating statistics, production expenditures, real estate values, foreign-owned agricultural land, machinery, state facts, world agriculture, historical statistics, food consumption and expenditures, estimates of soil erosion impact, fertilizer use, chemical use, aquaculture, international agriculture, rural development, crops, livestock)
   http://www.mannlib.cornell.edu/cgi-bin/subj.cgi?ag

National Agricultural Statistics Service (U.S. Department of Agriculture)
   http://www.usda.gov/nass/#NASS

National Marine Fisheries Service
   http://www.esdim.noaa.gov/

Pesticide Fact File
   DIALOG (file 306)

RiceWeb
   http://www.riceweb.org

U.S. State Fact Sheets (Economic Research Service, U.S. Department of Agriculture)
   http://www.econ.ag.gov/epubs/other/usfact/

World Agricultural Outlook Board (world agricultural supply and demand, projections for major agricultural commodities, trade, farm income, consumer food prices, crop estimates)
   http://www.mannlib.cornell.edu/cgi-usda/agency.cgi?waob

Astronomy
Canadian Astronomy Data Centre (data from the Hubble Telescope)
   http://cadcwww.dao.nrc.ca/

Frequencies for Interstellar Molecular Microwave Transitions (for reference in astronomic observation in the microwave and millimeter wavelengths)
   http://physics.nist.gov/PhysRefData/

NSSDC OMNIWeb (solar wind magnetic field and plasma data, energetic proton fluxes, geomagnetic and solar activity indices)
   http://nssdc.gsfc.nasa.gov/omniweb/ow.html

The NASA Astrophysics Data System (includes International Ultraviolet Explorer (IUE) Observing Log data, astronomical data catalogs of star and galaxy observations— this is a mirror site of the Strasbourg Astronomical Data Center)
   http://ads.harvard.edu/

NASA /GSFC Space Physics Data Facility (Coordinated Data Analysis Web)
   http://cdaweb.gsfc.nasa.gov/cdaweb/istp_public/

NSSDC (National Space Science Data Center)
   http://nssdc.gsfc.nasa.gov/

Orbital Mechanics Calculators
   http://liftoff.msfc.nasa.gov/academy/rocket_sci/orbmech/orbmech.html

Planet and Asteroid Data Calculator
   http://orange.mcs.dundee.ac.uk:8080/Test/astronomy/planets/PlanTime.htm

The Princeton Pulsar Group (radio pulsar parameters)
   http://pulsar.princeton.edu/

Solar Wind Information
   http://www.sel.noaa.gov/wind/windinfo.html

Strasbourg Astronomical Data Center (information about astronomical objects collected by observatories around the world—spectrographic, astrometric, photometric, radio and far infrared, high-energy data)
   http://cdsweb.u-strasbg.fr/

Sunrise/Sunset/Twilight and Moonrise/Moonset/Phase (U.S. Naval Observatory)
   http://tycho.usno.navy.mil/srss.html

Theoretical Nuclear Properties for Astrophysics
   http://t2.lanl.gov/data/astro/molnix96/molnix.html

Twelve Year Planetary Ephemeris: 1995-2006 (NASA)
   http://planets.gsfc.nasa.gov/TYPE/TYPE.html

Chemistry and Materials
Adhemix (properties of adhesives and glues)
   Questel (file ADHEMIX)

Aluminum Fracture Toughness Database (plane strain fracture toughness and notch tensile strength for aluminum alloys)
   STN (file ALFRAC)

Aluminum Standards and Data from the Aluminum Association Database (aluminum alloys—properties, composition)
   STN (file AAASD)

ASMDATA (materials—composites, alloys, plastics, and metals—properties, specifications, composition)
   STN (file ASMDATA)

Beilstein Online (physical, chemical, mechanical, electrical, magnetic optical properties of organic compounds)
   DIALOG (file 390)
   STN (file BEILSTEIN)

Chapman and Hall Chemical Database (molecular weight, melting, freezing, and boiling points, solubility, relative density, optical rotation, dissociation constants)
   DIALOG (file 303)

Chemical Catalogs Online (commercially available chemicals, their suppliers, properties, and prices)
  STN (file CHEMCATS)

CHEMSAFE (safety characteristics of flammable substances)
  STN (file CHEMSAFE)

CHEMTOX Online (physical and chemical data, toxicity of regulated and toxic substances)
  DIALOG (file 337)

COPPERDATA (physical and mechanical properties of copper alloys)
  STN (file COPPERDATA)

Corrosion (effects of over 600 agents on metals, carbon, glass, plastics, rubbers)
  Orbit (file CORROSION)

DETHERM (thermophysical data relating to chemical industry processes—properties of pure compounds and mixtures)
  STN (file DETHERM)

DIPPR (physical properties for commercially important chemicals and substances)
  STN (file DIPPR)

DOSE (chemicals and effects, properties, toxicity)
  SilverPlatter

Gmelin Handbook of Inorganic and Organometallic Chemistry (physical and chemical properties of inorganic and organometallic compounds)
  STN (file GMELIN)

HODOC (CRC Handbook of Data on Organic Compounds)
  STN (file HODOC)

Inorganic Crystal Structure Database (crystal lattice parameters, density, atomic parameters, and temperature factors for inorganic compounds)
  STN (file ICSD)

International Plastics Selector (properties and flammability of plastics)
  STN (file IPS)

Janssen Chemical Catalog (properties of industrial and research chemicals)
  Questel (file JANSSEN)

Joint Army-Navy-Air Force Database (thermochemical properties of inorganic substances and organic substances with one or two carbons)
  STN (file JANAF)

Kirk-Othmer Encyclopedia of Chemical Technology (includes more than 6000 tables)
  BrainWave
  DIALOG (file 386)

Material Safety Data Sheets
gopher://gopher.chem.utah.edu/11/MSDS

Material Safety Data Sheets from the Canadian Centre for Occupational Health and Safety (physical properties, fire and explosion data, ingredients for American and Canadian products used in Canadian workplaces)
STN (file MSDSCCOHS)
STN Easy (file MSDS-CCOHS)

The Merck Index Online (molecular weight, physical and toxicity data)
BrainWave
DIALOG (file 304)
Questel (file MRCK)
STN (file MRCK)

METALCREEP (creep and rupture stress properties of aluminum alloys and steels)
STN (file METALCREEP)

Metals Datafile (mechanical and physical properties of ferrous and nonferrous alloys)
Orbit (file MDF/I)
STN (file MDF)

Minimal Risk Levels for Hazardous Substances (Agency for Toxic Substances and Disease Registry) (physical and chemical properties, toxicology of pesticides and industrial chemicals)
http://atsdr1.atsdr.cdc.gov:8080/mrls.html

National Research Council Canada Metals Crystallographic Data File (crystal lattice parameters, density, atomic parameters, and temperature factors for metals and intermetallic phases)
STN (file CRYSTMET)

NIST Chemistry WebBook (thermodynamic and ion energetics data)
http://webbook.nist.gov/chemistry/

NIST Structural Ceramics Database (properties of alumina, aluminum nitride, beryllia, boron nitride, silicon carbide, silicon nitride, and zirconia)
STN (file NISTCERAM)

NISTTHERMO (thermochemical properties of inorganic substances and organic substances containing one or two carbon atoms)
STN (file NISTTHERMO)

Occupational Health Services Material Safety Data Sheets
DIALOG (file 332)

PDLCOM (Test data on chemical compatibility and environmental stress crack resistance of plastics)
STN (file PDLCOM)

PLASPEC Materials Selection Database (properties and characteristics of plastic materials)
 BrainWave
 DIALOG (file 321)
 STN (file PLASPEC)

POLYMAT (data on commercially available plastic materials)
 STN (file POLYMAT)

Polymer Online (molecular, physical, mechanical, biological properties of polymers)
 BrainWave
 DIALOG (file 322)

Registry of Toxic Effects of Chemical Substances (toxicity data for drugs, agrochemicals, and commercially important substances)
 DataStar (file RTEC)
 DIALOG (file 336)
 STN (file RTECS)

SPECINFO (spectral data for organic compounds)
 STN (file SPECINFO)

TRCTHERMO (thermodynamic data for 7000 compounds)
 STN (file TRCTHERMO)

WebElements (Periodic Table—atomic weight, chemical data, physical data, nuclear and electronic information, crystallographic information, and more. There is a "ChemPuter" at this site, which allows you to calculate element percentages, electron counts, reaction yields, isotope patterns, oxidation state, VSEPR, and MLXZ)
 http://www.shef.ac.uk/uni/academic/A-C/chem/web-elements/

Environment
ASAPII Publications (a variety of full-text sources containing material relating to the environment)
 LEXIS-NEXIS (file ASAPII in ENVIRN Library)

ATSDR/EPA Top 20 Hazardous Substances
 http://atsdr1.atsdr.cdc.gov:8080/cxcx3.html

ATSDR/EPA Priority List of Hazardous Substances
 http://atsdr1.atsdr.cdc.gov:8080/popdocs.html

Energy Information Administration—Global Warming and Greenhouse Gas Emissions
 http://www.eia.doe.gov/environment.html

Energy Information Administration—Environmental Effects of the Utility Sector/ Transportation Sector
 http://www.eia.doe.gov/environment.html

Energy Information Administration—Environmental Legislation and Its Impacts
http://www.eia.doe.gov/environment.html

Enviroline (abstracts)
BrainWave
DataStar (file ENVN)
DIALOG (file 40)
Orbit (file ENVIRO)

EPA Journal
Electric Library
LEXIS-NEXIS (file EPAJNL in ENVIRN Library
ProQuest Direct

Environmental Technologies (market research and export information for environmental technologies for the U.S. and selected countries)
http://www.ita.doc.gov/envirotech/emps.html

Global Environment Outlook-1 Report
http://www.unep.org/unep/eia/geo1/

Greenwire (environmental statistics, including state and world roundups)
LEXIS-NEXIS (file GRNWRE in ENVIRN Library)

Handbook of International Economic Statistics (comparative pollution information)
http://www.odci.gov/cia/publications/pubs.html

Hazardous Substances Data Bank (properties, toxicity, and effects of chemicals)
STN (file HSDB)
Telnet to National Library of Medicine's TOXNET system at toxnet.nlm.nih.gov—
you must be a registered user

National Environmental Data Referral Service (points to data sets held by government and academic and private organizations)
http://www.esdim.noaa.gov/

Nuclear Regulatory Commission (storage and disposal of nuclear waste, licenses for handling nuclear materials, types of usage, safety inspections)
http://www.nrc.gov/

Toxic Chemical Release Inventory (TRI)
Telnet to toxnet.nlm.nih.gov—you must be a registered National Library of
Medicine online services user

VISTA Emergency Response Notification System (discharges of hazardous substances)
LEXIS-NEXIS (file ERNS in ENVIRN Library)

VISTA National Priority List of Hazardous Waste Sites (rankings for ground water, standing water, air, and overall)
LEXIS-NEXIS (file NPLIST in ENVIRN Library)

VISTA Toxic Chemical Release Inventory (release of toxic chemicals into the environment by certain companies as reported to the EPA)
    LEXIS-NEXIS (file TRIS in ENVIRN Library)

Wall Street Journal Interactive Edition Publications Library, Environment Publications category

Ziff Newsletters (environment newsletters)
    LEXIS-NEXIS (files ZEV1 and ZEV2 in ENVIRN, MARKET, and NEWS Libraries)

Geology

Geological Time Machine
    http://www.ucmp.berkeley.edu/help/timeform.html

National Earthquake Information Center (earthquakes, deaths, magnitudes, Richter and Modified Mercalli scales)
    http://wwwneic.cr.usgs.gov/neis/general/handouts/general_seismicity.html

Mineral Resource Surveys Program (U.S. Geological Survey)
    http://minerals.er.usgs.gov/

National Geophysical Data Center
    http://www.esdim.noaa.gov/

Tsunami Database (National Geophysical Data Center)
    http://www.ngdc.noaa.gov/seg/hazard/tsudb.html

VolcanoWorld (eruptions, explosivity index, deaths)
    http://volcano.und.nodak.edu/vwdocs/current_volcs/current.html

Oceanography

Interactive Marine Observations (NOAA) (tides, marine weather, sea state data)
    http://www.nws.fsu.edu/buoy/

NOAA Coastal and Estuarine Oceanography Branch Tide Predictor
    http://www.opsd.nos.noaa.gov

National Oceanographic Data Center
    http://www.esdim.noaa.gov/

OLLD Data Resources (National Ocean Service) (water levels, tides)
    http://www.olld.nos.noaa.gov/data_res.html

U.S. Coastal Tide Tables
    http://www.zephyrs.com/tide.htm

WWW Tide and Current Predictor (University of S. Carolina)
    http://tbone.biol.sc.edu/tide/sitesel.html

Physics

The 1986 CODATA Recommended Values of the Fundamental Physical Constants (National Institute of Standards and Technology)
  http://physics.nist.gov/PhysRefData/

Atlas of the Spectrum of a Platinum/Neon Hollow-Cathode Lamp for Ultraviolet Spectrograph Calibration (National Institute of Standards and Technology)
  http://physics.nist.gov/PhysRefData/

Atomic Model Data for Electronic Structure Calculations (National Institute of Standards and Technology)
  http://math.nist.gov/DFTdata/

Atomic Spectroscopic Database (atomic energy levels, wavelengths, and transition probabilities)
  http://aeldata.nist.gov/nist_atomic_spectra.html

International Atomic Energy Agency (includes Atomic and Molecule Data Information System (AMDIS), Power Reactor Information System (PRIS), Global Network of International System of Units (SI)
  http://physics.nist.gov/Divisions/Div840/SI.html

Nuclear Data Information System (nuclear physics data)
  http://www.iaea.or.at/

Review of Particle Properties (Lawrence Berkeley Laboratory)
  http://pdg.lbl.gov/

Wavenumber Tables for Calibration of Infrared Spectrometers (National Institute of Standards and Technology
  http://physics.nist.gov/PhysRefData/

X-Ray Attenuation Coefficients and Mass Energy-Absorption Coefficients for Materials of Dosimetric Interest (basic quantities used in calculations of penetration and energy deposition by photons in biological, shielding, and other materials)
  http://physics.nist.gov/PhysRefData/

Weather and Climate

CLIMVIS (graphs and/or tabular data—historic, worldwide)
  http://www.ncdc.noaa.gov/onlineprod/drought/xmgr.html

Federal Meteorological Handbook
  http://www.nws.noaa.gov/oso/oso1/oso12/metartaf/fmh1/fmh1toc.htm

Global Network of Isotopes in Precipitation (hydrogen and oxygen isotope content in precipitation)
  http://iaea.or.at/programs/ri/gnip/gnipmain.htm

Meteorological Conversion for Common Values (temperature, height, wind speed)
http://www.nws.mbay.net/convert.html

National Climatic Data Center (historical weather data)
http://www.ncdc.noaa.gov/ncdc.html
http://www.esdim.noaa.gov/

National Snow and Ice Data Center (select Full Text Search or Design Your Own Search Interface)
http://www.esdim.noaa.gov/

NOAA Climate Table (U.S. monthly mean temperature and precipitation)
http://www.nws.noaa.gov/climate.shtml

NOAA Weather Radio Frequencies
http://www.nws.noaa.gov/noaaradio.shtml

NWS Climate Table (average monthly temperature and precipitation tables for U.S. cities)
http://www.nws.noaa.gov/climatex.shtml

World Meteorological Organization (metasite for meteorological and oceanographic information; for oceanographic, choose the Integrated Global Ocean Services System Products Bulletin, Highlights and/or Data Products)
http://www.wmo.ch/

CASE STUDIES

Case Study 9-1: Agricultural Water Use

Purpose: This case study shows how to follow a trail from a logical starting point to a source that gives a better answer. It also demonstrates the variety of agricultural information available through two major institutions: Cornell University's Mann Library and the U.S. Bureau of the Census.

Question: How much water is used for agricultural purposes in the U.S.?

Likely sources: Cornell's Mann Library Gateway: Index by Subject: Agriculture, because it offers a wealth of agricultural statistical information on a variety of topics.

Access points used: Links

System: Web site

I decided to start with the Mann Library (Cornell) Home Page: Gateway: Index by Subject: Agriculture at http://www.mannlib.cornell.edu/cgi-bin/subj.cgi?ag. This fabulous metasite provides a good choice of resources.

The top of the site listed major categories, including Agricultural Economics and Crops. The only heading that looked promising was General which proved to be the right choice for irrigation and related subjects. None of the information quite answered the question, but there was a link to a Farm and Ranch Irrigation Survey that supplemented the 1982 Census of Agriculture. Having discovered this survey and now knowing that the Census of Agriculture addresses the topic of irrigation, I thought that perhaps the Census of Agriculture might have the information I wanted.

I went to the Census of Agriculture at http://www.census.gov/econ/www/ag0100.html. As I scrolled down the page to read about the census, I saw a link to Farm and Ranch Irrigation Survey. Good! I selected that heading and then the View button. I could also have chosen Download or Images, but I'd rather have instant gratification in text-only form.

I was told that the reports were in PDF format. I skimmed the links to see which tables I might want. As is so often the case, many of the tables were broken down by category, but one looked as though it would have aggregated information that would answer the question: Estimated Quantity of Water Applied by Source: 1994 and 1988.

FIGURE 9-1.
The Census Bureau's Farm and Ranch
Irrigation Survey, Table 10

Table 10. **Estimated Quantity of Water Applied by Source: 1994 and 1988**
(Excludes irrigation data for Alaska, Hawaii, and abnormal and horticultural specialty farms)

Geographic and water resources areas	Water applied from all sources			Wells				
				Total			Only source	
	Acres irrigated	Acre-feet applied	Average acre-feet per acre	Farms	Acres irrigated	Acre-feet of water applied	Farms	Acres irrigated
TOTAL								
Conterminous United States...... 1994...	46 418 380	79 627 392	1.7	104 732	28 816 442	39 429 089	82 775	22 473 31
1988....	46 199 161	84 182 177	1.8	111 582	26 774 017	40 465 419	92 139	21 762 17
27 leading irrigation States..... 1994...	45 591 076	79 092 930	1.7	101 305	28 330 359	39 151 291	79 971	22 075 83
1988....	45 180 948	83 456 023	1.8	107 400	26 276 495	40 129 250	88 527	21 345 22
17 Western States .... 1994...	32 053 028	66 119 390	2.1	66 897	16 731 924	28 640 077	49 459	11 839 92
1988....	37 188 846	72 897 539	2.0	65 915	20 122 568	32 572 800	70 653	16 266 73
All other States....... 1994...	827 304	534 463	.6	3 427	486 183	277 798	2 804	397 48
1988....	1 018 213	726 154	.7	4 282	497 522	336 169	3 612	416 94
1994 DATA								
Arizona..................	752 019	3 310 359	4.4	1 339	340 306	1 145 973	1 053	154 27
Arkansas................	2 853 929	3 196 019	1.1	5 012	2 581 893	2 838 666	4 384	2 182 61
California................	7 245 487	22 474 499	3.1	29 105	3 876 870	9 821 489	20 936	1 631 90
Colorado................	2 998 888	5 241 741	1.7	3 815	1 357 765	2 120 104	2 037	931 57
Florida..................	1 416 019	1 922 166	1.4	6 272	746 071	842 427	5 823	587 38
Georgia.................	619 536	325 009	.5	1 753	450 029	256 444	1 493	364 09
Idaho...................	3 183 733	6 023 644	1.9	4 268	1 307 686	2 189 793	2 053	749 59
Illinois..................	271 725	168 518	.6	798	251 551	156 244	766	237 19
Kansas..................	2 501 925	3 336 027	1.3	4 817	2 446 930	3 241 405	4 559	2 338 95
Louisiana...............	820 816	865 335	1.1	2 016	557 431	636 457	1 730	460 91

All tables are in PDF format and require the Adobe Acrobat Reader.

There was nothing telling the size of the PDF file, so I just had to take a chance. In fact, it turned out to be a mere 41K bytes. In it was indeed the answer. In 1994, 79,627,392 acre-feet of water were applied for agriculture in the coterminous United States. The table even broke down usage by acre, so I knew that the average was 1.7 acre-feet per acre, down from 1.8 acre-feet in 1988.

FIGURE 9-2.

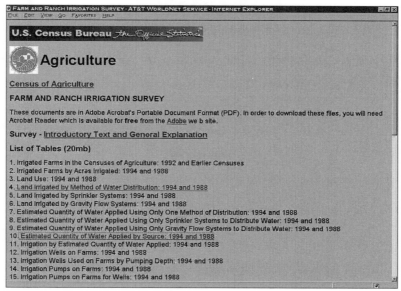

*Even though the data is broken down by source, we can use the totals
to answer the question.*

Lessons learned:

√ Even when the first obvious source doesn't answer the question, it might lead you to a more appropriate one that does.

√ Always have the Adobe Acrobat Reader configured to work with your browser. You never know when you will encounter a PDF file.

Case Study 9-2: Boiling Points of Chemical Substances

Purpose: This case study demonstrates how to use STN's Numeriguide to choose a database. It also shows how to compensate for variations in definition used in different database records.

Question: Which chemical substances have boiling points between 50 and 52 degrees Celsius under standard conditions?

Likely sources: In this case, I didn't worry about the individual sources. I knew that STN offers a number of databases that cover physical properties. I let the system tell me which sources were best.

Access points used: Fields

System: STN

First I needed to decide which file to use. I went into STN's Numeriguide to see which files cover boiling points. After entering Numeriguide, I typed e boiling point/ph. PH is the field for Property Hierarchy. I performed this step to make sure I had the right terminology. The statement says, in effect, "Show me all terms in the boiling point hierarchy so that I can choose the right one on which to search."

The system responded with a number of terms, including *boiling point, boiling point—pressure derivative, boiling point of mixture,* and *boiling point constant.* I selected simply *boiling point.*

FIGURE 9-3.
The STN NUMERIGUIDE Indicating STN Files That Contain Boiling Points

FQ	FQ Type S=search D=display	Default Search Unit (*)	File
BP	S,D	C	BEILSTEIN, GMELIN
BP	S,D	K	DIPPR, TRCTHERMO
BP	S,D	degC	HODOC, HSDB, MRCK
BP	S	K	JANAF
BP.P	S	Torr	BEILSTEIN, GMELIN
BP.P	S	mmHg	HODOC, MRCK
BP.P	S	bar	TRCTHERMO
BP.TX	S		HSDB
BP			CHEMSALFE, DETHERM

(*) Original file units. For more information, use the HELP UNITS message in the specific file.

NTE	BEILSTEIN - At specified pressure.
NTE	CHEMSAFE - BP searchable only in /PROP field.
NTE	DETHERM - BP searchable only in /PROP field.
NTE	DIPPR - At 1 atm pressure.
NTE	HODOC - At 760 mm Hg (1 atm) unless otherwise noted.
NTE	TRCTHERMO - At 1 atm (1.01325 bar) pressure unless otherwise noted.

There were three files that expressed boiling points in degrees Celsius. I didn't *have* to use one of them, since I could convert to any system I wanted, but it would be easier if I did. I selected one which does use degrees Celsius: HODOC, the CRC Handbook of Data on Organic Compounds. My choice was also based on scope and, in this case, the scope of HODOC is appropriate to the question.

After entering the HODOC database, I typed s 50-52 deg C/bp to search for compounds with a boiling point from 50 to 52 degrees Celsius. Since the file already expresses temperature in degrees Celsius, I could have left off deg C, but it doesn't hurt to include it. Had I chosen a file that expresses temperature in a different system, I would have to have included the deg C, or else changed the values by using the SET command.

I got 127 hits. I might have assumed that there are 127 compounds for which the boiling point falls between 50 and 52 degrees C, but I would have been wrong. Here's what was going on:

- Each record displays boiling point in degrees C next to the pressure at which that boiling point is measured. After examining but two records, I could see that not

---

all the records displayed the same pressure. Did that matter? Yes. Boiling point varies as pressure varies.

- Standard pressure is 760 mmHg, meaning 760 millimeters of mercury. (One has to know this and also needs to know that pressure affects boiling point in order to evaluate and correct the data. Again, definitions are critical.)

The first record I got was for Registry Number 61764-94-1, with a boiling point of 50 degrees C at 12 mmHg, not at 760 mmHg. Therefore, this compound boils at 50 degrees C at a very low pressure.

I only wanted records for which the boiling point is between 50 and 52 degrees C at standard pressure! I had to search again, this time specifying that the pressure must be 760 mmHg. I typed s L5 (P) 760 mmhg/bp.p. L5 was the set number within which the 127 records fell. P stands for proximity; it is an operator that indicates that the items must appear on the same line of a table, which pressure and boiling point always do, since the value of the boiling point is dependent upon the pressure at which it is measured. The expression bp.p is the field code for the pressure at which boiling point is measured.

This strategy gave me 14 items out of the 127 for which boiling point is between 50 and 52 degrees Celsius at *standard pressure*. That's a lot fewer than the 127 results from my incorrect original search.

Lessons learned:

√ Definitions are important! Always ask yourself "Under what conditions is this information valid? Are there any indicators in the data that the information may not be valid?"

√ STN provides two important tools for properties hunting. One is Numeriguide, which helps you choose a database to search. The second is the ability to specify the system of measurement you desire, either on a statement-by-statement basis, or globally (by using the SET command).

Finding Historical Statistics

U nearthing historical statistics can be a fascinating endeavor that evokes images of 19th-century industrialists, green-eyeshaded clerks, Scottish thanes, dust-bowl refugees, and all manner of denizens of the past. A cursory trip through *Historical Statistics of the United States, Colonial Times to 1970* (a hard-copy source) is to the historically inclined what a used-book store is to a bibliophile—an experience where time stops, sensory input is repelled, and the mind revels.

Finding U.S. historical statistics often involves mining government records and censuses. In so doing, the researcher can't help tracing the evolution of government agencies. The Office of Road Inquiry, for example, was created in 1894 and became the Federal Highway Administration in 1966—but only after a series of other incarnations. You'll see unfamiliar names like Federal Power Commission, Business and Defense Services Administration, and others long since defunct or superseded.

It's not always easy to know which agency now holds the records, so historical research may involve an offline component. For example, the WPA (Works Progress Administration) building permit statistics are now available through the Bureau of Labor Statistics. There is some logic to that, since the WPA involved labor, but it also sponsored public works projects, which could be considered housing, transportation, and conservation, and could just as easily fall within the purviews of agencies dealing with those subjects. Or, the records could reside in the National Archives, which comprises the richest storehouse of U.S. government records anywhere.

When you're in pursuit of historical statistics, it's helpful to know that sometimes Congress issues reports, such as the 1934 Splawn Report, which is technically called *Report on Communication Companies*. If you can find copies of these reports, you'll have access to a wealth of historical information. They are not likely to be online, though you may identify them through two databases—CIS (Congressional Information Service) and ASI (American Statistics Index)—or by browsing through the online catalogs of university and other major libraries.

Scholars make historical statistics available through dissertations, articles, and books, often published by university presses. For example, an article called "The Building Industry and Business Cycles" in the *Journal of Business of the University of Chicago* (William H. Newman, vol. 8, no. 3, pp. 63-71) offers an index of new building permit values from 1875 to 1933 (table, page 627; citation, page 615). Harvard

University Press publishes a series called *Harvard Economic Studies*, which explicates and relies upon various types of historical economic statistics. A 1934 doctoral dissertation by John R. Riggleman at Johns Hopkins University, called *Variations in Building Activity in U.S. Cities*, traces urban construction trends.

Account books and all kinds of records have always been sources of historical material and statistics. You may be able to identify some of this material by using databases such as America: History and Life, Dissertation Abstracts, and Humanities Abstracts Full Text.

If you look through *Historical Statistics of the United States, Colonial Times to 1970*, you'll see the names of various statistics providers, including not just government agencies, but also journals, private companies, and analysts. For example, the construction section cites the following as contributing various construction cost indices between 1913 and 1970 (page 627):

- American Appraisal Co.

- Department of Commerce

- Associated General Contractors

- E.H. Boeckh

- Engineering-News Record (still extant, now called ENR)

- Department of Agriculture, Economic Research Service

- George A. Fuller Co.

- Handy-Whitman Public Utility

Or how about this: a company called J.F. Dewhurst & Associates published a book in 1955 called *America's Needs and Resources, A New Survey (1849-1952)*; it contributes the astonishing measure of total U.S. horsepower, broken down by work animals, automotive, factories, mines, railroads, vessels, farms, windmills, electrical generating plants, and aircraft!

Companies like the Bell System and Western Union also contribute valuable information, such as toll phone rates, numbers and frequency of phone calls, numbers of wires sent, and so on.

Magazines like *The Futurist* (available via Electric Library and ProQuest Direct) sometimes run comparisons of then and now, such as "Popular Brands in 1923 still Popular in 1993."

As fascinating as the process of digging for historical statistics is, it can also be fraught with heartbreak and frustration. Fire, war, flood, and other disasters have left the historical record incomplete. Large portions of records from the 1890 U.S. Census succumbed to fire; the War of 1812 destroyed other important U.S. papers.

Fortunately, much data does survive, including that from the U.S. Census of 1790. Did you know that George Washington presided over a country of about 4,000,000 people? (In reality, the number was greater than that, because slaves were counted as only 3/5 of a person, and the only Native Americans counted were those who lived off reservations and paid taxes to the U.S. government.) The following tally was made for the 1790 Census:

- Free white males of 16 years and upwards, including heads of families: 813,365
- Free white males under 16 years: 802,127
- Free white females, including heads of families: 1,556,628
- All other free persons: 59,511
- Slaves: 697,697

Here are some other interesting historical statistics, offered from the book *Census: 190 Years of Counting America* by Dan Halacy (Elsevier/Nelson Books, 1980):

- The first Biblical census was conducted by Moses. In the year 1491 B.C. there were 603,555 Israelite men aged 20 and over.
- The population count in Rome in 435 B.C. was 117,319 citizens, including women and children.
- The official population of France in 1781 was counted as 24,802,500. However, this number was arrived at through sampling and is considered somewhat inaccurate.
- The first census in Russia began in 1897 and was completed in 1905. It showed that there were almost 130 million people in the country.

SPECIAL PITFALLS OF HISTORICAL STATISTICS

When you look at statistics over time, you encounter problems of consistency and equivalency. Perhaps the formula, method, or survey procedure that was used at one time was changed at another time. Or classifications (the definitions of things counted) might have changed. Compilers of historical statistics may make adjustments to compensate for these changes. Always read the documentation that goes with the data to see what has been done, how, where, and when. Adjustments are as subject to error and dispute as data collection methods.

TYPES OF DATA

Any kind of statistic can be an historical one. The farther back in time you go, however, the less readily available statistics become. The following types of 20th-century U.S. historical statistics are the easiest to come by:

Vital statistics

Government and military spending

Military strengths and losses

Economic statistics

Industries, including:

Broadcasting

- Radio and television stations, sets, advertising expenditures, mobile transmitters, etc.

Communications

- Telegraph and telephone rates, revenues, facilities, traffic, conversation frequency and duration, etc.

Construction and housing

- Dwellings
- Prices of buildings and construction materials
- Ages of buildings
- Tenure of homes
- Vacancy rates
- Mortgage debt
- Housing starts
- Foreclosures
- Mortgage status (mortgaged or not)

Energy

- Fuel consumption
- Production
- Raw material consumption

Manufacturing

- Consumption of selected commodities
- Depreciation
- Horsepower ratings
- Inventories
- Orders
- Production and production capacity
- Shipments
- Value of output

Transportation

- Air traffic and aeronautics (route mileage, fuel consumption, aircraft speeds, accidents, revenue, etc.)

- Merchant marine (vessel tonnage, value of waterborne imports and exports, cargo tonnage, shipbuilding, persons entering the U.S. by ship, etc.)
- Railroads (equipment, revenues, taxes, fuel, railroad mileage and passenger traffic, capital expenditures, etc.)
- Roads and highways (passenger and freight traffic, costs, revenues, mileages of various types of roads and streets, highway debt, speeds traveled, gas taxes, etc.)
- Vehicles

KEY PRODUCERS

Producers of historical data are often the same as the producers of the original surveys or records. However, in some cases, material has been synthesized and/or organized by others, including database producers.

Original producers include:

- U.S. government agencies and former agencies, such as the Bureau of the Census, Department of Commerce, Federal Communications Commission (FCC), Geological Survey, National Archives and Records Administration (NARA)
- Local and regional governments
- Trade associations
- International agencies
- Private firms, such as the National Bureau of Economic Research

Synthesizers include:

- Universities and scholars
- Journals and newspapers
- Encyclopedia and other reference source publishers
- Historical societies

TYPES OF SOURCES

You will find historical statistics gathered and reported in these sources:

- Almanacs
- Encyclopedias
- Historical journals
- Statistical compilations such as the Statistical Abstract of the U.S.
- Newspapers
- Books
- Dissertations

BEST PLACES TO LOOK

The following sources cover, in a single listing, not just U.S. history in the 20th century, but all varieties of world history in all time periods. A separate listing follows for economic history sources. Many of these resources will require a little extra work to use. You might have to read the documentation to decipher the meanings of columns and codes. Some data sets are so large that they must be downloaded, and they require special software to analyze. The result is worth the work, though—some of this material is priceless!

Historical data is not exclusive to the types of sources listed here. You will also find time series and historical statistics in economic, financial, population, and other databases. Sometimes the same source that covers historical data will include forecasts as well.

NOTE: A wonderful new searchable system called JSTOR is being developed at the University of Michigan (http://www.jstor.org). This miracle contains old (back to the 19th century, in some cases) scholarly journals in the fields of economics, history, population studies, political science, anthropology, ecology, Asian studies, philosophy, sociology, and mathematics. Prices are high and not affordable by individuals, but developers plan to offer a plan for "the rest of us" in the future. You can take a test drive at the Web site. Don't miss this one!

General
America: History and Life (American history; abstracts only)
    DIALOG (file 38)

Archival Data Online Repository, University of Wisconsin (variety of archival data sets covering many different topics, including urban racial disorders in the 1960s, slave movement in the 18th and 19th centuries, Russian Imperial bureaucracy in the 18th and 19th centuries, French old regime bureaucrats in the 17th and 18th centuries, census and property survey for Florentine domains and the city of Verona in 15th-century Italy, plus more modern studies of Wisconsin, etc.)
    http://dpls.dacc.wisc.edu/archive.html

Britannica Online (search the index for your topic, then look for tables; good for war casualties and military strength; subscription required)
    http://www.eb.com

Collier's Encyclopedia
    Cognito!
    Electric Library
    Encarta Online Library

Columbia Encyclopedia
    Cognito!
    Encarta Online Library

FAOSTAT Forestry Statistics Database (country populations, food aid)
    http://www.fao.org/waicent/forestry.htm

FEDSTATS (federal government agency statistics locator)
  http://www.fedstats.gov

Historical Abstracts (world history; abstracts only)
  DIALOG (file 39)

Historical Demographic, Economic, and Social Data for the United States 1790-1860 (Harvard University)
  http://icg.harvard.edu/census/

The HistoryNet (The National Historical Society) (world and American history, aviation and technology history, military history, women's history)
  http://www.thehistorynet.com

Integrated Public Use Microdata Series 1850-1990 (U.S.) (Minnesota Historical Census Projects. This source covers the entire U.S., not just Minnesota.)
  http://www.hist.umn.edu/~ipums/

Inter-university Consortium for Political and Social Research (ICPSR) (older surveys of U.S. and international education)
  http://www.icpsr.umich.edu/archive1.html

Labor Statistics Project (with working conditions, living standards, household economy, family demography; this site also has abstracts of studies available online at other sites and also offline and lists of machine-readable databases available by request—scope is worldwide economic, social, and demographic history)
  http://www.eh.net/Databases/

National Environmental Data Referral Service (climate, oceanography, geophysics, snow and ice, marine fisheries, health; scope is worldwide; includes historical data—*much of the data is offline).*
  http://www.esdim.noaa.gov/

Penn World Tables (population, economy, 1950-1992)
  http://www.nber.org/pwt56.html

Population Index: Office of Population Research Princeton University (leads to offline sources)
  http://opr.princeton.edu/

Population Timeline (Paul Ehrlich and The Population Bomb)
  http://www.pbs.org/population_bomb/time.html

Segregation Data 1890-1990 (National Bureau of Economic Research)
  http://www.nber.org/segregation.html

United Nations Population Division (world population from year 0 projected to 2150)
  gopher://gopher.undp.org/00/ungophers/popin/wdtrends/histor

U.S. Counties Population Trends (Missouri State Census Data Center 1960-1994)
http://www.oseda.missouri.edu/cgi-bin/uiccont?/mscdc/reports/poptrends@secure

Economic History

Consumer Expenditure Survey Abstracts (National Bureau of Economic Research)
http://www.nber.org/ces_cbo/

Dow Jones Historical Data (EconWPA)
http://econwpa.wustl.edu/eprints/data/papers/9603/9603001.abs

Dow Jones Industrial Average Closing Values from 1900 to 1993 *(huge!)*
http://lib.stat.cmu.edu/datasets/djdc0093

Economic and Trade Data by Country, 1983-1993
http://www.clark.net/pub/lschank/trade-data.txt

Economic History Services Databases (U.S. population 1790-1980); also the Historical Economic Report of the President 1959-1996 (National Bureau of Economic Research)
http://www.nber.org/databases/erp97/

Economic Time Series Page (University of Alabama at Birmingham)
http://bos.business.uab.edu/data/data.htm (metasite of economic and financial time series—primarily U.S.)

FRED (Federal Reserve Economic Data) Database Index (U.S. economic and financial time series)
http://www.stls.frb.org/fred/dataindx.html

Gray and Bartelsman Manufacturing Industry Productivity Database (National Bureau of Economic Research)
http://www.nber.org/pub/productivity

Highlights of U.S. Foreign Trade
http://www.clark.net/pub/lschank/highlights-trade.txt

Historical Labor Statistics Project (working conditions, living standards, family economy)
http://cs.muohio.edu/Databases/Labor/

Imports by SIC category 1958-1992 (National Bureau of Economic Research)
http://www.nber.org/pub/feenstra

National Bureau of Economic Research (citations to papers available offline—U.S. economic history for the last 200 years)
http://www.nber.org/index.html

NBER Macro History Database (National Bureau of Economic Research data covering pre-World War I and interwar economies of the U.S., UK, France, and Germany)
http://www.nber.org/databases/macrohistory/contents/index.html

Trade Balances 1987-1994
   http://www.clark.net/pub/lschank/trade-balance.txt

Tradeline (historical securities, mutual funds, bonds, foreign exchange rates, options, indexes, U.S. and international)
   Dow Jones News/Retrieval

U.S. Business Cycle Expansions and Contractions 1854-1991 (National Bureau of Economic Research)
   http://www.nber.org/cycles.html

The U.S. Nuclear Weapons Cost Study Project (Brookings Institution) (cost of building, managing, dismantling the atomic bomb, spending on nuclear weapons, weapons tests and stockpiling)
   http://www.brook.edu/FP/PROJECTS/NUCWCOST/WEAPONS.HTM

U.S. Foreign Trade Highlights (Office of Trade & Economic Analysis U.S. Department of Commerce)
   http://www.ita.doc.gov/industry/otea/usfth/hili.html

U.S. Trade Overview
   http://www.clark.net/pub/lschank/trade-outlook.txt

SPECIAL SEARCH TIPS

- Go first to the place you'd find current statistics on the topic. Lots of producers furnish tables with information going back from a few to many years.

- Time series are formatted as tables rather than within text. Since most full-text sources still exclude tables, go to a statistical compendium or database rather than to a news or journal article. Using `time series` as a search term may be effective.

CASE STUDIES

Case Study 10-1: Military Casualties

Purpose: This case study demonstrates how to find statistics using a database that supplies only abstracts.

Question: How many Soviet casualties were there in World War II?

Likely sources: Historical journals

Access points used: Full text; index terms

System: DIALOG (file 39: Historical Abstracts)

   In order to conduct an effective search, you need something to grab onto. There are no special attributes, such as codes, in the Historical Abstracts database, so I knew I either needed to experiment with full text or find some index terms that would help confine results to material with statistics.

Using the word *casualties* (together with a description of the war and the country) might have worked, but that strategy would not guarantee numbers. I could easily have ended up with phrases no more specific than "...there were heavy casualties." However, it turned out that using the term *statistics*, whether as an index term or part of the full text, was an excellent strategy. Here's what I did:

I entered s casualties and statistic? and (soviet? or russian?) and (world()war()ii or second()world()war) and got 11 hits.

Notice that I did not limit to articles in English. That is because in this database all abstracts are in English, regardless of the language of the article.

See two of the items in Figure 10-1, edited for brevity.

Most of the eleven items retrieved in this search were on target.

FIGURE 10-1
Two Records from Historical Abstracts

```
DIALOG(R)File 39:Historical Abstracts
(c) 1997 ABC-CLIO. All rts. reserv.

SOVIET MILITARY LOSSES IN WORLD WAR II.
Bacon, Edwin
Journal of Slavic Military Studies (Great Britain) 1993 6(4): 613-633.
ABSTRACT: Two Soviet commissions (1988-89) have released conflicting and
incomplete estimates of the staggering Soviet military losses in men and
equipment during World War II, placing total casualties at more than 8
million, almost half of which may have died after surrendering.
DESCRIPTORS: Statistics ; USSR ; World War II ; Casualties ; 1941-1945
```

Comment: Both statistics *and* casualties *are used as index terms.* Casualties *also appears in the text.*

```
DIALOG(R)File 39:Historical Abstracts
(c) 1997 ABC-CLIO. All rts. reserv.

Ratio of loss of life and military equipment on the eastern front during
World War II
O SOOTNOSHENII POTER' V LIUDIAKH I BOEVOI TEKHNIKE NA SOVETSKO-GERMANSKOM
FRONTE V KHODE VELIKOI OTECHESTVENNOI VOINY
 Sokolov, Boris Vadimovich
 Voprosy Istorii (USSR) 1989 (9): 116-126.
NOTE: Based on Soviet and German primary and secondary sources; 45 notes.
LANGUAGE(s): Russian.
ABSTRACT: A comparative statistical report on Soviet and German military and
civilian casualties and material losses suffered in 1941-45. Soviet battle
casualties totalled about 11 million, while Germany and its allies lost some
three million on the eastern front, a ratio of 3.7:1, and the Soviets lost
twice as many planes and tanks as Germany. The main reason for this
disproportionately high ratio was Stalin's disregard for human lives, the mass
purges of 1937-38 which wiped out a major part of the Red Army high command
down to the ranks of regimental commanders, and the suppression of personal
initiative-replaced by blind obedience to Stalin's often incompetent military
orders. (N. Frenkley )
DESCRIPTORS: World War II; Germany; USSR; Casualties; Military capability;
1941-1945; Eastern front
```

Comment: Notice that statistical *is used in the text, but* statistics *is not an index term.* Casualties *appears in both text and indexing. Note too that, while the article is in Russian, the statistics can still be gleaned from the English abstract.*

Lessons learned:

√ Searching full text is most efficient when there is some kind of "hook" available, such as an index term or word indicating the presence of numeric data within the text.

√ Articles in languages other than English may still be useful to English speakers who don't know the original language if there are English-language abstracts.

Case Study 10-2: Fuel Prices

Purpose: This case study illustrates the importance of statistical compendia, especially when looking at data over time. It also shows the wealth of information provided by the U.S. Energy Information Administration.

Question: How does the price of a gallon of gasoline in 1997 compare to prices in the past?

Likely sources: Newspapers; U.S. Energy Information Administration

Access points used: Links

System: Web site

I could have looked in newspapers for the years I wanted, but that would have been a real chore, and I probably would have spent a lot of time flailing around. Tables are likely to be excluded from the full text, and individual prices could be hard to pinpoint. Instead I decided to try the Energy Information Administration (http://www.eia.doe.gov), since it publishes lots of statistics and time series.

FIGURE 10-2

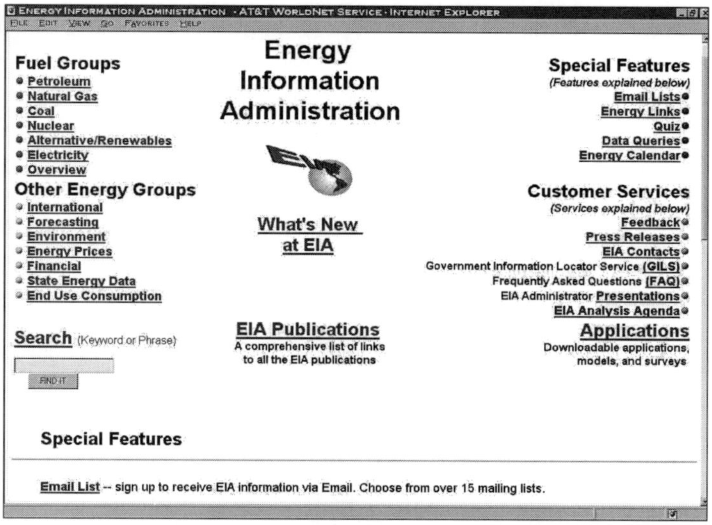

Energy prices are found under Other Energy Groups on the Energy Information Administration's excellent Web site.

The welcome page offered a category called Energy Prices. I had my choice of Crude Oil, Petroleum Products, Natural Gas, and so on. I went to the chart for Petroleum Products and from there chose Gasoline-Retail on an Annual basis.

FIGURE 10-3
Petroleum Product Prices at the Energy Information Administration Site

Petroleum Products

Energy Price Series	Weekly	Monthly	Annual	State Level	Short-Term Projection	Mid-Term Projection
Gasoline	X, TC	X, TC	X, TC	TC	X, TC	PDF, TC
- Wholesale	X, TC	X, TC	X, TC	TC	NA	NA
-Retail	X, TC	X, TC	X, TC	TC	NA	NA
Diesel Fuel	X, TC	X, TC	TC	TC	X, TC	PDF, TC
- Wholesale	X, TC	X, TC	X, TC	NA	NA	
-Retail	X, TC	X, TC	X, TC	NA	NA	NA
Distillate (Heating Oil)	X, TC	X, TC	TC	TC	X, TC	PDF, TC
- Wholesale	X, TC	X, TC	X, TC	TC	X, TC	NA
-Retail	X, TC	X, TC	X, TC	TC	NA	NA
Jet Fuel	X, TC	X, TC	X, TC	X, TC	NA	PDF, TC
Residual Fuel	X, TC	X, TC	X, TC	X, TC	X, TC	PDF, TC
Propane	X, TC	X, TC	X, TC	TC	NA	PDF, TC

Natural Gas

Energy Price Series	Weekly	Monthly	Annual	State Level	Short-Term Projection	Mid-Term Projection
Wellhead	NA	X,TC	TC	TC	X,TC	PDF, TC
City Gate	NA	X,TC	TC	TC	NA	PDF, TC
Residential	NA	X,TC	TC	TC	X,TC	PDF, TC
Commercial	NA	X,TC	TC	TC	NA	PDF, TC

I got a terrific chart going back to 1973, showing Leaded, Unleaded, Unleaded Premium, and All Types. Figures are annual from 1973 to 1993, then monthly.

So, what did I have?

In 1973, a gallon of leaded regular gasoline cost just $.388! Those were the days—except that we couldn't buy unleaded. The next year—the year of the embargo—the price jumped to $.532. That seemed high, but it never fell to that level again. In 1976 we began to see unleaded gas, and regular cost $.614 a gallon. Prices jumped in 1980—unleaded

FIGURE 10-4
Historical Retail Gasoline Prices

Table 9.4 Motor Gasoline Retail Prices, U.S. City Average
(Cents per Gallon, Including Taxes)

	Leaded Regular	Unleaded Regular	Unleaded Premium	All Types a
1973 Average......	38.8	NA	NA	NA
1974 Average......	53.2	NA	NA	NA
1975 Average......	56.7	NA	NA	NA
1976 Average......	59.0	61.4	NA	NA
1977 Average......	62.2	65.6	NA	NA
1978 Average......	62.6	67.0	NA	65.2
1979 Average......	85.7	90.3	NA	88.2
1980 Average b.....	119.1	124.5	NA	122.1
1981 Average......	131.1	137.8	c 147.0	135.3
1982 Average......	122.2	129.6	141.5	128.1
1983 Average......	115.7	124.1	138.3	122.5
1984 Average......	112.9	121.2	136.6	119.8
1985 Average......	111.5	120.2	134.0	119.6
1986 Average......	85.7	92.7	108.5	93.1
1987 Average......	89.7	94.8	109.3	95.7
1988 Average......	89.9	94.6	110.7	96.3
1989 Average......	99.8	102.1	119.7	106.0
1990 Average......	114.9	116.4	134.9	121.7
1991 Average......	NA	114.0	132.1	119.6
1992 Average......	NA	112.7	131.6	119.0
1993 Average......	NA	110.8	130.2	117.3
1994 Average......	NA	111.2	130.5	117.4
1995 January.....	NA	112.9	132.4	119.0
February..	NA	112.0	131.6	118.1
March.....	NA	111.5	130.6	117.3
April.....	NA	114.0	132.5	119.7
May.......	NA	120.0	138.3	125.6
June......	NA	122.6	141.1	128.1
July......	NA	119.5	138.4	125.2
August....	NA	116.4	135.7	122.2
September.	NA	114.8	133.2	120.6
October...	NA	112.7	131.5	118.5
November..	NA	110.1	129.2	116.1
December..	NA	110.1	129.0	116.0

regular was $1.245—and continued high until 1986, when unleaded regular dropped back to $.927.

Prices didn't exceed a dollar again until 1989, when unleaded regular jumped to $1.021. In April of 1996, they soared to $1.251, the first time they'd been that high since 1981, when unleaded regular cost $1.378. A footnote with the 1981 entry says that, in that year, the Bureau of Labor Statistics changed the weights used to calculate average prices. From 1981 forward, gasohol is included in the average for All Types. However, I was looking not at All Types, but at Unleaded Regular, and Leaded Regular before that, so the footnote didn't affect the figures above.

Lessons learned:

√ Always read the footnotes to determine whether they apply to the data in which you're interested.

√ Because they concentrate the data in one place, statistical compendia can be better sources for tracing numbers over time than newspapers that originally published the data year by year.

√ You cannot always predict whether the year(s) you want will be included in a time series, even if the general time period in question is covered.

√ Time intervals to which the data applies may vary within a table (that is, the data may go by year, then by month; or every five years for a while, then by year).

Finding Public Opinion and Trend Statistics

The primary methods of gathering public opinion data are surveys and polls. Polling data may take various forms, such as a database of the actual questions and responses, summary statements ("5% of those asked about such-and-such believe thus-and-so"), or tables. In any case, pay close attention to the wording—it may cast light on the validity of the survey. When you can see the question, you can often learn what's really being measured, how accurately the results were reported, and how valid the study may be.

For example, the following question comes from a Harris poll (Harris 1977 American Economy Survey No. 7783).

Date 5/77: Compared to a few years ago, do you feel that (READ LIST) among teenagers has been increasing a great deal, only some, or hardly at all?

Smoking of marijuana:

Responses: A great deal/Only some/Hardly at all/Not sure

Percent	Responding
70.40%	A great deal
20.10%	Only some
5.20%	Hardly at all
4.3%	Not sure

Number of valid cases 1616

Note that this question asks whether the respondent *thinks* marijuana smoking has risen. The question has to do with perception, not fact. The survey is one of public *opinion*, not personal behavior. If this item were incorrectly reported, one might conclude that marijuana smoking was actually up, not just that people *thought* such behavior had increased. *NOTE: You can find this survey cited at the Institute for Research in Social Science at the University of North Carolina, IRSS Study Number S7783 (http://www.irss.unc.edu/tempdocs/13:11:15:1.htm).*

Contrast the previous question with this one from Harris Study No. 912091:

Thinking of all the time you were smoking, which comes closest to describing the number of cigarettes you usually smoked in an average day—fewer than five cigarettes a day, about half a pack, about a pack, about a pack and a half, about two packs, or more than two packs a day?

Responses: Fewer than five cigarettes/About half a pack/About a pack/About a pack and a half/About two packs/More than two packs/Don't smoke every day, smoke only occasionally/Not sure

Percent	Responding
15.10%	Fewer than five cigarettes
25.90%	About half a pack
31.20%	About a pack
15.10%	About a pack and a half
6.90%	About two packs
5.00%	More than two packs a day
0.30%	Don't smoke every day, smoke only occasionally
0.50%	Not sure

Number of valid cases: 378

This question measures *behavior*, not attitude. Note also that the number of valid cases is far smaller than for the previous question, which may cast doubt on the validity of the survey as a whole.

Let's say these studies have been written up in a newspaper article. A likely wording for the first survey results might be "According to a recent survey, 90.5% of respondents believe marijuana use among teenagers is increasing." This figure, 90.5%, is the addition of the categories "A great deal" and "Only some." However, both of those categories indicate that the respondent *thinks* marijuana use is increasing. (To be completely accurate, one should probably throw in the 5.2% who said "Hardly at all.")

My goodness—it looks as though almost everyone thinks teenage marijuana use is increasing! However, consider this:

- The poll didn't measure whether use actually *is* increasing.

- The poll didn't even ask if the respondent thought marijuana use is going down or staying the same (in other words, the question was leading and likely to produce positive results)

- Our hypothetical reporter lumped together two categories as if they were one, to create an even stronger impression than the actual responses showed.

Now, let's consider a possible reporting of the second question. Let's say our reporter wrote "In a recent survey of smokers, 31.2% of respondents admitted to smoking a pack a day." What do we know from this hypothetical wording? Or perhaps the question should be: What do we *not* know from this? We don't know if most smokers smoke more or less than a pack a day. We don't know how many people failed to answer at all. And we know nothing about the validity of the survey (there were only

378 valid cases). (By the way, we're only *assuming* that the survey addressed smokers, based on the lack of choices indicating that the person doesn't smoke at all.)

The questions themselves provide a fair amount of context. For more, we need to examine the survey methodology. However, *reported* statistics often fail to include all the information needed to evaluate validity. Moral of the story: if the figures are critical to your task, dig deeper. Try to find other data to corroborate or refute your numbers. Prefer sources with tables showing the actual survey results. And always consider the source!

TYPES OF DATA

The following types of data contribute to public opinion and trend statistics:

- Attitudes about social issues like abortion, crime, divorce, teenage pregnancy, smoking, drug and alcohol use, sex
- Attitudes about government and elected officials
- Attitudes about other people and groups
- Behavior, such as how leisure time is spent, smoking, alcohol and drug use, sex, driving habits, spending habits, and other lifestyle factors

KEY PRODUCERS

Key producers frequently include broadcast and print polling organizations, such as ABC News or the *Washington Post*, or a joint venture between the two. They also include:

- *Atlanta Journal-Constitution*
- CNN
- NBC
- *New York Times*
- *Los Angeles Times*
- *USA Today*

Private polling companies

- American Demographics
- The Gallup Organization
- Louis Harris and Associates
- Roper Center for Public Opinion Research

University- or research-affiliated polling organizations

- Institute for Social Research, University of Michigan
- Inter-university Consortium for Political and Social Research
- National Opinion Research Center

TYPES OF SOURCES

You will find public opinion and trend statistics collected and reported in:

- Reports and surveys
- Newspaper articles
- Magazine articles
- Web sites

BEST PLACES TO LOOK

Public opinion surveys are often reported through the news media, so if you don't find what you need through primary sources, be sure to check newspapers. Following is a directory of mostly primary sources of public opinion surveys and their online locations:

The Abortion Report (polls about abortion)
    LEXIS-NEXIS (file ABTRPT in CMPGN, EXEC. LEGIS, and NEWS Libraries)

California Poll Codebook Search (back to 1955)
    http://gort.ucsd.edu/iassist/calpoll2.html

Europa (European Public Opinion)
    http://europa.eu.int/en/comm/dg10/infcom/epo/polls.html

The Gallup Organization
    http://www.gallup.com/

GSS Reports—Topical Reports
    http://www.icpsr.umich.edu/gss/report/t-report/repttndx.htm

GSSDIRS Trend Tables
    http://www.icpsr.umich.edu/gss/cdbkmap.htm

ICPSR (Inter-university Consortium for Political and Social Research) (fee required for most data, but not all)
    http://www.icpsr.umich.edu/index.html

Institute for Research in Social Science (UNC)
    http://www.irss.unc.edu/data_archive/

Japan Economic Newswire Plus (includes Japanese public opinion polls)
    BrainWave
    DIALOG (file 612)
    Dow Jones News/Retrieval
    LEXIS-NEXIS (file JEN in multiple libraries)
    Wall Street Journal Interactive Edition Publications Library

Louis Harris and Associates, The Harris Poll (general poll, public policy issues, politics)
    http://www.techsetter.com/harris/html/home.html

The Monitoring the Future Study
  http://www.isr.umich.edu/src/mtf/index.html

National Archive of Criminal Justice Data
  http://www.icpsr.umich.edu/NACJD/index.html

National Election Studies
  http://www.umich.edu/~nes/

The National Election Studies NES Guide to Public Opinion and Electoral Behavior
(includes opinion on public policy issues; tables and graphs)
  http://www.umich.edu/~nes/nesguide/nesguide.htm

National Opinion Research Center (General Social Survey conducted on an ongoing
basis; used extensively by social scientists)
  http://www.norc.uchicago.edu

The Pew Research Center for the People and the Press
  http://www.people-press.org/

Princeton University Survey Research Center (Terrific metasite for public opinion data)
  http://www.princeton.edu/~abelson/index.html

Public Opinion Online (U.S. public opinion surveys back to 1936; includes consumer
preferences as well as attitudes about issues of public interest)
  DIALOG (file 468)
  LEXIS-NEXIS (file RPOLL in MARKET and NEWS Libraries)

Public Perspective (general public opinion and demographics from The Roper Center)
  LEXIS-NEXIS (file PUBPER in MARKET and NEWS Libraries)

Public Pulse (what Americans are thinking, doing, and buying)
  LEXIS-NEXIS (file PPULSE in MARKET and NEWS Libraries)

Roper Center for Public Opinion Research
  DIALOG (file 468)
  LEXIS-NEXIS (file RPOLL)
  http://www.lib.uconn.edu/RoperCenter/

Social Change Reports
  http://www.icpsr.umich.edu/gss/report/s-report/reptsndx.htm

Sourcebook of Criminal Justice Statistics
  http://www.albany.edu/sourcebook/

SPECIAL SEARCH TIPS

- Poll and public opinion data can masquerade under various names. Look for these
  key words:
    Attitude(s)

Media research
Poll(s)
Public opinion
Report
Social and economic data
Social science data
Survey (research)

- When searching full text, use the terms *poll*, *report*, *survey*, and *study*.

CASE STUDY

Case Study 11-1: Attitudes Toward Female Beauty

Purpose: This case study illustrates how to search the Public Opinion Online database for survey data. It also shows how careful and thoughtful one needs to be when evaluating and analyzing the data.

Question: What do Americans consider physically attractive in a woman?

Likely sources: Public Opinion Online

Access points used: Full text; fields (for gathering all the questions in the study)

System: DIALOG (file 468)

I started this search by typing s standards and beauty and got 0 hits. I tried another term s attractiveness and this time got 32 hits. To make sure these items related to women, I entered s s1 and women. The result was 6 hits.

Three of these six items seemed relevant, all focusing on specific body parts. For those of you who can't contain your curiosity, see the results, which are longish, but interesting indeed, in Figure 11-1.

These were intriguing results, particularly since I had no idea how many men *vs.* women were in the sample. It's important to know that, and it's also important to know what the other questions in the survey were like. What did respondents perceive as the purpose of the study? How willing would they be to give truthful answers? How comfortable? The only way to find out more about the sample is to look up the methodology for the survey, which is not included in this database. However, from here we *can* see what all the questions were.

To gather all the questions for this survey, I typed s oc=abc and sb=960327, where oc is the organization code and sb is the beginning date of the survey. Even though the date is displayed with the month first, you must search by year, month, day. I found this out the hard way when sb=03/27/96 didn't work. I finally EXPANDed on sb= to see how dates are formatted.

From my search statement, I got 20 hits, which means that there were 20 questions in this survey. DIALOG's Format 6 allowed me to display just the questions. The other

FIGURE 11-1
Three Questions from a Public Opinion Survey

Three out of 20 questions in a survey conducted by ABC News in March of 1996, by telephone. Data provided by the Roper Center for Public Opinion Research; 600 adults were surveyed. It is important to look at the other questions in this survey to judge the results.

1. All other things being equal, how important do you think the size of women's breasts are to her overall physical attractiveness—very important, somewhat important, somewhat unimportant, or very unimportant?

Very important	10%
Somewhat important	45
Somewhat unimportant	27
Very unimportant	17
Don't know/no opinion	2

2. What about you? When you look at a woman in terms of physical attractiveness, which part of her body is most important to you—her face, her hair, her breasts, her buttocks, or her legs?

Face	64%
Hair	10
Breasts	4
Buttocks	5
Legs	7
Other (vol.)	2
All equal (vol.)	6
None (vol.)	2
Don't know/no opinion	1

3. The following questions may seem a little sensitive or embarrassing, but they are for a story on ABC News 20/20 with Barbara Walters and Hugh Downs. The story is on whether body shape affects the way people view women. Remember your answers to these questions and all others are confidential. Just your best guess, when the average man looks at a woman in terms of physical attractiveness, which part of her body is most important to him—her face, her hair, her breasts, her buttocks, or her legs?

Face	40%
Hair	2
Breasts	31
Buttocks	11
Legs	9
Other (vol.)	1
All equal (vol.)	4
None (vol.)	*
Don't know/no opinion	3

Question Notes: * = less than .5 percent

questions were about political party affiliation (2), women's attractiveness (15), and Presidential politics (3).

This turned out to be a very interesting survey for critical analysis. When I saw all the questions, I realized that many of them were aimed at women, having to do with their attitudes about the size of their own breasts and how that fact has affected their body image. Some of the questions could be directed at men as well, asking about what the respondent perceives as attractive. There was also a question about what the respondent thought men's preferences are.

I suspect most of the respondents were women with medium-sized breasts. Consider these facts:

- Most of the *respondents* thought breast size isn't very important, but they believed that men think it *is* important. *(Comment: Unless men are willing to admit that they're out of step with the rest of their sex, then most of the respondents must have been women.)*

- Most of the respondents considered their own breast size medium. *(Comment: If that's true, then most respondents must have been women.)*

- Most respondents found medium-size breasts to be the most attractive. *(Comment: Since we know that most of the respondents were women, and we know most of the respondents had medium-size breasts, this answer isn't surprising.)*

I am very suspicious of both the sample and the significance of the results. Not all questions could have been asked of all respondents (men wouldn't have been asked about the impact of their own breast size on their body image, for example). Also, the answers sound very much like women's attitudes, but not like men's. How else can one explain the discrepancy between respondents saying that breast size isn't very important, but that they think that men think it is important? My conclusion: This survey *may* be an accurate representation of attitudes of women with medium-size breasts, but certainly not of the population as a whole.

Lessons learned:

√ Dates may be formatted in databases in unexpected ways.

√ It is important that all questions in a survey pertain to all respondents.

√ Examining all the questions in a public opinion survey is important to determine consistency, anomalies in methodology, and the possible motivation/truthfulness of the respondent in answering specific questions.

√ Don't extrapolate results of an opinion poll to the population at large unless you're sure the sample represents the general population. It would not be fair to report on common standards of female attractiveness based on this poll, which is probably biased in favor of the opinions of women with medium-size breasts.

Finding Political and Government Statistics

Everyone has an opinion about politics and government. Some gather data to support their opinions or provide material for action. Data about politics and government comes from many sources, including the following:

- Journalists
- Attorneys
- Government documents
- Survey research
- Public interest groups
- Political parties
- Congressional disclosure forms
- Congressional, state, and local oversight agencies
- The Clerk of the U.S. House of Representatives (keeps the official statistics on federal elections)
- The Current Population Survey conducted by the Census Bureau (ferrets out information on registration and voting)
- The Office of Management and Budget (publishes the U.S. budget)
- The Treasury Department (provides fiscal figures, including receipts and expenditures, based on financial records)
- The Office of Personnel Management (collects payroll data from all U.S. government agencies, except the CIA, National Security Agency, and Defense Intelligence Agency)
- Other government agencies

TYPES OF DATA

Statistics related to these types of data are important in politics and government:

- Government budgets and spending
- Government programs
- Government agencies and employees
- Military spending

- Military forces and demographics
- Entitlement spending
- Elections
- Characteristics of the electorate
- Registration, voting, and voting districts
- Congress and its voting records
- Campaigns and campaign finance
- Political parties
- Elected officials and their staffs
- Laws and legislation

KEY PRODUCERS

While government agencies often gather and report statistics, other public and private organizations may repackage and add value to some of the data. In addition, many outside agencies compile their own statistics about government and politics. Look for data from:

- Almanac of American Politics, published by The National Journal
- Federal Election Commission
- A Matter of Fact database
- National Election Studies (NES) within the Center for Political Studies, University of Michigan's Institute for Social Research
- State and local governments (links collected at http://lcweb.loc.gov/global/state/stategov.html)
- U.S. Congress
- U.S. Department of Health and Human Services and its agencies
- U.S. Office of Management and Budget
- U.S. Department of Defense

TYPES OF SOURCES

You'll find political and government statistics reported in the following types of sources:

- Almanacs
- Newspapers and wire services
- Government publications
- Think tank reports
- Watchdog groups and journals
- Campaign finance filings
- Web sites

BEST PLACES TO LOOK

Sources for government and political statistics are abundant. The following directory of sources and their locations includes categories for campaign finance; congress and legislation; congressional districts; defense; elected officials; elections; government spending, programs, and employment; and state and local governments, in addition to the general listing. And don't overlook newspapers after checking those sources below.

Collections
LEXIS-NEXIS APOLIT Library (Associated Press Political Service)
LEXIS-NEXIS BNA Library (Bureau of National Affairs)
LEXIS-NEXIS CMPGN Library
LEXIS-NEXIS EXEC Library
LEXIS-NEXIS LEGIS Library

General
ASI (American Statistics Index) (for *identifying* statistical publications produced by the U.S. government; not generally full text)
    DIALOG (file 102)
    Scheduled to be on LEXIS-NEXIS in 1998, including selected full text

Almanac of American Politics (Congressional districts, representatives, state voting and registration patterns)
    LEXIS-NEXIS (file AMPOL in multiple libraries)

BNA Daily News from Washington (banking, antitrust, pensions and benefits, environment, product liability, securities law, toxics law, trade, federal contracts, labor, bankruptcy, trademarks and copyrights, patents, occupational health)
    BrainWave
    DIALOG (file 655)

The Brookings Review
    Dow Jones News/Retrieval
    ProQuest Direct
    Wall Street Journal Interactive Edition Publications Library

Cato Journal
    ProQuest Direct

CIS (covers publications of Congress, including hearings, reports, etc.; while only an index, this source may be the only one to lead to certain statistical material)
    DIALOG (file 101)
    LEXIS-NEXIS (file CISINX in CODES, GENFED, and LEGIS Libraries)

FactSearch
    FirstSearch

GPO Monthly Catalog (bibliographic file, but leads to studies, reports, fact sheets, statistical series, etc.)
DIALOG (file 66)

Information Please Almanac
Cognito!
Encarta Online Library

A Matter of Fact (multidisciplinary)
FirstSearch (file FactSearch)
SilverPlatter
(plus others, see p. 4)

PAIS International (Public Affairs Information Service) (political science, law and crime, economics, government, international relations, business, finance, as they relate to public policy)
DataStar (file PAIS)
DIALOG (file 49)

Wall Street Journal Interactive Edition Publications Library, Government & Politics Publications category

The Washington Post
BrainWave
DIALOG (file 146)
Dow Jones News/Retrieval
LEXIS-NEXIS (file WPOST in NEWS Library)
Wall Street Journal Interactive Edition Publications Library

World Almanac
Electric Library
FirstSearch

World Almanac of U.S. Politics
Electric Library

Campaign Finance

Campaign Summary Reports (financial statements for incumbents and challengers)
LEXIS-NEXIS (file CMPSUM in CMPGN and LEGIS Libraries)

Center for Responsive Politics (campaign finance)
http://www.crp.org/index.html-ssi

Congressional Political Action Committee Report (PAC contributions to members of Congress)
LEXIS-NEXIS (file PAC in CMPGN, ENTERT, and LEGIS Libraries)

Federal Election Commission (elections and voting statistics, financial information about candidates, PACs, and parties)
    http://www.fec.gov

Federal Election Commission Recent Releases (rankings of PACs by spending, House and Senate members by spending)
    LEXIS-NEXIS (file FECREL in CMPGN Library)

PAC Summary Reports (PAC financial statements)
    LEXIS-NEXIS (file PACSUM in CMPGN Library)

Political Finance & Lobby Reporter (PAC expenditures)
    LEXIS-NEXIS (file PFLRPT in CMPGN, EXEC, LEGIS, and NEWS Libraries)

Congress and Legislation

Congressional Committee Vote Report (Congressional committee members' voting records and counts)
    LEXIS-NEXIS (file COMVTE in CMPGN and LEGIS Libraries)

Congressional Committee Votes Archive (past Congressional committee voting records)
    LEXIS-NEXIS (file CVTARC in CMPGN and LEGIS Libraries)

Congressional Floor Votes Archive
    LEXIS-NEXIS (file VOTARC in CMPGN and LEGIS Libraries)

Congressional Observer Publications (Congressional votes)
    http://www.proaxis.com/~cop/

Congressional Vote Report (includes total and partisan tallies as well as individual votes)
    LEXIS-NEXIS (file VOTES in CMPGN and LEGIS Libraries)

Congressional Record Abstracts (roll call votes from 1981 through November 1993 only)
    DIALOG (file 135)

CQ's American Voter (Congressional member voting records, including committee votes)
    http://voter96.cqalert.com

CQ's VoteWatch (floor votes)
    http://www.pathfinder.com/@@OcZlGwUA8YpxPbzt/CQ/

Thomas (Congressional roll call votes later than November 1993)
    http://thomas.loc.gov

Congressional Districts

Congressional District/State Profile Report (demographics, election histories, industry, and employment for each district)
    LEXIS-NEXIS (file DIS/ST in BUSREF, CMPGN, and LEGIS Libraries)

Defense

Armed Forces Newswire Service (defense budget)
> Dow Jones News/Retrieval
> Wall Street Journal Interactive Edition Publications Library

Britannica Online (subscribers only; for military strengths around the world, search the index under "United States Army, The," and look for tables)
> http://www.eb.com

The Center for Defense Information (arms trade database, military spending)
> http://www.cdi.org/

Current Status of the Navy
> http://www.navy.mil/

Defense & Foreign Affairs' Strategic Policy (standard arms price index covers prices for military hardware)
> LEXIS-NEXIS (file DFA in EXEC, MARKET, NEWS, NSAMER, and
>> WORLD Libraries)

Defense Electronics
> LEXIS-NEXIS (file DEFELC in MARKET and NEWS Libraries)

Defense News (U.S. and international defense industry statistics)
> Dow Jones News/Retrieval
> LEXIS-NEXIS (file DEFNEW in NEWS Library)
> Wall Street Journal Interactive Edition Publications Library

Defense Week (military budget)
> Dow Jones News/Retrieval
> Wall Street Journal Interactive Edition Publications Library

Department of Defense (defense budget)
> http://www.dtic.mil/defenselink/

Department of Defense, Allied Contributions to the Common Defense
> http://www.dtic.mil/defenselink/pubs/allied_contrib95/index.html

Department of Defense Procurement Statistics, Procurement and Economic Information Division
> http://web1.whs.osd.mil/peidhome/peidhome.htm

Department of Defense Statistical Information Analysis Division (manpower, casualties, payroll trends, contracts)
> http://web1.whs.osd.mil/mmid/mmidhome.htm

Department of the Navy—Highlights of the Budget
> http://navweb.secnav.navy.mil/pubbud/9899/highbook/high_intro_u.html

For Your Eyes Only (arms sales, terrorism; partially excerpted on Soldier of Fortune Web site)
   http://www.sofmag.com/archive/ws/index.html

United States Air Force Library Fact Sheets (specifications for equipment; information on organizations within the Air Force, the Air Force in Operation Desert Storm, space equipment)
   http://www.af.mil/news/indexpages/fs_index.html

United States Navy Factfile (specifications of Navy equipment, including costs)
   http://www.chinfo.navy.mil/navpalib/factfile/ffiletop.html

Elected Officials

Congressional Honoraria Contributions (honoraria contributions to members of Congress by organizations, including PACs)
   LEXIS-NEXIS (file HONORA in CMPGN, ENTERT, and LEGIS Libraries)

Congressional Honoraria Receipts Report
   LEXIS-NEXIS (file MEMHON in CMPGN and LEGIS Libraries)

Congressional Legislative Record (major recent floor votes, member ratings by public interest groups)
   LEXIS-NEXIS (file MLEGIS in CMPGN and LEGIS Libraries)

Congressional Member Financial Disclosures
   LEXIS-NEXIS (file MEMFD in CMPGN and LEGIS Libraries)

Congressional Member Financial Report (includes opponents' financial statements)
   LEXIS-NEXIS (file MEMFIN in CMPGN and LEGIS Libraries)

Congressional Political Action Committee Report (PAC contributions to members of Congress)
   LEXIS-NEXIS (file PAC in CMPGN, ENTERT, and LEGIS Libraries)

Roll Call (richest members of Congress, House and Senate races, policy briefings)
   LEXIS-NEXIS (file ROLLCL in CMPGN, LEGIS, and NEWS Libraries)

Elections

Associated Press Campaign News (results of polls, elections, primaries, conventions, and caucuses)
   LEXIS-NEXIS (file CAMPGN in APOLIT and CMPGN Libraries)

Associated Press Election Wire (election results)
   LEXIS-NEXIS (file APELCT in CMPGN, NEWS, and TOPNWS Libraries)

Associated Press Political Service
   Dow Jones News/Retrieval
   Wall Street Journal Interactive Edition Publications Library

California Journal
  LEXIS-NEXIS file CAJRNL in CAL, CMPGN, EXEC, LEGIS, and NEWS Libraries)

Campaign Central
  http://www.clark.net/ccentral/

Cook Political Report (political races, including polls)
  LEXIS-NEXIS (file CKRPT in CMPGN and NEWS Libraries)

The Hotline (polls and races around the U.S.)
  LEXIS-NEXIS (file HOTLNE in CMPGN Library)

The Jefferson Project (election results, straw polls)
  http://www.voxpop.org/jefferson

Roll Call (richest members of Congress, House and Senate races, policy briefings)
  LEXIS-NEXIS (file ROLLCL in CMPGN, LEGIS, and NEWS Libraries)

Government Spending, Programs, and Employment

Consolidated Federal Funds Report (federal expenditures or obligations for grants, salaries, wages, procurement contracts, direct payments, loans, and insurance for the states, District of Columbia, and U.S. territories)
  http://www.census.gov/ftp/pub/govs/www/cffr.html

Federal Government Employment Data (U.S. Census Bureau)
  http://www.census.gov/ftp/pub/govs/www/apesfed.html

Federal Spending Stateside and Beyond
  http://www.clark.net/pub/lschank/web/fedspend.html

The Green Book Overview of Entitlement Programs
  http://aspe.os.dhhs.gov/

Office of Management and Budget: Budget Publications and Economic Report of the President (includes historical expenditures back to the 1920s)
  http://www.access.gpo.gov/su_docs/budget/index.html

U.S. Budget (summary of President's budget proposal)
  LEXIS-NEXIS (file BUDGET in EXEC Library)

State and Local Governments

Census of Governments (federal, state, and local governments)
  http://www.census.gov/ftp/pub/govs/www/index.html

Census State Data Centers (state-level data centers)
  http://www.census.gov/sdc/www/

Finance Data for the Largest Cities in the U.S. (U.S. Census Bureau)
http://www.census.gov/ftp/pub/govs/www/city50.html

Finance Data for the Largest Counties in the U.S. (U.S. Census Bureau)
http://www.census.gov/ftp/pub/govs/www/cou50.html

Local Government Employment and Payroll Data (U.S. Census Bureau)
http://www.census.gov/ftp/pub/govs/www/apesloc.html

State and Local Government Finance Estimates by State (U.S. Census Bureau) (covers
from 1988 to 1993)
http://www.census.gov/ftp/pub/govs/www/estimate.html

State Government Employment and Payroll Data by State (U.S. Census Bureau)
http://www.census.gov/ftp/pub/govs/www/apesst.html

State and Local Governments Meta-Indexes
http://lcweb.loc.gov/global/state/stategov.html

State Tax Collection Data by State (U.S. Census Bureau)
http://www.census.gov/ftp/pub/govs/www/statetax.html

CASE STUDY

Case Study 12-1: Government Spending

Purpose: This case study illustrates the difficulty of finding information one hears
bandied about every day.

Question: What percentage of the U.S. federal budget is spent on defense? On entitlements? On foreign aid?

Likely sources: The Office of Management and Budget, which publishes the budget;
the U.S. Treasury Department, which tracks expenditures; newspapers, which report
on government expenditures

Access points used: Full text

System: LEXIS-NEXIS (MAJPAP file)

Because I suspected that data on government Web sites might be formatted as long
spreadsheets that would make it hard to pick out which line items pertain to each category, I started with newspapers; these I knew would present the information in cap-
sulized form.

There were several considerations affecting my strategy:

- It's best to search several newspapers at once rather than trying one paper at a time.
- Because LEXIS-NEXIS charges by the search, I started broad so I wouldn't have
  to start over and incur additional charges.

- I confined the date to recent articles since I was interested in the current breakdown. (I could have used the CURRNWS file, which is limited to the last two years, but the coverage is so broad there that the system would have to search through all kinds of irrelevant sources.)

In the MAJPAP file, I typed `budget w/4 (u s or united states) w/10 (defense or entitlement* or foreign w/1 aid) and date aft 9/1/96`.

FIGURE 12-1

This strategy may have been overly restrictive, but it did answer the foreign aid part of the question. I got passages in which the terms *budget* and *United States* are in different sentences, such as:

> "Either way, foreign aid will continue to be less than 1 percent of the budget. The United States is fourth in overseas assistance and flat last among industrial nations as a fraction of GNP...."

I also got:

> "In fact, the United States devotes less than 1 percent of its budget to foreign aid."

A restrictive strategy on LEXIS-NEXIS answers the foreign aid portion of the question. We need to broaden the search to address the defense and entitlement angles better, however.

I was surprised the system found the second story, since *budget* and *United States* were not within four words of each other. The *1* must not be considered a word, and *of* is a stop word in this system. Perhaps *its* is too.

All but one of the other ten stories also treated foreign aid; one was about defense but didn't answer the question. To redo the search more broadly, leaving out foreign aid, I type `budget w/15 (u s or united states) w/15 (defense or entitlement*) and date aft 9/1/96` and got 75 hits. After narrowing (using the FOCUS feature) with `percent, per cent,` or `portion`, I got records that provided the following types of information:

- Proposed total for military spending for 1998, which is 3 percent less than the 1997 appropriation by Congress. (Comment: There was no comparison with total budget.)
- Breakdown of the defense budget itself and comparison with total defense budget.
- Exactly what I was looking for, but within the context of a letter to the editor. (Comment: Letters are not reliable sources. I could have excluded them,and perhaps I should have.)
- Percentage of decline in the military budget. (Comment: Military is another word I could try next time if I need to.)
- Portion of GDP (Gross Domestic Product) represented by military spending.

I was looking for patterns like "Defense spending represents x percent of the federal budget," but I didn't find anything resembling that. If such a sentence existed, I would have found it with my strategies. Or would I? I used the term (u s or united states) so that I wouldn't get the budgets of other countries. But most stories in American newspapers will assume The U.S. aspect and perhaps not use the term. I needed to go broader, leaving out reference to the U.S.

I tried again, with budget w/15 (defense or entitlement*) and date aft 9/1/96. Too many hits resulted over 1000 documents. I searched again, with more restrictions. Typing budget w/6 federal w/10 (defense or entitlement*) and date aft 9/1/96 gave me 239 hits. I FOCUSed on percent or per cent to narrow further and retrieved 128 items. That was still a lot, but I was loath to narrow too much.

The results still danced around the question until I got to a quote from Senator Pete Domenici, who claimed that half the budget is consumed by entitlements and 18 percent by defense. This information was close to what I wanted (although I wondered if *half* is exactly 50%), but with all due respect to Senator Domenici, I wanted to verify his numbers.

I kept going. Story number 18, from *The Rocky Mountain News* of February 11, 1997, was an editorial stating that entitlements make up 53 percent of the budget. Now I was getting somewhere. While editorial writers can be wrong, they have research departments and editors to check their facts, so they can be considered fairly reliable. However, my experiences in the editorial library at a major newspaper left me with just enough doubt to want to verify even further.

Story number 30, from *The Kansas City Star* of January 18, 1997, finally gave me what I wanted on the entitlement angle: "In 1970 entitlement spending claimed only 37 percent of the federal budget, according to the Congressional Budget Office. That figure had climbed to more than 47 percent in 1985. Last year it was above 55 percent." I knew that by that the writer meant somewhere between 55 and 56 percent rather than somewhere between 55 and 100 percent, though the sentence worded in an ambiguous way.

Story number 72 at last confirmed Senator Domenici's claim. The *Journal of Commerce* from November 7, 1996 said, "In 1995, 65 percent of the $1.5 trillion federal budget went automatically to entitlements and interest on the national debt, leaving 35 percent for all discretionary spending, including 18 percent for defense." Even though these figures referred to 1995 rather than 1996, since they represented a "second opinion," I was willing to accept them.

Lessons learned:

√ Information relating to budgets can be cut many ways, not all of which can be allowed for when formulating a strategy.

√ It's important to verify information that may come from biased or partisan sources.

√ An abundance of information on a topic may make the desired angle difficult to pinpoint.

√ Consider eliminating letters to the editor and editorials when searching newspapers.

Finding Sports, Entertainment, and Arts Statistics

S ports, entertainment, and the arts cover a very broad territory. Data include information from individual owners or teams, producers, distributors, and from groups or associations of those participating in, selling to, or observing the activity. Some samples include:

- Reports from trade associations, such as the American Booksellers Association
- Sales figures reports, such as bestseller lists
- Reports from theaters, record or video stores, sports arenas
- Reports from radio stations
- Surveys of TV viewers

TYPES OF DATA
You can find the following types of statistics about sports, entertainment, and the arts:

General
- Prices of movie, theater, concert, and sporting event tickets
- Attendance figures at movies, theaters, concerts, and sporting events

Art
- Earnings of artists and those in art-related occupations
- Numbers and financial status of galleries
- Prices of art

Film and Television
- Film and theater box office grosses
- Television and radio ratings
- Revenue from commercials, commercial prices
- Earnings of those in the film, radio, television, and theater industries

Music
- Air play (radio stations)
- Concert grosses
- Earnings of musicians and those in music-related occupations
- Top-selling music

Publishing
- Author and publisher earnings
- Magazine circulations
- Book sales

Sports
- Sports standings, records, and scores
- Earnings of athletes, coaches, and team owners
- Sporting event grosses and attendance

KEY PRODUCERS

Much sports, entertainment, and arts information is gathered and reported by the trade press and associations, including:

- Association of American Publishers
- BASELINE (producers of entertainment industry information)
- *Billboard*
- Book Industry Study Group
- *Editor & Publisher*
- Nielsen Media Research/A.C. Nielsen
- *Publishers Weekly*
- *Variety*
- Sports organizations like the NCAA, National Football League, National Basketball Association, National Hockey League, etc.

TYPES OF SOURCES

You will find sports, entertainment, and arts statistics reported in the following:

- Almanacs
- Encyclopedias
- Newspapers
- Trade journals and newspapers
- Yearbooks

BEST PLACES TO LOOK

Unlike the subjects in other chapters, sports, entertainment, and arts are well-covered by many types of sources: those provided by traditional online vendors and also those contributed by Web-based media organizations, associations, and almanac and encyclopedia publishers. Trade journals are particularly important sources for broadcasting, film and video, and publishing. This directory of major sources and their locations covers general sources first and is followed by categories for broadcasting, film and video, music, publishing, and sports.

Collections

LEXIS-NEXIS Entertainment Library (ENTERT)

LEXIS-NEXIS SPORTS Library

General

A Matter of Fact (multidisciplinary)
 FirstSearch (file FactSearch)
 SilverPlatter
 (plus others; see p. 4)

Amusement Business
 LEXIS-NEXIS (files MARS and PROMT in MARKET Library; file ASAPII in
  NEWS Library)
 ProQuest Direct

BPI Entertainment Newswire (concert grosses, ticket prices—including sports, top singles, top albums, top videos, box office charts)
 Electric Library
 LEXIS-NEXIS (file BPIENT in ENTERT Library)

FEDSTATS (federal government agency statistics locator)
 http://www.fedstats.gov

IAC Magazine Database
 DIALOG (file 47)
 DataStar (file MAGS)

Information Please Almanac
 Cognito!
 Encarta

Top Ten Awards Books, Movies, and Videos
 LEXIS-NEXIS (files AWARDS, BSTSLR, TOPMOV, and TOPVID in
  ENTERT Library)

Wall Street Journal Interactive Publications Library, Media & Entertainment Publications category

World Almanac
  Electric Library
  FirstSearch

Ziff Newsletters (entertainment)
  LEXIS-NEXIS (file ZET1 in ENTERT, MARKET, and NEWS Libraries)

NOTE: Most newspapers online exclude sports statistics found in tabular form.

Broadcasting

Asian Mass Communication and Information Centre
  http://irdu.nus.sg/amic/

Broadcasting
  DIALOG (file 148)

Broadcasting & Cable
  Dow Jones News/Retrieval
  Wall Street Journal Interactive Publications Library

Broadcasting/Cable TV Industry Reports
  LEXIS-NEXIS (file BRORPT in ENTERT Library)

Cable World
  Dow Jones News/Retrieval
  LEXIS-NEXIS (files MARS and PROMT in MARKET Library, abstracts only)
  Wall Street Journal Interactive Publications Library

Communications Daily
  Dow Jones News/Retrieval
  LEXIS-NEXIS (file COMDLY in ENTERT Library)
  Wall Street Journal Interactive Publications Library

Electronic Media (ratings, sales, financial information)
  Dow Jones News/Retrieval
  LEXIS-NEXIS (file EMEDIA in ENTERT, MARKET, NEWS, and PEOPLE Libraries)
  Wall Street Journal Interactive Publications Library

Hollywood Reporter (box office grosses, TV ratings)
  Dow Jones News/Retrieval
  LEXIS-NEXIS (file THR in ENTERT Library)
  Wall Street Journal Interactive Publications Library

Los Angeles Times
  DIALOG (file 630)
  Dow Jones News/Retrieval
  LEXIS-NEXIS (file LAT in multiple libraries)
  Wall Street Journal Interactive Publications Library

New Media Markets (cable TV, radio, satellites: market shares, prices, growth rates, consumer spending and attitudes)
    Dow Jones News/Retrieval
    LEXIS-NEXIS (file NEWMED in ENTERT, MARKET, NEWS, UK, and
        WORLD Libraries)
    Wall Street Journal Interactive Publications Library

Satellite TV Finance
    Dow Jones News/Retrieval
    LEXIS-NEXIS (file STVFIN in ENTERT Library)
    Wall Street Journal Interactive Publications Library

Television Digest
    DIALOG (files 16, 148, 636, 771, 772)
    Dow Jones News/Retrieval
    LEXIS-NEXIS (file TVDIG in ENTERT, MARKET, and NEWS Libraries)
    Wall Street Journal Interactive Publications Library

Top Ten Plex (top television shows and TV movies of all time)
    http://www.gigaplex.com/10top/10tv.htm

Film and video
BASELINE Box Office Grosses
    LEXIS-NEXIS (file GROSS in ENTERT Library)

BASELINE Latest Grosses
    LEXIS-NEXIS (file LGR in ENTERT Library)

Billboard (top video rentals)
    Electric Library
    LEXIS-NEXIS (file BILLBD in ENTERT Library)
    ProQuest Direct

Box Office Grosses
    LEXIS-NEXIS (file GROSS in ENTERT Library)

The Cinema Connection (worldwide TV ratings and film box office)
    http://www.socialchange.net.au/TCC/Awards_and_Box_Office/index.html

Daily Variety (Note: Not all tables with grosses, ratings, top rentals, etc. are included in the database, but you can find some grosses in the text; `film boxoffice report` works as a search term)
    Dow Jones News/Retrieval
    LEXIS-NEXIS (file DLYVTY in ENTERT Library)
    Wall Street Journal Interactive Publications Library

Hollywood Reporter (box office grosses, TV ratings)
> Dow Jones News/Retrieval
> LEXIS-NEXIS (file THR in ENTERT Library)
> Wall Street Journal Interactive Publications Library

Internet Movie Database Business Information (grosses, budgets, rental revenues, release dates)
> http://us.imdb.com/Sections/Business/Index/

Latest Box Office Grosses (grosses from the previous weekend)
> LEXIS-NEXIS (file LGR in ENTERT Library)

Los Angeles Times
> Dow Jones News/Retrieval
> LEXIS-NEXIS (file LAT in multiple libraries)
> Wall Street Journal Interactive Publications Library

New Media Markets (market shares, prices, growth rates, consumer spending and attitudes)
> Dow Jones News/Retrieval
> LEXIS-NEXIS (file NEWMED in ENTERT Library)
> Wall Street Journal Interactive Publications Library

Screen Finance
> Dow Jones News/Retrieval
> LEXIS-NEXIS (file SRNFIN in ENTERT Library)
> Wall Street Journal Interactive Publications Library

Service Annual Survey
> http://www.census.gov/svsd/www/sas.html

Variety (some film grosses in the full text)
> Dow Jones News/Retrieval
> LEXIS-NEXIS (file VARTY in ENTERT Library)
> Wall Street Journal Interactive Publications Library

Video Marketing News
> Dow Jones News/Retrieval
> Wall Street Journal Interactive Publications Library

Video Store
> DIALOG (files 16 and 570)
> Dow Jones News/Retrieval
> LEXIS-NEXIS (files MARS and PROMT in MARKET Library)
> Wall Street Journal Interactive Publications Library

Video Week
  Dow Jones News/Retrieval
  LEXIS-NEXIS (file VIDWK in ENTERT Library)
  Wall Street Journal Interactive Publications Library

Music
Billboard (albums, including by genre (Billboard 200); air play, including by genre; search for byline `weekly` with your subject terms)
  Dow Jones News/Retrieval
  Electric Library
  LEXIS-NEXIS (file BILLBD in ENTERT Library)
  ProQuest Direct
  Wall Street Journal Interactive Publications Library

Charts All Over the World (radio charts, sales charts, air play—various countries; links to other charts)
  http://www.lanet.lv/misc/charts/

MusicPlex (best-selling albums of all time)
  http://www.gigaplex.com/music/top25.html

Music Trades
  DIALOG (file 148)
  Dow Jones News/Retrieval
  LEXIS-NEXIS (file ASAPII in NEWS Library)
  Wall Street Journal Interactive Publications Library

Publishing
Advertising Age
  DIALOG (files 16, 570, 799)
  Dow Jones News/Retrieval
  LEXIS-NEXIS (file ADAGE in BUSFIN, ENTERT, MARKET, NEWS, and
      PEOPLE Libraries)
  Wall Street Journal Interactive Publications Library

Adweek's Marketing Week
  DIALOG (files 16, 148, 570)

American Booksellers Association
  http://www.bookweb.org/reference/

Baker & Taylor (book prices, units shipped)
  http://www.baker-taylor.com

Census of Manufactures
  http://www.census.gov/econ/www/ma0100.html

Census of Retail Trade
  http://www.census.gov/econ/www/retmenu.html

Editor & Publisher Magazine
  DIALOG (files 88 and 148)
  Dow Jones News/Retrieval
  LEXIS-NEXIS (file EPMAG in NEWS Library)
  ProQuest Direct
  Wall Street Journal Interactive Publications Library

Facts About Newspapers (Newspaper Association of America) (readership, advertising, sections read, both Canadian and American; includes historical statistics)
  http://www.naa.org/info/Facts/

Folio
  DIALOG (file 148)
  Dow Jones News/Retrieval
  Wall Street Journal Interactive Publications Library

Publishers Weekly
  DIALOG (files 47, 88, 148)
  Dow Jones News/Retrieval
  Wall Street Journal Interactive Publications Library

Subtext (financials in article form)
  http://www.bookwire.com/subtext/

Ulrich's International Periodicals Directory
  DIALOG (file 480)
  LEXIS-NEXIS (file ULRICH in BUSREF Library)

NOTE: Many publishing industry statistics are not yet online. Important producers include the Association of American Publishers (http://www.publishers.org), R. R. Bowker (http://www.bowker.com), and Book Industry Study Group (http://www.bookwire.com/bisg). For extensive lists and a few online statistics, see Book Industry Study Group at http://www.bookwire.com/bisg/research-resources/. Resources include those dealing with education, college, library and specialized markets, printing, and new media as well as trade books.

Sports

@Bat (The Official Site of Major League Baseball)
  http://www.majorleaguebaseball.com

ASAP Publications
  LEXIS-NEXIS (file ASAPII in SPORTS Library)

Britannica Online (see Major Team and Individual Sports: Major Team Sports: name of sport, such as baseball: History: Professional baseball, or other name of sport: records and statistics)
  http://www.eb.com

Britannica Sporting Record : The Olympic Games
  http://sports.eb.com

ESPNet Sportszone (fee)
  http://espnet.sportszone.com/

GolfWeb
  http://www.golfweb.com

Information Please Sports Almanac
  Cognito!
  Encarta Online Library

Leisure/Recreation Industry Reports
  LEXIS-NEXIS (file LEIRPT in ENTERT Library)

Olympics Factbook
  LEXIS-NEXIS (file OLYFAC in BUSREF and SPORTS Libraries)

The Sporting News
  Dow Jones News/Retrieval
  LEXIS-NEXIS (file TSN in MARKET, NEWS, SPORTS Libraries)
  ProQuest Direct
  Wall Street Journal Interactive Publications Library

The Sports Network (an extremely useful metasite for anyone interested in sports statistics, with individual player and team stats and records, match-ups, team rankings, report cards, divisional/conference/interleague records, attendance stats, and much more. Coverage includes professional, college and minor league baseball, football, hockey, men's and women's basketball, soccer (MLS, International, World Cup, CONCACAF), auto racing (NASCAR, Indy, art, Formula), golf (PGA, LPGA, Seniors, Nike, European Tour), horse racing (thoroughbred, harness), boxing, and men's and women's tennis.
  LEXIS-NEXIS (file SPONET in NEWS, TOPNWS, and SPORTS Libraries)
  http://www.sportsnetwork.com

CASE STUDIES

Case Study 13-1: Movie Budget

Purpose: This case study illustrates how to find business information pertaining to a movie. It also shows that systems aren't always logically designed, and proves that you sometimes have to get creative to answer questions.

Question: How much money was spent to make the movie "Independence Day"?

Likely sources: Internet Movie Database

Access points used: Links

System: Web site

The resource list in this chapter lists the Internet Movie Database Business Information site as a source for movie budgets, so I decided to give that a try. Until recently, this kind of information was very expensive to find. You either had to take a chance that it had been published in the *Los Angeles Times* or the entertainment trade publications, or you had to use expensive movie databases like the BASELINE series (which still provide great information and good value for the price).

The site is at http://us.imdb.com/Sections/Business/Index/. There, the Help told me that, to find movie budgets, I needed to search or browse by movie title, then click on a link that would get me to business information for the production.

I found an interesting bug at this site. When I went to the Business Section Browser, I was given the option to search or to browse by title, by letter of the alphabet, or by year. When I searched on "Independence Day," I got nothing. However, when I browsed through the letter "I," I found the movie. The Help facility was circular and didn't explain why I could find the movie by browsing but not by searching.

At the site, budget, grosses, and admissions were listed. The budget for the movie was a cool $75 million—a pittance (see Figure 13-2).

FIGURE 13-1

A great resource with a straightforward-looking interface is a little trickier than meets the eye. When I searched for "Independence Day" I found nothing, but browsing worked.

Lessons learned:

√ Interesting Web sites are being developed that can lessen dependence on older or more expensive sources.

√ You can't always depend on logical design or useful Help for a system. Sometimes you just have to be creative and try different strategies.

Case Study 13-2: Movie Attendance

Purpose: This case study illustrates a successful search of the same source on three different systems to find information about people's entertainment habits.

Question: How many and/or what percentage of U.S. adults go to the movies on a regular basis?

Likely sources: American Demographics, because it tracks spending and lifestyle attributes.

Access points used: Full text; individual journal; industry category

Systems: LEXIS-NEXIS; Web site; Wall Street Journal Interactive Publications Library

LEXIS-NEXIS FILE AMDEM

In LEXIS-NEXIS, I selected the AMDEM file in the NEWS Library for American Demographics and typed (movie! or film!) and (attend! or go!) and date aft 1/1/95. The exclamation point is the symbol for truncation and allowed me to pick up any words starting with the characters before it. I limited by date because I wanted recent material. I did not use the term *adult* because that might have narrowed the search too much, leaving out articles that didn't discriminate by age. It also might have restricted the search to sex movies.

I got 42 hits. The citation for number 12, from December of 1996, read as follows:

Tomorrow's Markets; Pg. 4. 1563 words. Going to the Movies; Young adults are the movie industry's best customers. But slow population growth and declining rates of movie attendance make them a shrinking market for movie theaters into the next century.

This article was a strong contender. Even though it focused on *young adults*, I reasoned it might include information about other adult markets (see Figure 13-4).

It did! It said:

*Adults aged 18 to 24 are significantly more likely to **go** to the **movies** at least once a month, at 34 percent, compared with 20 percent for all adults. They are more often*

FIGURE 13-2

Business Information for Independence Day (1996)

Budget
$75m

Opening Weekend
$50.2m (USA) (4 July 1996) (2282 screens)

Gross
ESP 1,797,301,907 (Spain)
$797.9m (worldwide)
$491.8m (Non-USA)
£35.694m (UK) (13 October 1996)
£31.193m (UK) (15 September 1996)
£16.034m (UK) (18 August 1996)
JPY 3,766,488,300 (Japan) (26 January 1997)
JPY 3,514,563,300 (Japan) (19 January 1997)
JPY 2,859,214,700 (Japan) (5 January 1997)
JPY 2,418,449,700 (Japan) (29 December 1996)
JPY 1,829,112,200 (Japan) (22 December 1996)
JPY 1,450,228,900 (Japan) (15 December 1996)
JPY 850,881,900 (Japan) (8 December 1996)
£36.8m (UK)
$306.124m (USA) (15 December 1996)
$306.052m (USA) (8 December 1996)
$305.891m (USA) (1 December 1996)

Some titles don't carry this much information in the Internet Movie Database, but we're lucky. We get budget, grosses, and admissions for "Independence Day."

FIGURE 13-3

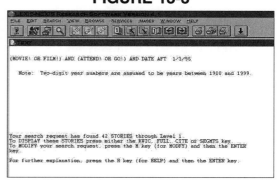

```
LEXIS-NEXIS Research Software Version 4. 1
FILE  EDIT  SEARCH  VIEW  BROWSE  SERVICES  IMAGES  WINDOW  HELP

TEXT

(MOVIE! OR FILM!) AND (ATTEND! OR GO!) AND DATE AFT  1/1/95

   Note: Two-digit year numbers are assumed to be years between 1900 and 1999.




Your search request has found 42 STORIES through Level 1.
To DISPLAY these STORIES press either the KWIC, FULL, CITE or SEGMTS key.
To MODIFY your search request, press the M key (for MODFY) and then the ENTER
key.
For further explanation, press the H key (for HELP) and then the ENTER key.
```

A broad search strategy yields 42 hits on LEXIS-NEXIS.

FIGURE 13-4

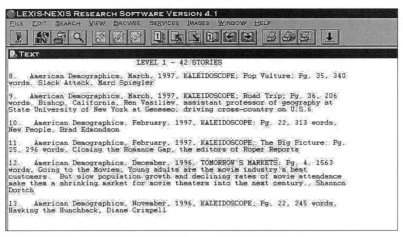

The 12th item from the LEXIS-NEXIS search looks like a good prospect because it mentions movie attendance in the title.

*than twice as likely as the population as a whole to have seen specific **movies** in the past month, according to Mediamark Research. They also make up disproportionate shares of the audience for most films viewed in theaters. People aged 18 to 24 are 13 percent of Mediamark's sample population, but 34 percent of those who **go** to the **movies** at least once a month.*

But even better, at the end of the article was a super table entitled "Projected Thousands of Adults Who **Attend Movies** At Least Once a Month, By Age, 1996, 2000, 2006, and 2010, and Percent Change, 1996-2000 and 2006-2010." The chart was broken down into 6 age ranges and All Adults. The sources listed were Mediamark Research, Census Bureau, and American Demographics. And the table was included in the full text!

Note that all my search terms were present except *film*. Had I used the term *adult* I still would have found this article. I also would have succeeded had I specified that (movie! or film!) had to be within a few words of (attend! or go!) instead of just appearing in the same record, but that wasn't necessary.

Wall Street Journal Interactive Edition Publications Library (http://interactive.wsj.com)

In the Wall Street Journal Interactive Publications Library, I could confine the search to American Demographics alone, or I could search the Marketing Publications category. I decided to try both.

Within the Marketing Publications category, I selected Advanced Search and then the Marketing box. I filled in the Look for Words in Full Article box with (movie$ or film$) and (go$ or attend$), selected Date range 01/1/95 to 05/21/97, and asked the system to sort headlines by relevance and to display them as the full article. Note that $ is the symbol for truncation and that 5/21/97 was the date I performed the search.

The American Demographics article that I found previously was number eight on the list.

FIGURE 13-5
The Advanced Search Screen from the Wall Street Journal Interactive Edition Publications Library

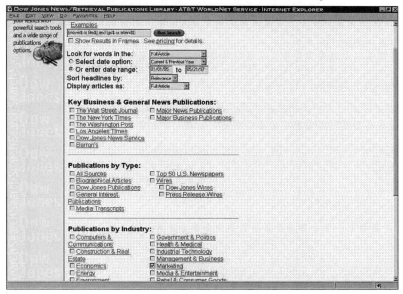

To compare strategies, I went back to the search screen to try American Demographics only. Keeping the same dates and other parameters, I typed:

```
(movie$ or film$) and (go$ or attend$) and demographics.so.
```

This statement indicated that I wanted the terms to appear in any source with the word *demographics* in its name. This time, my article was number one, and all the hits came from American Demographics.

American Demographics Web Site (http://www.demographics.com)
This site is considered shareware, meaning that if you try it and like it, you buy a subscription. If you order online, the annual price if $59—not bad if you do a lot of demographic or market research. The price also gets you a hard copy subscription.

I went to the Search Facility link under Research Tools; then under the Editorial Archives link, I selected American Demographics Magazine. This brought me to the search box, where I typed (movie or film) and (attend or go). In this system, the search engine automatically looks for longer words starting with the same letters. You can also use a minus sign before a variable to act as a NOT, so I tried to exclude early dates by putting in -1994 -1993 -1992 -1991 -1990, but it didn't work!

This search did bring up the same item that I found in the LEXIS-NEXIS search that is printed on p. 228. The wording was different from that of the LEXIS-NEXIS cite, but the value of the content was still recognizable.

Lessons learned:

√ Thinking out of the box is important. Although American Demographics isn't defined as an entertainment source, it had the answer I was looking for. Think about the approach your question takes as well as the general topic area it covers. (This was as much a question on how people spend their time and money as a question on the entertainment industry.)

√ If you can identify a specific source that is likely to answer the question (such as American Demographics), try that first before going broader.

√ Don't automatically discount article titles that are slightly skewed from the angle you want—the article may go on to cover what you need.

√ Even when you search the same source using the same strategy, if you're searching different systems, you will probably get different numbers of results and different wordings.

Finding Legal and Crime Statistics

C rime data comes from reports by law enforcement and criminal justice agencies, such as the FBI, local police departments, bureaus of corrections, etc. However, not all agencies report, and those that do report don't necessarily count in ways consistent with each other.

Because not all crimes result in arrests and/or convictions, observations are important auxiliary sources of statistics. According to Regina Schekall, a statistics buff and California Certified Crime Analyst-to be who sponsors the excellent Crime Statistics Site (http://www.crime.org), observations fall into two categories: direct and experimental. Direct observations involve monitoring known criminals or high-risk areas. Experimental observations consist of staged crimes followed by observation of the witnesses.

Reports from victims are gathered through the use of victimization surveys conducted by the U.S. Department of Justice and other organizations.

Reports from offenders help to round out the picture. Researchers gather offender data by interviewing prison inmates; by establishing relationships with offenders and participating in their world; and by sampling the general population in the attempt to identify and get information from offenders.

TYPES OF DATA

An enormous amount of data contributes to the field of legal and crime statistics. Some of the contributors are listed below under the categories of attorneys and law offices, legal education, courts and judges, crime, criminals, law enforcement, and corrections.

Attorneys and law offices

- Numbers of attorneys by type of practice, geographical area, etc.
- Demographics of attorneys
- Fees charged by attorneys; income of attorneys
- Publications by attorneys
- Demographics of law office personnel
- Earnings of law office personnel
- Computer use in law offices
- Law office expenditures

Legal education

- Demographics of law students
- Law schools, law school professors
- Computer use in law schools
- Bar examination
- Continuing education for attorneys

Courts and judges

- Court case processing time
- Number of cases per jurisdiction
- Numbers of cases of particular types
- Court costs
- Numbers and types of judges
- Judges' salaries
- Demographics of judges
- Demographics of court personnel
- Earnings of court personnel
- Budgets and expenditures of courts
- Jury demographics
- Jury behavior
- Jury selection

Crime

- Crime numbers and rates
- Drug-related crimes
- Crimes committed using guns
- White collar crime, computer crime
- Retail crime
- Violent crime
- Dollar amounts of stolen goods, drugs sold, etc.
- Locations of crimes
- Arrests
- Prosecutions
- Plea bargaining
- Confessions
- Types of evidence

- Bail
- Demographics of victims

Criminals

- Demographics of criminals, jail and prison inmates; numbers of prisoners in solitary confinement, on death row, with AIDS, etc.
- Convictions and acquittals
- Sentences assigned
- Sentences served
- Prison populations
- Recidivism
- Executions

Law enforcement

- Numbers of law enforcement personnel; sizes of agencies and departments
- Budgets of law enforcement agencies
- Funding of law enforcement agencies
- Shootings by law enforcement personnel
- Police brutality
- Law enforcement personnel killed in the line of duty
- Law enforcement personnel salaries
- Law enforcement personnel pensions
- Demographics of law enforcement personnel
- Computer use in law enforcement
- Stolen property recovered

Corrections

- Demographics of corrections personnel
- Earnings of corrections personnel
- Computer use in corrections
- Corrections budgets and expenditures
- Corrections funding

KEY PRODUCERS

Government at all levels, and research and university centers gather and produce statistics in the legal and criminal area. They include:

- Bureau of Justice Statistics, U.S. Department of Justice

- Criminal justice research centers (such as the Hindelang Criminal Justice Research Center at the University of Albany, which publishes the Sourcebook of Criminal Justice Statistics)
- Federal Bureau of Investigation
- State and local law enforcement agencies
- Statistical Abstract of the U.S.

TYPES OF SOURCES
You will find legal and crime statistics gathered and reported in various reports and statistical compendia.

BEST PLACES TO LOOK
Web-based sources dominate the legal and crime area, particularly due to the involvement of government agencies, universities, and international organizations. However, don't forget almanacs and professional journals. This directory lists sources and locations for general legal statistics and in the specific areas of courts, crime, lawyers, and prisons.

General
ASI (American Statistics Index) (for *identifying* statistical publications produced by the U.S. government)
  DIALOG (file 102)
  Scheduled to be on LEXIS-NEXIS in 1998, including selected full text

FEDSTATS (federal government agency statistics locator)
  http://www.fedstats.gov

Information Please Almanac
  Cognito!
  Encarta

A Matter of Fact (multidisciplinary)
  FirstSearch (file FactSearch)
  SilverPlatter
  (plus others; see p. 4)

NCJRS (National Criminal Justice Reference Service)
  DIALOG (file 21)

State and Local Government
  http://www.piperinfo.com/state/states/html (search here for attorney general for a
    list of links to all AG sites, some of which have statistics)

World Almanac
  Electric Library
  FirstSearch

Courts

Administrative Office of the U.S. Courts (caseloads of U.S. courts and Supreme Court—look for reports and press releases)
http://www.uscourts.gov/

Caseload Highlights (National Center of State Courts)
http://www.ncsc.dni.us/research.htm

Facts About the American Civil Justice System (American Bar Association) (tort filings, caseloads and types of cases, product liability cases, numbers of lawyers in some countries)
http://www.abanet.org/media/factbook.html

Statistical Abstract of the United States
http://www.census.gov/stat_abstract

Crime

Bureau of Justice Statistics
http://www.ojp.usdoj.gov/bjs/

Crime Statistics Site by Regina Schekall (international links, national and state links, county and city links—a phenomenal metasite)
http://www.crime.org

Facts About the American Criminal Justice System (American Bar Association)
http://www.abanet.org/media/factbook.html

Federal Bureau of Investigation Uniform Crime Reports
http://www.fbi.gov/homepage.htm

National Archive of Criminal Justice Data
http://www.icpsr.umich.edu/NACJD/index.html

National Institute of Justice
http://www.ncjrs.org/nijhome.htm

Sourcebook of Criminal Justice Statistics
http://www.albany.edu/sourcebook/

UNCJIN (United Nations World Crime Survey)
http://www.ifs.univie.ac.at/~uncjin/wcs.html

Uniform Crime Reports (arrests, crimes reported—by state, county, or total)
http://www.lib.virginia.edu/socsci/crime/

Lawyers

LEXIS-NEXIS LEGNEW Library (news about the U.S. legal industry and legal profession)

National Archive of Criminal Justice Data (demographics of lawyers, attitudes toward lawyers, sizes of firms, types of practices)
http://www.icpsr.umich.edu/NACJD/index.html

Statistical Abstract of the U.S.
http://www.census.gov/stat_abstract

U.S. Bureau of Justice Statistics (prosecutors)
http://www.ojp.usdoj.gov/bjs/

U.S. Bureau of Labor Statistics (for attorney salaries, search on attorneys or lawyers)
http://stats.bls.gov

Prisons
Federal Bureau of Prisons Quick Facts (inmate and staff demographics, number of institutions, type of offense, length of sentence and stay—includes total sentenced and unsentenced populations back to 1964)
http://www.bop.gov/facts.html

Statistical Abstract of the United States Law Enforcement, Courts, and Prisons
http://www.census.gov/stat_abstract

CASE STUDIES

Case Study 14-1: Terrorism

Purpose: This case study illustrates how to search Web sites of government agencies for crime statistics. It also highlights the variability of data formats (HTML, PDF, ASCII, etc.) and the importance of being prepared to deal with any one of them. The study shows that, even when you know which agency is responsible for a particular subject, you still have to be creative to find the desired information.

Question: What are the latest figures on terrorist incidents in the U.S.?

Likely sources: FBI; Bureau of Justice Statistics at http://www.ojp.usdoj.gov/bjs/

Access points used: Links; titles; index terms

System: Web site

Since terrorism falls within the jurisdiction of the FBI, I thought of the Uniform Crime Reports put out by the FBI. The version of Uniform Crime Reports on the FBI Web site is a 7 megabyte PDF file, not something I cared to tangle with, so I looked for something easier to work with. There is an interactive series of screens at the University of Virginia's site at http://www.lib.virginia.edu/socsci/crime/. However, after looking there, I discovered that the Uniform Crime Reports *does not* cover terrorism.

Next I tried the Bureau of Justice Statistics, which offers a wide selection of crime statistics (http://www.ojp.usdoj.gov/bjs/). Here's the list of topics:

- Crimes and Victims
- Drugs and Crime

- Criminal Offenders
- Law Enforcement
- Prosecution
- Courts and Sentencing
- Corrections
- Expenditure and Employment
- Criminal Record Systems
- Special Topics
- Other Sources

I considered the Crimes and Victims link but concluded it might be too broad. Instead I started with Special Topics. There were three categories under Special Topics:

- Criminal Justice, General
- Firearms and Crime
- The World Factbook of Criminal Justice Systems

Under Criminal Justice, General, there were links to the 1994 and 1995 Sourcebook of Criminal Justice Statistics as well as some off-topic material. I chose the 1995 edition and followed a link to the Sourcebook itself at http://www.albany.edu/sourcebook.

There was a clickable listing of sections, and also a link to Searching by Keywords. I chose the latter (see Figure 14-3).

I was given the choice of searching the index, tables and figures, or looking at PDF files. I started with the tables and figures by typing `terrorism` in the box and pressing Submit.

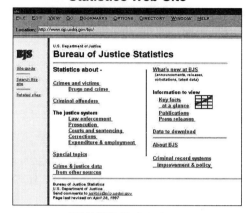

FIGURE 14-1
The Bureau of Justice Statistics Web Site

FIGURE 14-2

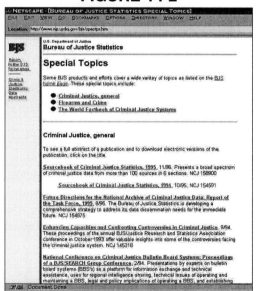

The Special Topics section in the Bureau of Justice Statistics includes the Sourcebook of Criminal Justice Statistics.

The result was 1 hit: "Casualties resulting from international terrorism involving U.S. citizens, by type of casualty, 1981-95." This wasn't really what I wanted. I wanted terrorist incidents in the U.S.

I went back and picked the Search the Index link. The page had a listing of index terms, and the word *terrorism* leaped out at me. I didn't need to search it—I just clicked on the term.

FIGURE 14-3

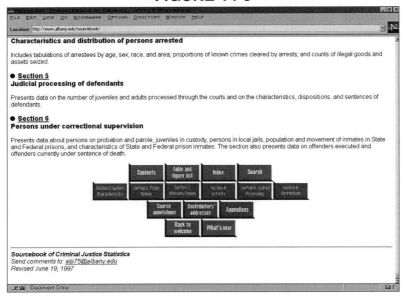

Navigate through the Sourcebook of Criminal Justice Statistics using options such as Contents, Table and Figure List, Index, and Search.

Bingo! The second entry was "Terrorist incidents, by type of incident and target, United States, 1982 - 94 (aggregate)." There was a link to a 4K Acrobat file—small. I clicked on it.

After the page loaded in Acrobat, I magnified it (it was too small to read in its normal state), and saw that the total for 1982 to 1994 was 177 incidents. There were 142 bombings, 4 malicious destructions of property, 2 acts of sabotage, 4 hostile takeovers, 8 arsons, 11 kidnapping/assault/alleged assassinations/assassinations, 5 robberies/attempted robberies, and 1 hijacking. The table did not break the incidents down by year. The source was listed as the Federal Bureau of Investigation, but not the Uniform Crime Reports.

Lessons learned:

√ Sometimes the obvious place to look is the wrong one.

√ Searching by keywords doesn't always pick up relevant material. (I searched figures and tables for `terrorism`, but I didn't find the table of Terrorist Incidents, even though it was there.) Browsing is an equally important strategy.

√ Don't take No for an answer—until you reach the point of diminishing returns.

Case Study 14-2: Number of Lawyers

Purpose: This case study demonstrates searching full text for information that is hard to describe. It shows the dual meanings of terms like *attorney* and *practice*. It

---

demonstrates the importance of terms like "study" and "survey" when searching full text and it highlights the complementary relationship between full-text sources and statistical compendia.

Question: How many lawyers are there in the United States?

Likely sources: American Lawyer; other law profession journals and newsletters; Statistical Abstract of the U.S.

Access points used: Full text; narrowing search field to a particular journal

System: LEXIS-NEXIS (file American Lawyer in LEGNEW Library); Web site

In the LEXIS-NEXIS LEGNEW Library, AMLAWR file, I typed (lawyers or attorneys) w/2 practic! w/6 united states. This statement was designed to find statements along the lines of "There are x number of lawyers practicing in the United States."

FIGURE 14-4

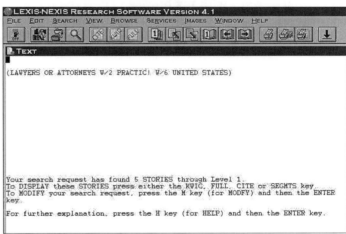

This simple search statement on LEXIS-NEXIS should find items that include wording such as "There are x number of attorneys practicing in the United States."

One item from my results read "Of the 618,000 lawyers practicing in the United States....", but it's from 1987. This excerpt showed that the strategy is sound, but the data was too old.

Next I tried a FREE-STYLE search: How many attorneys are there in the United States? And I tried the following FREESTYLE search, with not much luck: How many lawyers practice in the United States? Then I went back to command searching: (attorneys or lawyers) w/3 (number or rise or increase or swell!) and date aft 1/1/95.

I encountered the following red herrings:

- *Attorney* is often used in *attorney general.*

- *Practice* turns up in *private practice.*

- Measures are expressed in ways other than raw numbers, such as "it has been reported that about two thirds of all the lawyers in the world are in the United States...." and "The total active lawyer population rose 11.5 percent from 1988 to 1991...."

Without angles to search for, such as pay, or salary, or incidence, I was very much dependent upon how the text was worded, and it wasn't worded correctly here. I gave up this tactic and tried another strategy.

The Statistical Abstract of the U.S. usually includes various labor statistics. Sometimes they're too general to answer specific questions, but I was willing to try. I went hopefully to Stat Abs at http://www.census.gov/stat_abstract. Once there, I could select Law Enforcement, Courts, and Prisons; or Labor Force, Employment, and Earnings. I went with Labor Force, Employment, and Earnings because that category usually includes totals for particular occupations. (*NOTE: There is an online index to the Statistical Abstract, but it is an exact copy of the paper index, and lists topics by page only. I could look there for* lawyers *or* attorneys, *but that would only give me a vague idea where to look on the Web site, which is arranged by broad category, not page numbers.*)

The data was in PDF format, so it was a good thing that I had Adobe Acrobat Reader configured to work with my browser. Once the file was loaded, I used Acrobat's Find feature—the icon with the binoculars—to look for my keywords: *lawyers* and *attorneys*.

Table 637, Employed Civilians, by Occupation, Sex, Race, and Hispanic Origin: 1983 and 1995, had the answer. Under the section called Managerial and Professional Specialty, there was a row for Lawyers and Judges, and then a row for Lawyers alone. In 1995, the total number of employed lawyers was 894,000. (The column itself said 894, but at the top, the heading gave the key "Total employed (1,000)").

Lessons learned:

√ Even a perfect strategy won't work if the data isn't present.

√ Searching full text with terms that carry different meanings in various contexts can mislead.

√ When you need a national head count of people employed in a particular occupation, statistical compendia are often better sources than those offering full-text descriptions.

√ Sources that sound too general or comprehensive may nevertheless include the specific data you need in a small section.

√ Be sure to read codes and keys in tables with figures to make sure you interpret the numbers correctly.

Finding International Statistics

nternational statistics cover the same subjects as those described in the other chapters in this book, all of which deal predominantly with the United States. They are generally gathered by use of the same methodologies, that is, country-level statistics come from censuses, surveys, studies, and administrative records. They are also derived from that same data by the use of extraction programs, as well as for-mulae and algorithms. Problems of validity may be compounded when gathering infor-mation from more than one country because circumstances and definitions will vary by location and custom. Problems are further exacerbated when statistics are sought or compiled by multi- or intergovernmental units. Some contributors include:

- International and nongovernmental organizations
- Country statistical offices
- Banks and other financing institutions
- Private companies
- Trade associations and chambers of commerce

TYPES OF DATA
While any type of data described in the other chapters can be gathered at the national or international level, the most readily available types of country and world informa-tion include:

- Population and demographics
- Health and vital statistics
- Literacy
- Economic indicators
- Education

KEY PRODUCERS
National, regional, and intergovernmental agencies producing statistics include:

- Eurostat (Statistical Office of the European Communities)

- Statistical agencies of various national governments. For metasites encompassing these agencies on the Web, see:

  Statistical Agencies (International), U.S. Bureau of the Census
  http://www.census.gov/main/www/stat-int.html

  International Statistical Offices at the Office of National Statistics, UK
  http://www.ons.gov.uk/pages/links.htm

  Links to Statistical Agencies at the Management and Coordinating Agency, Japan
  http://www.stat.go.jp/1.htm

- United Nations and its agencies (Food and Agriculture Organization, International Monetary Fund, UNESCO, World Bank, etc.)
- Central banks
- U.S. Department of State
- Central Intelligence Agency

TYPES OF SOURCES

You will find international statistics gathered and reported in sources such as:

- Almanacs
- Encyclopedias
- Statistical compendia
- Yearbooks

BEST PLACES TO LOOK

As you might expect, North American and European information is easier to come by than statistics focusing on other parts of the world. Sources for other areas of the world are becoming more plentiful as the globe shrinks, but methodologies remain inconsistent and problematic everywhere. This directory is arranged with collections and specialized services first, followed by general sources and their locations, and then listings for specific subjects or regions, in this order:

- Africa
- Asia Pacific
- Business and Economy (General)
- Country Statistical Agencies
- Defense
- Demographics
- Environment
- Europe
- Industries
- International Agencies

- Latin America
- Middle East
- North America
- Russia and the Commonwealth of Independent States

Collections and Specialized Services

- LEXIS-NEXIS AUST Library (Australia)
- LEXIS-NEXIS CANADA Library
- LEXIS-NEXIS EUROPE Library
- LEXIS-NEXIS INVEST Library (regional financial and economic analyst reports)
- LEXIS-NEXIS MDEAFR Library (Middle East and Africa)
- LEXIS-NEXIS MEXICO Library
- LEXIS-NEXIS NSAMER Library (North and South America)
- LEXIS-NEXIS UK Library (United Kingdom/British Isles)
- LEXIS-NEXIS WORLD Library

General

ASAP Publications (these sources span various subjects including news, business, and finance)

  LEXIS-NEXIS (file ASAPII in the following groups: ASIAPC (ALLASI); EUROPE (ALLEUR); MDEAFR (ALLMDE); NSAMER (ALLNSA, CANADA, SAMER); WORLD (ALLWLD))

ASI (American Statistics Index) (for *identifying* statistical publications produced by the U.S. government)

  DIALOG (file 102)

Country Forecast (economic forecasts for the medium term)

  LEXIS-NEXIS (file BIFSVC in multiple libraries)

Country Report Service

  DataStar (file FSRI)

Country Reports (demographics, elections, business, economic indicators)

  LEXIS-NEXIS (many different file names in ASIAPC, EUROPE, MDEAFR, and NSAMER Libraries)

EIU Country Forecasts (five-year forecasts and historical)

  SilverPlatter

Infonation (economy, social indicators, population, geography, carbon dioxide emissions, literacy, school expenditures and enrollments, literacy, life expectancy, newspaper circulation, motor vehicles)

  http://www.un.org/pubs/cyberschoolbus/infonation

Information Please Almanac
  Cognito!
  Encarta

International Data Base, U.S. Bureau of the Census (demographics and socioeconomic statistics)
  http://www.census.gov/ftp/pub/ipc/www/idbnew.html

Kaleidoscope: Current World Data (overview of economy, people, media, population, armed forces, health care, transportation, communications, vital statistics for countries around the world)
  LEXIS-NEXIS (file KCWD in ASIAPC, BUSFIN, EUROPE, MDEAFR, NSAMER, and WORLD Libraries)

Library of Congress Country Studies
  http://lcweb2.loc.gov/frd/cs/cshome.html

Penn World Tables (population, economy, 1950-1992)
  http://www.nber.org/pwt56.html

UNESCO Statistical Yearbook (population, education, science, technology, research and development, libraries, media, publishing, cultural activities)
  http://unescostat.unesco.org

U.S. Department of State Information (includes report on state of human rights around the world, global issue fact sheets)
  LEXIS-NEXIS (file DSTATE in numerous libraries)

Wall Street Journal Interactive Publications Library, select one or more publications by region

World Almanac
  Electric Library
  FirstSearch

World Factbook
  Electric Library
  LEXIS-NEXIS (file WOFACT in multiple libraries)
  http://www.odci.gov/cia/publications/pubs.html

World Resources (World Resources Institute)
  http://www.wri.org/wri/wr-96-97/

Ziff Newsletters
  LEXIS-NEXIS (multiple files and libraries)

Africa
Africa News
  LEXIS-NEXIS (file AFRNWS in MDEAFR, NEWS, and WORLD Libraries)

African Population Database Documentation (United Nations Environment Programme; includes figures back to 1960)
  http://grid2.cr.usgs.gov/globalpop/africa/

ArabNet
  http://www.arab.net

Central Bank of Kenya
  http://www.arcc.or.ke/cbk.htm

Indian Ocean Newsletter (economies of countries on the eastern half of the African continent)
  LEXIS-NEXIS (file IONLR in MDEAFR, NEWS, and WORLD Libraries)

Asia Pacific

ASAPII Publications
  LEXIS-NEXIS (file ALLASI in NEWS Library)

Asia-Pacific Business Journals
  DIALOG (file 748)

Asia-Pacific News
  DIALOG (file 728)

Asia Population Database Documentation (United Nations Environment Programme)
  http://grid2.cr.usgs.gov/globalpop/asia/

Asian Development Bank
  http://www.asiandevbank.org

Business Asia (economic outlooks, vital statistics)
  LEXIS-NEXIS (file BUASIA in multiple libraries)

Business China (economic trends, vital statistics, market indicators in the People's Republic of China)
  LEXIS-NEXIS (file BUCHIN in multiple libraries)

China Hand
  LEXIS-NEXIS (file CHINAH in ASIAPC, BUSFIN, EUROPE, and WORLD Libraries)

Japan Economic Newswire Plus (Japanese economic indicators, industry association statistics, commodities and securities, public opinion polls)
  BrainWave
  DIALOG (file 612)
  Dow Jones News/Retrieval
  LEXIS-NEXIS (file JEN in multiple libraries)
  Wall Street Journal Interactive Publications Library

Japan News Wire (economic, corporate, industrial, and financial)
  DataStar (files JPNW, JPND)

Jiji Press Ticker Service (economic indicators, stocks, bonds, financial markets, etc. in Japan)
LEXIS-NEXIS (file JIJI in multiple libraries)

Reserve Bank of India
http://www.reservebank.com/

South China Morning Post (English-language newspaper published in Hong Kong)
DIALOG (file 726)
Dow Jones News/Retrieval
Wall Street Journal Interactive Publications Library

Xinhua (New China) News Agency (People's Republic of China economy, industry, trade, agriculture, sports, culture)
Dow Jones News/Retrieval
LEXIS-NEXIS (file XINHUA in multiple libraries)
Wall Street Journal Interactive Publications Library

Yomiuri Report from Japan (includes polls and surveys)
LEXIS-NEXIS (file RPTJAP in ASIAPC, EUROPE, MDEAFR, NEWS, and
WORLD Libraries)

Business and Economy (General)
Associated Banks of Europe Corporation (demographics, economic indicators, wages, prices, production for countries around the world)
LEXIS-NEXIS (file ABECOR in multiple libraries)

Business Update (latest economic performance of the ten largest Organization for Economic Cooperation and Development countries)
LEXIS-NEXIS (file BUSUPD in multiple libraries)

Country Briefings
Profound

Crossborder Monitor (business, economic, currency, and industry outlooks and trends around the world)
LEXIS-NEXIS (file BUSINT in multiple libraries)

Economist Intelligence Unit—Country Profiles (six-year retrospective of main macro-economic indicators)
LEXIS-NEXIS (file COUPRF in ASIAPC, BUSFIN, EUROPE, MDEAFR, NSAMER,
and WORLD Libraries)

EIU Country Reports (trade and economic data, industrial trends, economic outlook)
LEXIS-NEXIS (file COURPT in ASIAPC, BUSFIN, EUROPE, MDEAFR, NSAMER,
and WORLD Libraries)

EIU: The Economist Intelligence Unit (international trade, investment, finance, economics, equity markets, taxes)
  DIALOG (file 627)

EIU Tradewire (trade, leading markets, and general economy)
  http://www.i-trade.com/infosrc/eiu/eiuhome.shtml

Financial Times Full Text
  DIALOG (file 622)
  Dow Jones News/Retrieval
  Wall Street Journal Interactive Publications Library

Global Economic Outlook
  ProQuest Direct

Handbook of International Economic Statistics 1995
  http://www.odci.gov/cia/publications/pubs.html

IBC International Country Risk Guide (economic and political indicators)
  LEXIS-NEXIS (file IBCCRG in ASIAPC, BUSFIN, EUROPE, MDEAFR, NSAMER, and WORLD Libraries)

IBC Political Risk Service (economic forecasts)
  LEXIS-NEXIS (file IBCRPT in ASIAPC, BUSFIN, EUROPE, MDEAFR, NSAMER, and WORLD Libraries)

International Risk & Payment Review (risks of trading and investing in various markets; includes a risk indicator and rankings)
  DataStar (file IRPR)

Countryline Database
  Profound

WIS Country Data Forecasts (economic indicators for the last six years, the current year, and five years hence)
  LEXIS-NEXIS (file WISFOR in multiple libraries)

WIS Country Outlooks (economic, financial, and business indicators, historical data, and forecasts for two years)
  LEXIS-NEXIS (file WISOUT in multiple libraries)

World Financial Markets (Third World debt, world oil industry, foreign exchange, international monetary affairs, production, prices, forecasts)
  LEXIS-NEXIS (file WLDFIN in BANKS, BUSFIN, MARKET, NEWS, and WORLD Libraries)

.xls (economic indicators, demographics, exports and advertising expenditures by industry, retail sales, employment by industry; results in spreadsheet format)
  http://www.xls.com

Country Statistical Agencies

Here you'll find population, economic indicators, health, housing, education, manufacturing, industry, agriculture, labor, finance, geography, natural resources, climate, construction, trade, prices, wages, justice, tourism, elections, culture, income, and more.

Argentina Instituto Nacional De Estadistica y Censos (in Spanish)
http://www.indec.mecon.ar/default.htm

Australian Bureau of Statistics
http://www.statistics.gov.au/

Bolivia Business Online
http://www.boliviabiz.com/business/stats.htm

Brazilian Agency for Statistical, Geographic, Cartographic, Geodetic and Environmental Information
http://www.ibge.gov.br/english/e-home.htm

Bulgaria (National Statistical Institute of the Republic of Bulgaria) (in English)
http://www.acad.bg/BulRTD/nsi/index.htm

Canada (Statistics Canada) (in English and French)
http://www.statcan.ca/

Chile Instituto Nacional de Estadisticas (in Spanish)
http://www.conicyt.cl/servidores/ (selectINE)

Colombia Departmento Administrativo Nacional de Estadistica (DANE) (in Spanish)
http://www.sin.com.co/Clientes/DANE/

Commonwealth of Independent States (Interstate Statistical Committee of the Commonwealth; subscription required)
http://www.unece.org/stats/cisstat/mainpage.htm

Croatia (Republic of Croatia Central Bureau of Statistics) (in Croatian)
http://www.dzs.hr/

Cyprus Department of Statistics and Research (in English and Greek)
http://www.pio.gov.cy/update/

Czech Statistical Office
http://infox.eunet.cz/csu/csu_e.html

Denmark (Statistics Denmark)
http://www.dst.dk/internet/startuk.htm

Ecuador Instituto Nacional de Estadistica y Censos (in Spanish)
http://www4.inec.gov.ec/

Finland (Statistics Finland) (in Finnish and English)
http://www.stat.fi/sf/home.html

France (Institut National de la Statistique et des Etudes Economiques) (select the Publications link)
http://www.insee.fr

Germany Federal Statistical Office
http://www.statistik-bund.de/e_home.htm

Hong Kong Census and Statistics Department
http://www.info.gov.hk/censtatd/eindex.htm

Hungarian Central Statistical Office (in English and Hungarian)
http://www.ksh.hu/eng/homeng.html

India (Reserve Bank of India)
http://www.reservebank.com/

Indonesia Central Bureau of Statistics
http://www.bps.go.id/

Israel Central Bureau of Statistics
http://www.cbs.gov.il

Italy (Instituto Nazionale de Statistica) (in Italian)
http://petra.istat.it/

Jordan (Central Bank of Jordan)
http://www.cbj.gov.jo/

Japan Management and Coordination Agency
http://www.stat.go.jp/1.htm

Kenya (Central Bank of Kenya)
http://www.arcc.or.ke/cbk.htm

Korea (Republic Of) National Statistics Office (in English)
http://www.nso.go.kr/intro/e-intro.htm

Latvia Central Statistical Bureau (in English)
http://www.latnet.lv/ligumi/CSBL/

Lithuania Statistikos Departamentas (some in English)
http://www.std.lt/

Luxembourg STATEC (in French)
http://statec.gouvernement.lu/

Macau Census and Statistics Department (some in English)
http://macau.ctm.net/~dseccddi/ihome.htm

Malta Central Office of Statistics
http://www.magnet.mt/home/cos/

Mexico Instituto Nacional de Estadistica, Geografia e Informatica (INEGI) (in Spanish and English)
http://www.inegi.gob.mx/homeing/homeinegi/homeing.html

Netherlands (Statistics Netherlands) (in Dutch and English)
http://www.cbs.nl/index.htm

New Zealand (Statistics New Zealand)
http://www.stats.govt.nz/statsweb.nsf?OpenDatabase

Norway (Statistics Norway) (in Norwegian and English)
http://www.ssb.no/

Palestinian Authority
http://www.pcbs.org/

Peru Instituto Nacional de Estadistica e Informatica (in Spanish)
http://www.inei.gob.pe/

Poland Central Statistical Office
http://ciesin.ci.uw.edu.pl/

Quebec Bureau of Statistics (in French and English)
http://www.bsq.gouv.qc.ca/bsq/ang/bsq.html

Republic of Slovenia Statistical Office (in Slovenian and English)
http://www.sigov.si/zrs/letinde.html

Russia Goskomstat
http://feast.fe.msk.ru/koi/infomarket/emn/rating/gstat.html

Scotland General Register Office
http://www.open.gov.uk/gros/groshome.htm

Singapore (Statistics Singapore)
http://www.singstat.gov.sg/

Slovenia (Statistical Office of the Republic of Slovenia)
http://www.sigov.si/zrs/index_e.html

South Africa Central Statistical Service
http://www.css.gov.za/

Spain Instituto Nacional de Estadistica (some in English)
http://www.ine.es/

Sweden (Statistics Sweden) (in Swedish and English)
http://www.scb.se/indexeng.htm

Switzerland (Swiss Federal Statistical Office)
http://www.admin.ch/bfs/eindex.htm

Taiwan Ministry of Economic Affairs
http://www.moea.gov.tw/

Turkey State Institute of Statistics (in Turkish and English)
http://www.die.gov.tr/ENGLISH/index.html

United Kingdom Office for National Statistics
http://www.ons.gov.uk

Venezuela Oficina Central de Estadistica e Informatica (in Spanish)
http://www.ocie.gov.ve/

Defense

Defense Marketing International (defense budgets of countries)
  Dow Jones News/Retrieval
  Wall Street Journal Interactive Publications Library

Jane's Defence & Aerospace News/Analysis (defense industries and budgets both U.S. and non-U.S.)
  BrainWave
  DIALOG (file 587)

Periscope—Daily Defense News Capsules (defense budgets)
  Dow Jones News/Retrieval
  Wall Street Journal Interactive Publications Library

Demographics

Asian Mass Communication and Information Centre
  http://irdu.nus.sg/amic/

Global Population Distribution Database (United Nations Environment Programme)
  http://grid2.cr.usgs.gov/globalpop/1-degree/

Walden Country Reports (demographics and other major indicators)
  LEXIS-NEXIS (file COUREP in multiple libraries)

World Factbook
  Electric Library
  http://www.odci.gov/cia/publications/pubs.html

Environment

Europe Environment
  Dow Jones News/Retrieval
  LEXIS-NEXIS (file EURENV in EUROPE, MARKET, NEWS, and WORLD Libraries)
  Wall Street Journal Interactive Publications Library

Europe

Baltic News Service
   DataStar (files BNSA and BNSD)

Business Eastern Europe
   LEXIS-NEXIS (file BUEEUR in multiple libraries)

Business Europe
   LEXIS-NEXIS (file BUSEUR in multiple libraries)
   ProQuest Direct

Business News from Poland (wages, employment, imports/exports, market prices)
   LEXIS-NEXIS (file BNP in BUSFIN, EUROPE, NEWS, and WORLD Libraries)

DRT European Business Reports (Eastern European business)
   DataStar (file DRTE)

FT Reports: Eastern Europe (economics in Eastern Europe)
   DataStar (file FTEE)

German and European Market Statistics
   DataStar (file FAKT)

Times/Sunday Times (London) (company information, trade, industries, technology)
   DIALOG (file 710)
   Dow Jones News/Retrieval
   Wall Street Journal Interactive Publications Library

Industries

Africa Energy & Mining
   LEXIS-NEXIS (file AFRENM in MDEAFR, NEWS, and WORLD Libraries)

Asian Mass Communication and Information Centre
   http://irdu.nus.sg/amic/

Brokerline Database
   Profound

Europe 2000—Euro Stats & Facts
   DIALOG (file 636)
   LEXIS-NEXIS (file IACNWS in MARKET Library)

Foreign Agricultural Service (U.S. Department of Agriculture) (trade data and foreign market research reports; see especially the food market overview, which covers countries around the world. This is a great site for commodity-specific information.)
   http://fas.usda.gov

FT Reports: Energy and Environment (worldwide trends in oil, gas, coal, nuclear power, electricity, alternative energy)
   DataStar (file FTNV)

FT Reports: Financial Management and Insurance (worldwide trends in financial services and insurance)
  DataStar (file FTFM)

FT Reports: Industry (worldwide trends in the pharmaceutical and biotechnology industries)
  DataStar (file FTIN)

FT Reports: Technology (worldwide trends in communications, broadcasting, and media)
  DataStar (file FTTC)

Industry Scan (searches all Profound databases for your selected industry)
  Profound

International Energy Statistics (U.S. Energy Information Administration) (links to statistical information on the energy industries of various countries)
  http://www.eia.doe.gov/links.html

Office of Computers & Business Equipment (U.S. Department of Commerce) (market research on the computers and networking industries of various countries)
  http://inforserv2.ita.doc.gov/ocbe/ocbehome.nsf

World Tourism Organization
  http://www.world-tourism.org

International Agencies

Economic Commission for Latin America and the Caribbean
  http://www.eclac.cl/

Europa (The Statistical Office of the European Communities)
  http://europa.eu.int/en/comm/eurostat/eurostat.html

Food and Agriculture Organization of the United Nations
  http://www.fao.org/

Inter-American Development Bank
  http://www.iadb.org/

International Atomic Energy Agency, includes Atomic and Molecule Data Information System (AMDIS), Power Reactor Information System (PRIS), Global Network of Isotopes in Precipitation (GNIP, hydrogen and oxygen isotope content in precipitation), Nuclear Data Information System (nuclear physics data)
  http://www.iaea.or.at/

International Civil Aviation Organization (ICAO; see Publications, Electronic Documents, Information Kit for ICAO's 50th Anniversary for history of aviation statistics)
  http://www.cam.org/~icao/

International Labour Organization (statistics under construction)
http://www.ilo.org/

International Monetary Fund
http://www.imf.org/external/

International Telecommunication Union (equipment, routes, cellular markets, under-sea cables)
http://www.itu.ch/

International Trade Centre
http://www.intracen.org

OECD Statistics (Organisation for Economic Co-operation and Development)
http://www.oecd.org/std/

Organization of American States Trade Unit
http://www.sice.oas.org/

UNESCO (literacy, education, science and technology indicators, broadcasting)
http://www.unesco.org/

UNICEF (United Nations Children's Fund)
http://www.unicef.org/

United Nations Demining Database
http://www.un.org/Depts/Landmine/index.html

United Nations Department of Humanitarian Affairs (ReliefWeb) (financial tracking of humanitarian assistance; statistics and information about current and ongoing crises, including natural disasters and human conflicts)
http://www.reliefweb.int/

United Nations Economic Commission for Europe (in English and French)
http://www.unece.org/

United Nations Environment Programme
http://www.unep.org/ (see Global Environment Outlook reports at http://www.unep.org/unep/eia/geo/reports.htm#soe)

United Nations High Commissioner for Refugees
http://www.unhcr.ch/

United Nations Industrial Development Organization
http://www.unido.org/

United Nations International Drug Control Programme
http://undcp.org.index.html

United Nations Population Fund
  http://www.unfpa.org/

United Nations Statistics Division
  http://www.un.org/Depts/unsd/

World Bank
  http://www.worldbank.org/

World Food Programme (food aid statistics)
  http://www.wfp.org/

World Health Organization
  http://www.who.org/whosis/

World Meteorological Organization
  http://www.wmo.ch/

World Trade Organization (major source of international trade statistics; in English, French, and Spanish)
  http://www.wto.org/ (choose link International Trade)

Latin America
Business Latin America
  LEXIS-NEXIS (file BUSLAM in multiple libraries)

Chronicle of Latin American Economic Affairs
  LEXIS-NEXIS (file CHRLAT in NEWS, NSAMER, and WORLD Libraries)

Latin American News (industries in Latin America)
  DIALOG (file 749)

Latin American Newsletters (commodity prices, economies of Latin American and the Caribbean)
  LEXIS-NEXIS (file LAN in NEWS, NSAMER, UK, and WORLD Libraries)

Middle East
ArabNet
  http://www.arab.net

Central Bank of Jordan
  http://www.cbj.gov.jo/

Israel Ministry of Finance
  http://www.mof.gov.il/

Moneyclips (Middle East Newsfile) (Middle East demographic and economic statistics)
  DataStar (file CLIP)
  LEXIS-NEXIS (file MOCLIP in multiple libraries)

North America

Business Mexico
   LEXIS-NEXIS (file BUSMEX in BUSFIN, NEWS, NSAMER, and WORLD Libraries)
   ProQuest Direct

Canadian Business
   Dow Jones News/Retrieval
   LEXIS-NEXIS (file CANBUS in CANADA, NSAMER, WORLD, and NEWS Libraries)
   Wall Street Journal Interactive Publications Library

Canadian Business and Current Affairs Fulltext
   DIALOG (file 262)

Canadian Newspapers
   DIALOG (file 727)

SourceMex: Economic News and Analysis on Mexico (economy, industry, agriculture, social welfare)
   Dow Jones News/Retrieval
   LEXIS-NEXIS (file SRCMEX in NEWS, NSAMER, and WORLD Libraries)
   Wall Street Journal Interactive Publications Library

Russia and the Commonwealth of Independent States

Current Digest of the Post-Soviet Press (includes opinion polls as well as economics agriculture, sports, etc.
   LEXIS-NEXIS (file CDSP in EUROPE, NEWS, and WORLD Libraries)

Russian and CIS News (business and general news from Russia and the Confederation of Independent States)
   DataStar (files SVNW, SVND)

CASE STUDY

Case Study 15-1: Literacy Rates

Purpose: This case study shows how to search the Web site of a U.N. organization to compare information on the world's countries. It also illustrates that sometimes you have to rethink your question as you come across new information.

Question: Which countries have the highest and lowest literacy rates?

Likely sources: UNESCO, since this is the international organization responsible for education

Access points used: Links

System: Web site

I went to the UNESCO Web site at http://www.unesco.org. The opening screen had a link for Statistics, and also for Publications and Information Services. I tried the obvious first: Statistics.

This took me to UNESCO's Statistical Yearbook 1996. The first link, for Selected Indicators, said that it included adult illiteracy rates. *Illiteracy* is the opposite of *literacy*, so I figured that I should be able to get the information I needed here; I would just have to rephrase the question. I needed to find out which country had the highest percentage of people who could not read and which had the lowest percentage who could not read.

Indicators were divided by world region, then by country. This meant that I had to go through every country to find out which were the highest and lowest—a little tedious, but not unexpected. Fortunately the tables were in HTML, so I could skim them quickly.

The figures were divided

FIGURE 15-1

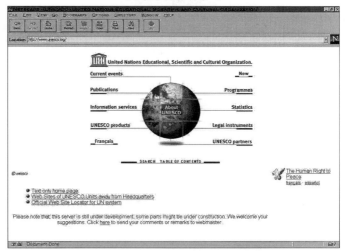

Note the Statistics link on UNESCO's Web Site.

FIGURE 15-2
UNESCO's Statistical Yearbook 1996

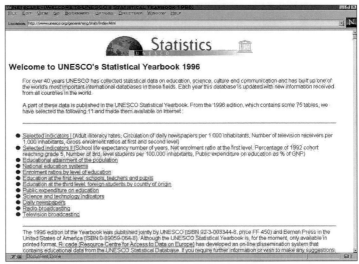

Adult illiteracy rates are found under the heading Selected Indicators.

into three sections: Male, Female, and Male/Female. I looked at Male/Female to get the full picture. I wanted the highest and the lowest numbers, for the highest illiteracy rate and the lowest illiteracy rate.

In Africa, the numbers for highest illiteracy were 80.8% in Burkina Faso and 86.4% in Niger. Everything else was below 70%. The lowest numbers were 18.2% illiteracy in South Africa, 14.9% in Zimbabwe, and 17.1% in Mauritius (see Figure 15-3).

FIGURE 15-3
Selected Indicators for Africa, Including Adult Illiteracy Rates

Africa.WSTIND2.e

Table on selected indicators

This table presents in a kind of overview a number of indicators in UNESCO'S fields of competence. The exact definitions and interpretation of these indicators are given in footnotes to the table.

Africa

Country	Adult illiteracy rates estimates 1995			Circulation of daily newspapers per 1.000 inhabitants 1994	Number of television receivers per 1.000 inhabitants 1994	Gross enrolment ratios at first and second level 1994		
	MF	M	F			MF	M	F
Algeria	38.4	26.1	51.0	46	79	84	89	79
Angola	...	...	...	11	6.6	45	...	...
Benin	63.0	51.3	74.2	2	5.5	40	54	26
Bostwana	30.2	19.5	40.1	24	17	93	91	96
Burkina Faso	80.8	70.5	90.8	0.3	5.5	25	31	19
Burundi	64.7	50.7	77.5	3	1.5	40	44	35
Cameroon	36.6	25.0	47.9	4	24	58	63	53
Cape Verde	28.4	18.6	36.2	-	3.4	83	85	81
Central African Republic	40.0	31.5	47.6	1	4.9	...	...	...

In North America, I saw that the highest number was 55%, in Haiti. Oops, then I noticed that there were lots of countries with dashes instead of numbers. This could have meant that the rate is 0, or it could have meant that the information isn't available. Countries with these entries included the Caribbean islands.

In South America, the highest numbers were 16.9% in Bolivia and 16.7% in Brazil. In Asia, the highest numbers were 72.5% in Nepal, 61.9% in Bangladesh, and 62.2% in Pakistan. In Europe, everything was dashes, and, in Oceania, the highest number was 27.8%, in Guinea.

From these numbers, one can conclude that the lowest literacy rates in the world are in Burkina Faso, Niger, Nepal, Bangladesh, and Pakistan. One can also conclude that it isn't a particularly useful question to ask which countries have the highest rates, since so much of the world *appears* to be 100% literate (and the best definition we get from the source is that *adult* illiterates over the age of 15 are counted and are expressed as a percentage of the total population in the corresponding age group).

Lessons learned:

√ Sometimes you have to reword or rethink your questions as you find out more about your subject and the way the data is organized.

√ Some information necessary for understanding the data may be missing from the site or publication.

√ Data may be arranged in a tedious fashion that is not useful to you (as by region and then by country) but you can often assemble the facts you need—it just takes longer to do it.

Finding Technology Statistics

Technology data may be gathered by scientists and engineers, professional and business associations serving them, regulatory agencies, and others. For example, energy data is contributed by power and gas companies, and the Energy Information Administration conducts surveys to find information such as residential energy consumption, conservation, prices, and so on.

Figures on computer usage may be gathered by survey or inferred partially or completely from sales data. Public filings with the Federal Communications Commission comprise one source of communications data. Industry surveys are used to compile financial data on companies, products, and technologies.

TYPES OF DATA
Here are some examples of the types of technology statistics you can find:

Communications
- Numbers, distribution of telephones, televisions, radios, and other communications devices
- Economics of communications

Computers
- Computer and information technology usage and distribution
- Numbers of computers and peripherals
- Economics of computers and software

Energy
- Scope and economics of solar, wind, geothermal energies
- Numbers and types of power plants, output generated
- Uses and penetration of nuclear technology
- Energy prices
- Emissions

Space

- Space vehicle specifications
- Space program and vehicle costs
- Space vehicle mileage and cargo hauled

Other

- Uses and penetration of laser technology
- Numbers, uses of various medical technologies
- Uses and deployment of biotechnologies
- Numbers, uses, distribution of robotic technologies

KEY PRODUCERS

Important producers of technology information include:

- Energy Information Administration, U.S. Department of Energy
- Statistical Abstract of the U.S.
- Federal Communications Commission (FCC)
- Publishers of newsletters and trade journals
- NASA
- Trade associations

TYPES OF SOURCES

You will find technology data reported in the following types of sources:

- Trade journals
- Newsletters
- Newspapers
- Statistical compilations and reports

BEST PLACES TO LOOK

Newsletters and trade journals are central to the reporting of technology statistics, though in the areas of energy and space technology, the U.S. government also does a fine job. As you might expect, computers are especially well-covered online. Biotechnology appears to be lagging as far as statistical reporting is concerned, but newspapers and the general business press can help here.

In addition to the general services and locations listed here, this Best Places to Look directory includes categories for biotechnology, communications, computers, energy, and space exploration.

Collections

- LEXIS-NEXIS CMPCOM Library (Computers and Communications
- LEXIS-NEXIS ENERGY Library
- LEXIS-NEXIS FEDCOM Library (Communications)
- LEXIS-NEXIS MKTRES Library (Market Research)

General

ASI (American Statistics Index) (for *identifying* statistical publications produced by the U.S. government)
    DIALOG (file 102)
    (Scheduled to be on LEXIS-NEXIS in 1998, including selected full text)

COMLINE Daily News Industrial Automation
    Dow Jones News Retrieval
    Wall Street Journal Interactive Publications Library

FEDSTATS (metasite for locating federally generated statistics)
    http://www.fedstats.gov

Financial Times Full Text
    DIALOG (file 622)
    Dow Jones News/Retrieval
    LEXIS-NEXIS (file FINTIME in multiple libraries)
    Wall Street Journal Interactive Publications Library

Science & Technology Data Canada
    http://www.cisti.nrc.ca/programs/indcan/slibrary/ststats.html

TableBase
    DataStar (file BTBL)
    DIALOG (file 93)
    http://www.tablebase.com

TECH-LINE Indicators Database (indicators calculated from patent data; technological strength and activity, technology cycle time, whether working at the leading edge, and whether high-quality technology for companies worldwide)
    LEXIS-NEXIS (file TECHLN in COMPNY Library)

Technology and Canada's Changing Manufacturing Sector
    http://www.cisti.nrc.ca/programs/indcan/slibrary/ststats.html

Wall Street Journal Interactive Publications Library (Industrial Technology Publications category)

Ziff Newsletters (biotechnology, computers/communications newsletters)
    LEXIS-NEXIS (multiple files and libraries)

Biotechnology

Biotech Business (newsletter)
  Dow Jones News/Retrieval
  Electric Library
  IAC InSite
  IAC InSite Pro
  Wall Street Journal Interactive Publications Library

Johns Hopkins University (host of the Genome Database)
  http://gdbwww.gdb.org/

McGraw-Hill's Biotechnology Newswatch
  LEXIS-NEXIS (file BIOTEC in NEWS Library)

National Center for Biotechnology Information (National Library of Medicine/National
Institutes of Health) (gene map of human genome, GenBank sequence database)
  http://www.ncbi.nlm.nih.gov/

Communications

Asian Mass Communication and Information Centre
  http://irdu.nus.sg/amic/

COMLINE Daily News Telecommunications
  Dow Jones News Retrieval
  Wall Street Journal Interactive Publications Library

Communications Week
  Dow Jones News/Retrieval
  Electric Library
  IAC InSite
  IAC InSite Pro
  Wall Street Journal Interactive Publications Library
  http://www.cmpnet.com/search/

Federal Communications Commission Annual Report (radio, television)
  http://www.fcc.gov/annual_report_95.html (or later)

Federal Communications Commission Second Annual Report and Analysis of Competitive
Market Conditions with Respect to Commercial Mobile Services
  http://www.fcc.gov/wtb/reports.html

Federal Communications Commission Statistics of Common Carriers (toll service revenues, penetration by state, historical rate tables, historical financial and economic
data, access lines, calls, minutes, financials of telephone companies, etc.)
  http://www.fcc.gov/Bureaus/Common_Carrier/Reports/FCC-State_Link/socc.html

Federal Communications Commission Long Distance Telephone Industry (market share, revenue, current and historical rates, household expenditures for telephone service, complaint rates, 800 and other special numbers, etc.)
http://www.fcc.gov/Bureaus/Common_Carrier/Reports/FCC-State_Link/ixc.html

Office of Telecommunications, International Trade Administration (cellular equipment and services, fiber optics, microwave, personal communications services, customer premises equipment, network switching and transmission equipment, satellites, search and navigation equipment, wireless, telecommunications; also selected non-U.S. countries)
http://www.ita.doc.gov/industry/tai/telecom/telecom.html

Statistical Abstract of the U.S.
http://www.census.gov/stat_abstract

Telephony
DIALOG (files 15, 148, 675)
Dow Jones News/Retrieval
LEXIS-NEXIS (file ASAPII in NEWS Library)
Wall Street Journal Interactive Publications Library

Wall Street Journal Interactive Publications Library (Computers and Communications Publications category)

.xls (forecasts and general industry statistics; results in spreadsheet format)
http://www.xls.com

Computers

CMPnet (multiple computer magazines, including *NetGuide, Electronic Buyers' News, Semiconductor Business News, Computer Reseller News, VARBusiness, Computer Retail Week, Information Week, Network Computing,* and *Communications Week,* among others)
http://www.cmpnet.com/search/

Communications Week
Dow Jones News/Retrieval
Electric Library
IAC InSite
IAC InSite Pro
Wall Street Journal Interactive Publications Library
http://www.cmpnet.com/search/

Computer Industry Forecasts
LEXIS-NEXIS (file CMPIND in BUSREF, CMPCOM, and MARKET Libraries)

Computer Industry Software, Services & Products
DataStar (file CISS)

Computer News Fulltext
   BrainWave
   DIALOG (file 674)

Computer Reseller News
   Dow Jones News/Retrieval
   Electric Library
   IAC InSite
   IAC InSite Pro
   LEXIS-NEXIS (file CRN in CMPCOM, MARKET, and NEWS Libraries)
   ProQuest Direct
   Wall Street Journal Interactive Publications Library
   http://www.cmpnet.com/search/

Computerworld
   DIALOG (files 15 and 674)
   Dow Jones News/Retrieval
   LEXIS-NEXIS (file CMPWLD in CMPCOM, MARKET, NEWS, and
        PEOPLE Libraries)
   ProQuest Direct
   Wall Street Journal Interactive Publications Library

Datamation
   DIALOG (files 47, 88, 148, 675)
   Dow Jones News/Retrieval
   LEXIS-NEXIS (files ASAPII and DATAMA in NEWS Library)
   Wall Street Journal Interactive Publications Library

Dealerscope
   DIALOG (files 15 and 148)
   LEXIS-NEXIS (ABI file in BUSFIN Library)

Electronic News
   Dow Jones News/Retrieval
   Electric Library
   IAC InSite
   IAC InSite Pro
   ProQuest Direct
   Wall Street Journal Interactive Publications Library

Information Access Company (IAC InSite, Computer InSite section)

MacWEEK
   Dow Jones News/Retrieval
   IAC InSite

IAC InSite Pro
Wall Street Journal Interactive Publications Library

Newsbytes News Network
http://www.newsbytes.com

Office of Computers & Business Equipment (U.S. Department of Commerce) (industry indicators, including historical information; trade and trends, computer equipment exports, earnings of software industry personnel, number of software establishments, hours worked, receipts)
http://infoserv2.ita.doc.gov/ocbe/ocbehome.nsf

PC Computing
Dow Jones News/Retrieval
IAC InSite
IAC InSite Pro
Wall Street Journal Interactive Publications Library

PC Week
Dow Jones News/Retrieval
IAC InSite
IAC InSite Pro
Wall Street Journal Interactive Publications Library

San Jose Mercury News
BrainWave
DIALOG (file 634)
Dow Jones News/Retrieval
IAC InSite
IAC InSite Pro
Wall Street Journal Interactive Publications Library
http://newslibrary.infi.net/sj/

Wall Street Journal Interactive Publications Library (Computers and Communications Publications category)

.xls (computer industry forecasts; results in spreadsheet format)
http://www.xls.com

Energy

The American Gas Association (natural gas industry statistics; subscription required; some of these statistics find their way into the Statistical Abstract of the U.S.)
http://www.aga.com

The American Petroleum Institute Basic Petroleum Data Book (annual petroleum statistics; subscription required)
http://www.api.org/index.htm

ASAPII Publications
   LEXIS-NEXIS (files AGENCY, COAL, OIL and UTIL in NEWS Library)

Coal (production, consumption)
   LEXIS-NEXIS (file COAL in ENERGY, MARKET, and NEWS Libraries)

Coal UK (UK purchases, production and imports, coal transportation, prices, company financials)
   Dow Jones News/Retrieval
   LEXIS-NEXIS (file COALUK in ENERGY, EUROPE, MARKET, NEWS, UK, and
      WORLD Libraries)
   Wall Street Journal Interactive Publications Library

Coal Week (prices, production, transportation, availability of coal in the U.S.)
   Dow Jones News/Retrieval
   LEXIS-NEXIS (file COALWK in ENERGY, MARKET, and NEWS Libraries)
   Wall Street Journal Interactive Publications Library

Coal Week International (prices, production, demand, transportation)
   Dow Jones News/Retrieval
   LEXIS-NEXIS (file COALIN in ENERGY, MARKET, NEWS, and WORLD Libraries)
   Wall Street Journal Interactive Publications Library

Electric Light & Power (top 100 utilities by financials and performance)
   Dow Jones News/Retrieval
   LEXIS-NEXIS (file ELP in NEWS, ENERGY, and MARKET Libraries)
   Wall Street Journal Interactive Publications Library

Electric Utility Week (fuel costs, utility rates)
   Dow Jones News/Retrieval
   LEXIS-NEXIS (file ELUTL in ENERGY and NEWS Libraries)
   Wall Street Journal Interactive Publications Library

Electrical World (power industry)
   DIALOG (file 624)
   Dow Jones News/Retrieval
   LEXIS-NEXIS (file ELECWD in ENRGY and NEWS Libraries)
   ProQuest Direct
   Wall Street Journal Interactive Publications Library

The Energy Daily (world oil supply and demand; also other forms of energy)
   Dow Jones News/Retrieval
   LEXIS-NEXIS (file ENGDLY in ENERGY, EXEC, LEGIS, MARKET, and
      NEWS Libraries)
   Wall Street Journal Interactive Publications Library

Energy Information Administration (U.S. Department of Energy) (fuels, forecasts, state data, prices, consumption, emissions, international, and time series)
   http://www.eia.doe.gov/ (See especially Feature Articles and Miscellaneous Items at http://www.eia.doe.gov/fuelelectric.html. Also see the EIA Interactive Query Facility at http://tonto.eia.doe.gov/eiaiq/index.html)

Energyline
   DIALOG (file 69)

Engineering and Mining Journal (prices of metals, ores, minerals, fuels)
   LEXIS-NEXIS (file EMG in ENVIRN and NEWS Libraries)

Foster Natural Gas Report (prices, consumption, industry statistics)
   Dow Jones News/Retrieval
   LEXIS-NEXIS (file FNGAS in ENERGY, MARKET, and NEWS Libraries)
   Wall Street Journal Interactive Publications Library

FT Energy Economist (statistics for all major energy sources)
   LEXIS-NEXIS (file ENRECO in ENERGY, MARKET, NEWS, UK, and WORLD Libraries)

Independent Power Report (worldwide power statistics)
   Dow Jones News/Retrieval
   LEXIS-NEXIS (file IPR in ENERGY, MARKET, and NEWS Libraries)
   Wall Street Journal Interactive Publications Library

Industrial Energy Bulletin (energy rates and prices)
   Dow Jones News/Retrieval
   LEXIS-NEXIS (file IEB in ENERGY, MARKET, and NEWS Libraries)
   Wall Street Journal Interactive Publications Library

Inside F.E.R.C.'s Gas Market Report (gas prices at all key pricing points)
   Dow Jones News/Retrieval
   LEXIS-NEXIS (file GASMKT in ENERGY and NEWS Libraries)
   Wall Street Journal Interactive Publications Library

International Coal Report (coal statistics)
   Dow Jones News/Retrieval
   LEXIS-NEXIS (file ICR in ENERGY, MARKET, NEWS, UK, and WORLD Libraries)
   Wall Street Journal Interactive Publications Library

International Gas Report
   Dow Jones News/Retrieval
   LEXIS-NEXIS (file IGASR in ENERGY, MARKET, MDEAFR, NEWS, UK, and WORLD Libraries)
   Wall Street Journal Interactive Publications Library

Nuclear Fuel (supplies and pricing of uranium and plutonium; includes forecasts)
  Dow Jones News/Retrieval
  LEXIS-NEXIS (file NUFUEL in ENERGY, MARKET, and NEWS Libraries)
  Wall Street Journal Interactive Publications Library

Nuclear News
  LEXIS-NEXIS (file NUNEWS in ENERGY, MARKET, NEWS, and
    PEOPLE Libraries)

Nucleonics Week (nuclear energy)
  Dow Jones News/Retrieval
  LEXIS-NEXIS (file NUWEEK in ENERGY, MARKET, and NEWS Libraries)
  Wall Street Journal Interactive Publications Library

Offshore
  Dow Jones News/Retrieval
  LEXIS-NEXIS (file OFFSHR in multiple libraries; ASAPII file in NEWS Library)
  Wall Street Journal Interactive Publications Library

Oil & Gas Journal
  DIALOG (files 15 and 148)
  Dow Jones News/Retrieval
  LEXIS-NEXIS (file OILGAS in multiple libraries)
  ProQuest Direct
  Wall Street Journal Interactive Publications Library

Pipe Line Industry
  DIALOG (file 148)
  LEXIS-NEXIS (file PLIND in NEWS Library)

Pipeline & Gas Journal
  Dow Jones News/Retrieval
  LEXIS-NEXIS (file PROMT in MARKET Library)
  Wall Street Journal Interactive Publications Library

Platt's International Petrochemical Report
  DIALOG (file 624)
  Dow Jones News/Retrieval
  Wall Street Journal Interactive Publications Library

Platt's Oilgram News
  DIALOG (file 624)
  Dow Jones News/Retrieval
  LEXIS-NEXIS (file PONEWS in ENERGY, MARKET, and NEWS Libraries)
  Wall Street Journal Interactive Publications Library

Platt's Oilgram Price Report
   DIALOG (file 624)
   Dow Jones News/Retrieval
   LEXIS-NEXIS (file PPRICE in ENERGY, MARKET, and NEWS Libraries)
   Wall Street Journal Interactive Publications Library

Power in Europe
   LEXIS-NEXIS (file PE in multiple libraries)

Public Utilities Fortnightly
   DIALOG (files 15 and 148)
   Dow Jones News/Retrieval
   LEXIS-NEXIS (ABI file in BUSFIN Library)
   Wall Street Journal Interactive Publications Library

Wall Street Journal Interactive Publications Library (Energy Publications Category)

World Oil
   DIALOG (file 148)
   Dow Jones News/Retrieval
   LEXIS-NEXIS (files ASAPII and WLDOIL in NEWS Library)
   Wall Street Journal Interactive Publications Library

NOTE: The Edison Electric Institute (http://www.eei.org) publishes the Statistical
Yearbook of the Electrical Utility Industry *(not online), from which some of the
material in the Statistical Abstract of the U.S. is drawn. Also, the Energy Information
Administration has links to energy companies and trade associations at http://www.
eia.doe.gov/links.html.*

Space Exploration
NASA (National Aeronautics and Space Administration) (missions and people in space)
   http://www.osf.hq.nasa.gov/spacemen.html

NASA Fact Sheets (budget, personnel, shuttle facts, space station facts)
   http://www.hq.nasa.gov/office/pao/NASA/fsheet_index.html

NASA FAQ (general questions, such as the temperature in space, weight of a space-
craft, cost of space shuttle, altitude/fuel/speed of shuttle, NASA's budget)
   http://www.nasa.gov/hqpao/q_a_subject.html

NASA—Satellites in Orbit
   http://www.osf.hq.nasa.gov/orbdata.html

NASA—U.S. Human Space Flights
   http://www.osf.hq.nasa.gov/flights.html

CASE STUDIES

Case Study 16-1: Number of 800 Numbers

Purpose: This case study illustrates the type of information available from the Federal Communications Commission. It also shows that data is presented in varying formats and that you should be ready with a variety of software programs with which to handle it.

Question: How many 800 telephone numbers are there in the U.S.?

Likely sources: Federal Communications Commission, which oversees the telecommunications industry

Access points: Links

System: Web site

The resources listed in this chapter indicate that the FCC provides data on 800 numbers at http://www.fcc.gov/Bureaus/Common_Carrier/Reports/FCC-State_Link/ixc.html. When I went to The Long Distance Telephone Industry site, I saw that the information I wanted was available in two forms: an 821KB file in PDF format, or a compressed file containing a Lotus spreadsheet and a WordPerfect document. The PDF would let me view the material instantly, so I opted for it.

FIGURE 16-1

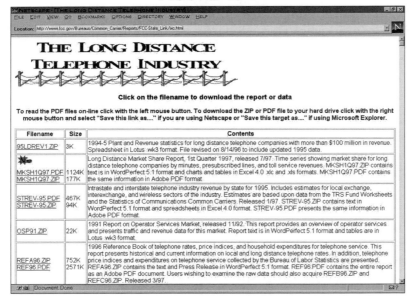

Files on this FCC site are available either in PDF format or as ZIPped files. To unzip a file, you need a utility such as PKZIP or WinZip. Once the .zip file is opened, you will probably need a specific word processing or spreadsheet program in order to read the data.

The PDF file took about 4 minutes to load in my copy of Adobe Acrobat Reader, which I had preconfigured as a helper application from my Web browser. In the left-hand Acrobat frame was a list of topics and tables. The first one that caught my eye was one that said "800 and 888 Service," so I clicked on that. The text was a short section defining 800 and 888 numbers and referring the reader to Table 14. I clicked on the icon for Table 14 and *voila!* There in the right-hand frame was the perfect information.

A table called "Telephone Numbers Assigned for 800 Service (Reported at End of Month Shown)" listed working 800 numbers, miscellaneous 800 numbers assigned, total 800 numbers assigned, and spare 800 numbers still available for each month from April of 1993 through April of 1997. The Miscellaneous category included numbers recently deactivated, suspended, and assigned but not yet activated.

FIGURE 16-2

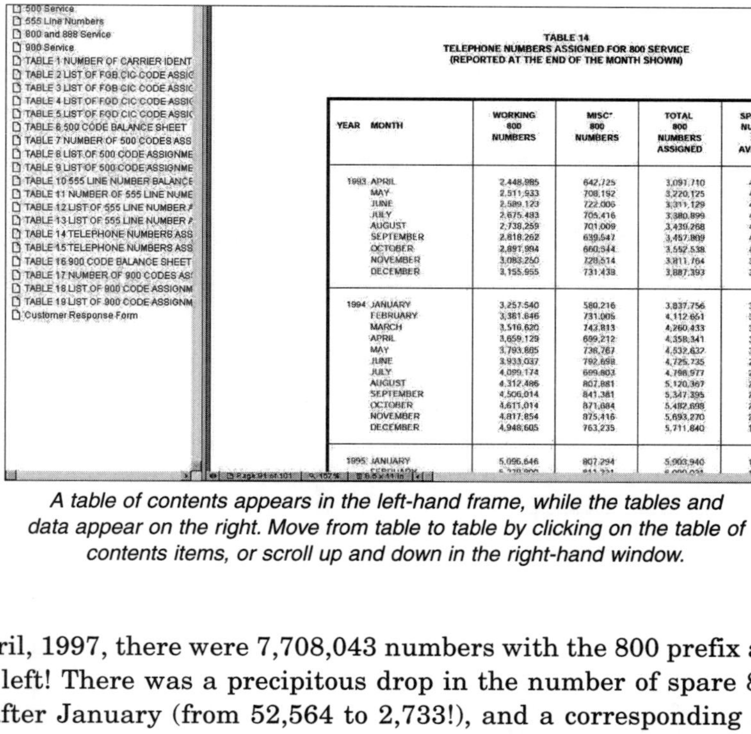

YEAR	MONTH	WORKING 800 NUMBERS	MISC* 800 NUMBERS	TOTAL 800 NUMBERS ASSIGNED	SPARE NUMB STIL AVAIL
1993	APRIL	2,448,985	642,725	3,091,710	4,61
	MAY	2,511,933	708,192	3,220,125	4,48
	JUNE	2,589,123	722,006	3,311,129	4,39
	JULY	2,675,483	705,416	3,380,899	4,32
	AUGUST	2,738,259	701,009	3,439,268	4,27
	SEPTEMBER	2,818,262	639,547	3,457,809	4,25
	OCTOBER	2,891,994	660,544	3,552,538	4,15
	NOVEMBER	3,083,250	728,514	3,811,764	3,89
	DECEMBER	3,155,955	731,438	3,887,393	3,92
1994	JANUARY	3,257,540	580,216	3,837,756	3,87
	FEBRUARY	3,381,646	731,005	4,112,651	3,59
	MARCH	3,516,620	743,813	4,260,433	3,44
	APRIL	3,659,129	699,212	4,358,341	3,35
	MAY	3,793,865	738,767	4,532,632	3,17
	JUNE	3,933,037	792,698	4,725,735	2,98
	JULY	4,099,174	699,803	4,798,977	2,91
	AUGUST	4,312,486	807,881	5,120,367	2,58
	SEPTEMBER	4,506,014	841,381	5,347,395	2,36
	OCTOBER	4,611,014	871,684	5,482,698	2,22
	NOVEMBER	4,817,854	875,416	5,693,270	2,01
	DECEMBER	4,948,605	763,235	5,711,840	1,99
1995	JANUARY	5,096,646	807,294	5,903,940	1,80

A table of contents appears in the left-hand frame, while the tables and data appear on the right. Move from table to table by clicking on the table of contents items, or scroll up and down in the right-hand window.

As of April, 1997, there were 7,708,043 numbers with the 800 prefix assigned and only 1,957 left! There was a precipitous drop in the number of spare 800 numbers available after January (from 52,564 to 2,733!), and a corresponding steep rise in the number of 800 numbers assigned between January and February. In my usual skeptical way, I wondered why, but looking at the figures for previous years, I could tell that this pattern seemed to hold true at the beginning of each year. My guess is that people tend to start new businesses and/or expand current ones with the changing of the calendar year, though there's no way to tell for sure from the data at hand.

Lessons learned:

√ Because you never know when you'll encounter a PDF file, you should always have Adobe Acrobat configured to work with your browser.

√ Keeping a variety of word processing and spreadsheet programs around may be beneficial, even if the programs are a little old. This site offered some files in WordPerfect 5.1 for DOS, hardly a state-of-the-art application. (You can often read older formats with newer software, however.)

√ Not every seeming anomaly in statistical data is a cause for alarm, but each one should be questioned.

Case Study 16-2: Laptop Sales

Purpose: This case study demonstrates that you can find great computer statistics in the trade magazines, often for free.

Question: How many laptop computers were sold in 1996?

Likely sources: Computer Reseller News

Access points used: Keywords

System: Web site

FIGURE 16-3

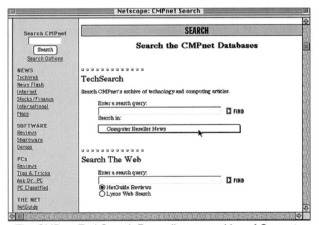

The CMPnet TechSearch Page allows searching of Computer Reseller News, among other publications.

There were many avenues through which to approach this question, but I though I'd start with a free source that offers searching of major industry magazines. CMP publishes *Computer Reseller News*, as well as *NetGuide*, *Communications Week*, *Information Week*, *Computer Retail Week*, and a variety of similar periodicals. The URL for the search page is http://www.cmpnet.com/search/.

There were multiple query boxes on the page, but the first one, TechSearch, targeted CMPnet's article archive, which was exactly what I wanted. (The other options let you search the entire Web, the TechCalendar, the TechEncyclopedia, a software archive, and a game archive.) In the TechSearch box, I entered `sales` and `1996` and `laptop` to retrieve articles that referred to sales in 1996 rather than some other year. However, it was also possible to get interim reports, such as "First quarter 1996," and the like.

Below the search box was a drop-down menu for specifying which journal to search, or All Journals. I set the choice to Computer Reseller News and clicked on Find.

The first article sounded promising. The date was June 2, 1997, so there was a good chance the article would include 1996 figures. Indeed, the opening sentence was "In 1996, notebooks became the dream machines of the computer industry." The article turned out to be exactly what I needed. The fourth paragraph began "The notebook market expanded faster than predicted, growing at a 23 percent clip with more than 1.7 million units shipped worldwide, according to Dataquest Inc., San Jose, Calif." When I put this information together with the first sentence, I could see that I was getting notebook sales figures for the year 1996.

The article used both the words *laptop* and *notebook*. I could have used both terms in the search—that would have been my fallback strategy had the answer not emerged on the first try.

I could have used an Advanced Search screen to limit the year of publication to 1997; that might have helped me narrow the statistics to those for 1996. However, CMP kept this facility (as well as its Help documentation) well hidden—there was no link to either on the main search screen.

Fortunately my broader strategy worked. In case yours doesn't, try the Advanced Search which is http://www.techweb.com/search/advsearch.html.

Lessons learned:

√ Trade journals are an important source of industry statistics. Look for Web sites sponsored by publishers. There may be archives available for free or at low cost.

√ Advanced search screens and even Help facilities may be well hidden on a system. Explore.

Finding Education Statistics

Data about education is collected by the Census Bureau in several ways: the decennial U.S. census, the monthly Current Population Survey, and the Census of Governments, which is conducted every five years. Surveys are also undertaken by other organizations, including:

- The National Center for Education Statistics
- Nongovernmental organizations, such as the National Education Association
- State governments
- The Bureau of Labor Statistics (data about the relationship between education and employment)

Data comes both from interviews of individuals and from administrative records kept by educational institutions and state and local agencies.

TYPES OF DATA
Some of the types of education statistics you can find are:

Curriculum and Achievement
- Curriculum
- Testing and test scores
- Grades
- Standards
- Vocational education
- English as a second language (ESL) and bilingual education
- Adult education
- Preschool
- Teaching methods
- Extracurricular activities
- School sports
- Literacy and numeracy
- Work-study programs

- Gifted and special education programs
- Professional education
- Technology and the schools

Finance

- School and higher education costs
- School funding
- School expenditures

Parents and Society

- Involvement of parents
- Parent attitudes
- Employers and the educational system
- General attitudes toward education

Schools

- Private, public, and religious schools
- School safety
- Home schooling
- Distance education
- Rankings of schools and universities
- School facilities
- Violence in schools
- School health issues
- Race relations and the schools
- Class size
- Year-round education
- School choice

Students

- Attitudes of students
- Demographics of students, teachers, and other personnel
- Dropout rates
- Graduation rates
- Disciplinary action
- Degrees granted

- Attendance
- Student interpersonal relations

Teachers and Administration
- Earnings and salaries of teachers and other personnel
- Labor issues
- Teacher attitudes
- Administrator attitudes
- Teacher training
- School boards
- School and academic libraries and librarians
- Counseling

KEY PRODUCERS
The primary producers of education statistics include:
- U.S. Department of Education, National Center for Education Statistics
- National Science Foundation
- UNESCO
- ERIC (Educational Resources Information Center)
- U.S. Bureau of the Census
- Statistical Abstract of the U.S.

TYPES OF SOURCES
You will find education statistics gathered and reported in the following types of sources:
- Reports
- Statistical compendia
- Surveys

BEST PLACES TO LOOK
Full-text sources are less important for education and library statistics than are statistical compendia, including those produced by various levels of government. However, you will find some material in the education research literature and also in professional journals for educators. Library organizations such as the American Library Association and the Special Libraries Association stay on top of conditions in their worlds as well.

American Library Association (numbers of libraries and librarians, largest libraries)
http://www.ala.org/library/larcfact.html

ASI (American Statistics Index) (for *identifying* statistical publications produced by the U.S. government)
  DIALOG (file 102)
  Scheduled to be on LEXIS-NEXIS in 1998, including selected full text

Association of Research Libraries (research libraries, salaries, law and medical libraries, preservation)
  http://www.arl.org

ERIC (encompasses RIE (Research in Education) and CIJE (Current Index to Journals in Education))
  BrainWave
  DIALOG (file 1)
  http://www.ed.gov/Search/eric.html

Chronicle of Higher Education
  ProQuest Direct
  http://chronicle.com

The Condition of Education 1996 (finance, salaries, outcomes, access to education, attainment, teacher work loads, enrollments, absenteeism and tardiness, demographics, test scores, college costs, dropouts)
  http://www.ed.gov/NCES/pubs/ce/ or
      gopher://gopher.ed.gov:10000/11/publications/majorpub/condition

Daily Report Card (state of U.S. schools)
  LEXIS-NEXIS (file RPTCRD in EXEC Library)

Digest of Education Statistics
  gopher://gopher.ed.gov:10000/11/publications/majorpub/digest

Education Week
  http://www.edweek.org/ (check the archives for articles)

Education Week: Quality Counts—U.S. and State Report Cards on the Quality of Education
  http://www.edweek.org/qc/

Educational Testing Service (nationwide, standardized tests; the family in education; adult literacy)
  http://www.ets.org/

Information Please Almanac
  Cognito!
  Encarta

A Matter of Fact (multidisciplinary)
  FirstSearch (file FactSearch)
  SilverPlatter
  (plus others; see p. 4)

National Center for Education Statistics: Compendium Digest of Education Statistics
http://nces.ed.gov/pubs

National Center for Education Statistics: Data and Surveys (numbers of schools and school districts, demographics, financial data, numbers of private schools/students/ teachers/graduates, school safety and discipline, post secondary education, faculty, recent college graduates, activities of high school students, skills and competencies, adult literacy, academic libraries, public libraries, school libraries, international comparisons)
http://nces.ed.gov/pubs/

National Center for Education Statistics: Education At A Glance (condition of education, access, school choice, achievement, adult education and literacy, community service, use of computers, college costs, safety and crime, curricula, disabled students, discipline, dropouts, economic outcomes, enrollment, extracurricular activities, funding, literacy, preschool, principals, staff, teachers)
http://nces.ed.gov/indihome.asp

National Center for Education Statistics: Learning About Education through Statistics
http://nces.ed.gov/pubs/96871.html

National Science Foundation (science enrollments, salaries of graduates, academic research and development spending, demographics of students)
http://www.nsf.gov

Peterson's Guides (private secondary education, undergraduate education)
http://www.petersons.com

School Finance Data (elementary, secondary, and post secondary schools)
http://www.census.gov/ftp/pub/govs/www/school.html

Special Libraries Association (demographics and salaries of special librarians)
http://www.sla.org

State Department of Education Agencies Meta-Site (links to state departments of education)
http://nces.ed.gov/sites.html

U.S. News & World Report (universities and graduate school rankings)
DIALOG (files 47, 88, 148)
Dow Jones News/Retrieval
Electric Library
LEXIS-NEXIS (file USNEWS in multiple libraries)
ProQuest Direct
Wall Street Journal Interactive Edition Publications Library
http://www.usnews.com/usnews/edu/

World Almanac
Electric Library
FirstSearch

CASE STUDY

Case Study 17-1: School Enrollment

Purpose: This case study illustrates that searching and browsing can yield completely different results. It also shows the importance of examining information *within* a table in addition to the title of a table. The data uncovered in this example proves that facts can contradict assumptions.

Question: How many K-12 children in the U.S. attend public schools *vs.* private schools?

Likely sources: National Center for Education Statistics (http://nces.ed.gov) because it collects a wide range of statistics about schools, students, and education in general

Access points used: Links; index terms; titles; full text (content of tables)

System: Web site

At the National Center for Education Statistics site, there was a link called statistics that led to a search page, a list of major statistical publications, and a subject index. Notice that these links were presented in text but not as one of the buttons. (See Figure 17-1.) You have to be diligent and meticulous to make sure you don't miss anything.

The subject index didn't mention *public schools* or *private schools*, but it did list a category for *enrollment*. Under *Enrollment* there were two tables: "Public School Student, Staff, and Graduate Counts by State, School Year 1993-94," and "School Enrollment Expected to Surpass Historic All-Time High from June of 1993."

FIGURE 17-1
The National Center for Education Statistics Web Site

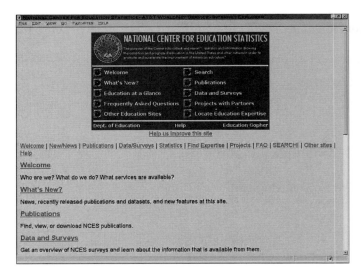

Neither of those sounded as though it would contain complete information, though I thought I might want to return to the former to compare it with a table of private schools later. Also, the figures were a little old.

I decided to try the search engine. I typed `private schools` and specified that this phrase should be in the title. I picked this term because I could think of no way to find the information I wanted without its being present. I could have added `public schools`, but I was afraid that might narrow the search too much if the wording were different. I assumed the title would refer to a table rather than a publication, but since I got no hits, that was probably wrong. Since the HELP function didn't define the scope of *title*, I did the search again, this time specifying that `private schools` should be in the contents rather than the title.

FIGURE 17-2
The National Center for Education Statistics Search Page

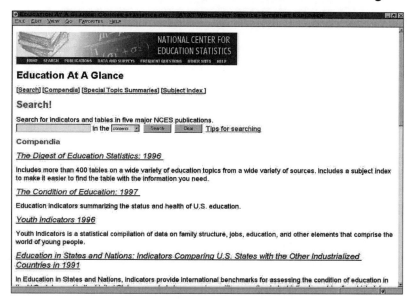

This time I got 55 hits. Some of the tables didn't have descriptive titles, but indicated only "Condition of Education 1997/Supplemental Table" followed by a table number. Others were clearly irrelevant for my purpose. However, there was one table called "The Condition of Education 1997/Elementary and Secondary School Enrollment." If this were broken down by public *vs.* private, it would be just what I was looking for (see Figure 17-3).

It was perfect: "Table 44-1: Elementary and secondary school enrollment in thousands, by control and level of school, with projections: Fall 1970-2007" showed yearly historical enrollments going back to 1970, and projections starting in 1997. In 1996, the total public school enrollment for K-12 was 45,700,000, or 88.8%; private school enrollment was 5,784,000, or 11.2%.

It was interesting that the percentage of enrollment in public schools (vs. private) hadn't gone down as dramatically as I would have thought. In 1970, public school enrollment was 45,894,000 or 89.5%; private school was 5,363,000, or 10.5%. A spot check of other years showed that the ratio was roughly the same. Overall enrollment in K-12 for both public and private was very much the same now (50,776,000 in 1995) as it was in 1970 (51,257,000).

FIGURE 17-3

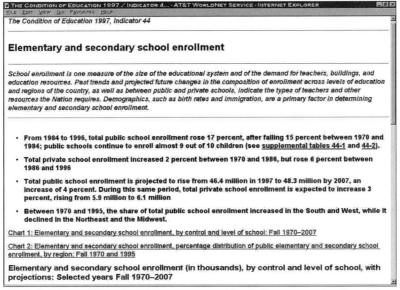

In the Condition of Education 1997, you can see historical, current, and projected data.

However, when I read the explanatory notes, I found that private school data for 1971-75, 1979, 1981-2, 1984, and 1986 was estimated! Also, I saw that, beginning in 1980, private schools were defined in a different way from before. In addition, some nursery school students had been included in the counts. Nevertheless, these were the official figures.

Lessons learned:

√ Watch for changing definitions and methodologies over time.

√ Browsing and searching complement each other; if one doesn't work, try the other method.

√ Go after your subject from various angles, including general, specific, and alternative terminologies. (In this case, the concept of *enrollment* was the point of entry, rather than public or private schools.)

Finding Transportation Statistics

Much transportation data is gathered by the U.S. government in its planning and regulatory roles. The U.S. Bureau of the Census conducts a commodity transportation survey of manufacturers every five years (part of the Census of Transportation, Communications, and Utilities), through which it collects information on characteristics of commodity shipments. The Bureau also conducts surveys that contribute to the Truck Inventory and Use Survey, and its Annual Survey of Manufactures includes information on the motor vehicle and equipment industry.

The Federal Aviation Administration, in its role as overseer of airports, airspace, and traffic control, gathers information on the use of airway facilities, air traffic, airmen, and aircraft production and registration.

The U.S. Department of Transportation licenses air carriers, and collects information about them in the course of the licensing process.

TYPES OF DATA
Some of the kinds of data you can find about transportation are:

General
- Transportation economics, including cost of labor, vehicles, fuel, etc.
- Transportation company market shares
- Transportation history

Facilities and equipment
- Miles of roads, highways, waterways
- Numbers of vehicles, aircraft, ships
- Capacities of vehicles
- Specifications for autos, trains, aircraft, ships
- Specifications for subways
- Cost and prices of vehicles

Usage
- Numbers of passengers and passenger miles for various modes of transportation
- Fuel usage

- Cargo transported
- Airport usage and traffic
- Road and highway traffic

Operations
- Safety and accidents
- Fares
- Road, highway, port, rail, subway, airport maintenance

Personnel
- Demographics and training of pilots, captains, drivers, etc.

KEY PRODUCERS

Many producers of transportation statistics are government-related, but private companies, associations, and publishers play a role as well. Some samples include:

- Air Transport Association of America
- Bureau of Transportation Statistics
- Federal Aviation Administration
- Federal Highway Administration
- Manufacturers of automobiles, aircraft, etc.
- Statistical Abstract of the U.S.
- U.S. Department of Transportation
- Ward's Communications

TYPES OF SOURCES

You will find transportation statistics gathered and reported in the following types of sources:

- Trade journals
- Statistical compendia
- Web sites

BEST PLACES TO LOOK

Transportation is one of the few areas addressed well both by the traditional online vendors and the Web sites of government and other organizations. Many of us take transportation for granted, so it's an eye-opener to discover how much of this information is out there. We just love our cars ... and our boats ... and our airplanes. This directory of Best Places to Look begins with sources and locations generally and proceeds through the following categories:

- Air
- Auto, Motorcycle, and Truck
- Rail
- Urban
- Water

General
ASAPII Publications
LEXIS-NEXIS (files AIR and AUTO in NEWS Library)

Bureau of Transportation Statistics State Transportation Analysis Tables—STAT (U.S. Department of Transportation) (highways, vehicle miles of travel, state expenditures for local roads, capital outlays, fatalities, crashes, air traffic, tax receipts, gasoline usage, vehicle registrations, pavement conditions, road mileage, government obligations, licensed drivers, etc.)
http://www.bts.gov/ntda/fhwa/

Census of Transportation, Communications, and Utilities (U.S. Bureau of the Census)
http://www.census.gov/prod/2/trans/93comflo/

Department of Defense Fact File (specifications for military equipment)
http://www.dtic.mil/defenselink/factfile/

FEDSTATS (federal government agency statistics locator)
http://www.fedstats.gov

Information Please Almanac
Cognito!
Encarta Online Library

Jane's Electronic Information System (weapons, aerospace, urban transport systems, avionics, rail)
http://www.btg.com/janes/

The Journal of Commerce (includes a special section on water, air, rail, and truck transportation)
DIALOG (file 637)

National Safety Council (accidents)
http://www.nsc.org

National Transportation Safety Board (accidents)
http://www.ntsb.gov

Standard & Poor's Daily News Reports (in addition to financial information, this file contains auto industry and airline industry statistics and business failures; use event names and event codes)
  DIALOG (file 132)

TableBase
  DataStar (file BTBL)
  DIALOG (file 93)
  http://www.tablebase.com

Transport Europe
  LEXIS-NEXIS (file EURTRN in EUROCOM, EUROPE, NEWS, TRANS, and
      WORLD Libraries)

Transportation Annual Survey (U.S. Department of the Census)
  http://www.census.gov/econ/www/se0800.html

Transportation Resources—Highway, Transit, and Rail System Information (fares, schedules, scope, mileage)
  http://dragon.princeton.edu/~dhb/systems.html

Transportation Statistics Annual Report (U.S. Department of Transportation; safety, economics, environmental impact and trends, freight movement, energy, airline industry)
  http://www.bts.gov/btsprod/

U.S. Department of Transportation (numbers of cars and planes, miles of roads and railroad track, numbers of airports, miles of waterways, etc.)
  http://www.bts.gov/

Wall Street Journal Interactive Publications Library (Transportation & Aerospace Publications category)

World Almanac
  Electric Library
  FirstSearch

Ziff Newsletters (transportation industry newsletters)
  LEXIS-NEXIS (file ZIP1 in multiple libraries)

Air

Aerospace America
  LEXIS-NEXIS (file AEROAM in MARKET, NEWS, and TRANS Libraries)

Aerospace Industries Association of America (sales, employment, the helicopter industry, executive compensation)
  http://www.access.digex.net/~aia/
  See http://www.access.digex.net/~aia/pubs.html for ordering information and
      titles of free statistical series available offline

Aerospace Propulsion (engine orders by company, platform, and customer for a five-year period)
> Dow Jones News/Retrieval
> LEXIS-NEXIS (file AERPRO in MARKET, NEWS, and TRANS Libraries)
> Wall Street Journal Interactive Publications Library

Aerospace Reports (aerospace industry)
> LEXIS-NEXIS (file AER in TRANS Library)

Air Safety Week
> Dow Jones News/Retrieval
> Wall Street Journal Interactive Publications Library

Air Transport Association of America (annual report of U.S. airline industry, passenger and cargo traffic, fuel cost and consumption, employment, industry earnings, safety, who flies and why—some historical)
> http://www.air-transport.org/data/

Air Transport World
> DIALOG (files 15 and 148)
> Dow Jones News/Retrieval
> ProQuest Direct
> Wall Street Journal Interactive Publications Library

Air Transportation Reports (air transportation industry)
> LEXIS-NEXIS (file AIRRPT in TRANS Library)

Airbus
> http://www.airbus.com

Airline Financial News
> Dow Jones News/Retrieval
> Wall Street Journal Interactive Publications Library

ATA Data and Statistics (airline safety, prices, fuel costs and consumption, passenger and cargo loads, employment)
> http://www.air-transport.org/data/

Aviation Daily
> Dow Jones News/Retrieval
> LEXIS-NEXIS (file AVDLY in MARKET, NEWS, and TRANS Libraries)
> Wall Street Journal Interactive Publications Library

Aviation Europe
> Dow Jones News/Retrieval
> LEXIS-NEXIS (file AVEUR in EUROPE, MARKET, NEWS, TRANS, and
>   WORLD Libraries)
> Wall Street Journal Interactive Publications Library

Aviation Week & Space Technology (includes fuel prices)
  DIALOG (file 624)
  Dow Jones News/Retrieval
  LEXIS-NEXIS (file AVWEEK in MARKET, NEWS, and TRANS Libraries)
  Wall Street Journal Interactive Publications Library

Bell Helicopter (helicopter specifications and history)
  http://www.bellhelicopter.com

Boeing (aircraft and space station specs and facts)
  http://www.boeing.com

BTS Transportation Indicators (domestic scheduled passenger service, domestic ton miles, domestic operating finances, also traffic and international operations)
  http://www.bts.gov/oai/

Business and Commercial Aviation
  DIALOG (file 148)
  Dow Jones News/Retrieval
  LEXIS-NEXIS (file BCA in NEWS, MARKET, and TRANS Libraries)
  Wall Street Journal Interactive Publications Library

Commodity Flow Survey (Bureau of Transportation Statistics)
  http://www.bts.gov/ntda/cfs/

FAA Administrators Factbook (accidents, incidents, hijacking, air traffic, airports, delays, air carrier activity, industry trends, space industry trends, active airmen and women)
  http://www.tc.faa.gov/ZDV/FAA/administrator/factbook.html

FAA Statistical Handbook of Aviation (traffic, airports, aircraft, expenses, civil airmen, accidents, imports/exports of aircraft)
  http://www.bts.gov/oai/faasha.html

Fatal Accident Reporting System Database (Bureau of Transportation Statistics)
  http://www.bts.gov/ntda/farsdb/

Flight International
  DIALOG (files 16, 80, 148, 772, 799)
  Dow Jones News/Retrieval
  LEXIS-NEXIS (file FLIGHT in MARKET, NEWS, TRANS, UK, and
    WORLD Libraries)
  Wall Street Journal Interactive Publications Library

Flightline
  DataStar (file FLIG)

Industry Financial Review (Office of Aviation Analysis) (airline quarterly financial reviews)
  http://www.dot.gov/ost/aviation/analysis.html

Jane's Airport Review
  DIALOG (file 587)
  Dow Jones News/Retrieval
  Wall Street Journal Interactive Publications Library

Landings (huge metasite covering airlines and airline history, airports, accident reports—much of the site is links, but there's content too)
  http://www.landings.com

Learjet Inc. (specifications and history)
  http://www.learjet.com/

McDonnell Douglas (specifications and history of McDonnell Douglas aircraft and helicopters)
  http://www.mdc.com

Military Aircraft Database (specifications, U.S. air-dropped bombs, aircraft strength and losses in World War II)
  http://www.csd.uwo.ca/~pettypi/elevon/gustin_military/

Northrop Grumman (commercial and military aircraft specifications)
  http://www.northgrum.com/

OAI International Air Passenger and Freight Statistics
  http://www.bts.gov/oai/international/index.html

Office of Aerospace, U.S. Department of Commerce (employment, value of shipments, capital expenditures, trade data, aircraft and parts, guided missiles and space vehicles, top export markets, top suppliers to the U.S., etc.)
  http://www.ita.doc.gov/industry/tai/green/aerhome.html

On-Time Statistics—BTS Office of Airline Information
  http://www.bts.gov/ntda/oai/

Raytheon (aircraft specifications)
  http://www.raytheon.com/rac/

Statistical Handbook of Aviation (Bureau of Transportation Statistics)
  http://www.bts.gov/ntda/shafaa/

Weekly of Business Aviation
  Dow Jones News/Retrieval
  LEXIS-NEXIS (file WBA in MARKET, NEWS, and TRANS Libraries)
  Wall Street Journal Interactive Publications Library

World Airline News
  Dow Jones News/Retrieval
  Wall Street Journal Interactive Publications Library

Auto, Motorcycle, and Truck

Automotive News (see especially Economic Forecast and Market Data Book sections)
DIALOG (files 16 and 570)
Dow Jones News/Retrieval
LEXIS-NEXIS (file AUTONW in MARKET, NWS and TRANS Libraries)
Wall Street Journal Interactive Publications Library

Automotive Industries (worldwide production by plant)
http://ai.chilton.net

Automotive Reports (automotive industry)
LEXIS-NEXIS (file AUT in TRANS Library)

Federal Highway Administration (annual highway statistics, motor fuel by states, traffic volume, vehicle miles of travel, toll facilities)
http://www.fhwa.dot.gov

Harley Davidson Motorcycles
http://www.harley-davidson.com/

Kelly Blue Book
http://www.kbb.com/

Modern Tire Dealer
DIALOG (file 148)
Dow Jones News/Retrieval
LEXIS-NEXIS (file ASAPII in NEWS Library)
Wall Street Journal Interactive Publications Library

Motor Carrier Financial and Operational Statistics (Bureau of Transportation Statistics)
http://www.bts.gov/ntda/mcs/

Motor Freight Transportation and Warehousing Survey (U.S. Bureau of the Census)
http://www.census.gov/svsd/www/tas.html

National Highway Traffic Safety Administration (economic cost of motor vehicle accidents, traffic accident facts)
http://www.nhtsa.dot.gov/

State Freight Transportation Profiles (Bureau of Transportation Statistics)
http://www.bts.gov/ntda/sftp/

Transborder Surface Freight Data (Bureau of Transportation Statistics)
http://www.bts.gov/ntda/tbscd/

Tires and Rubber Reports (Tires and rubber industry reports)
LEXIS-NEXIS (file TIR in TRANS Library)

Truck Inventory and Use Survey (Bureau of Transportation Statistics)
http://www.bts.gov/programs/tius/

Trucking Reports (trucking industry)
   LEXIS-NEXIS (file TRU in TRANS Library)

U.S. Department of Commerce Auto Industry Data (motor vehicle trade data, parts trade data, industry economic and financial data)
   http://www.ita.doc.gov/industry/basic/

Ward's Auto World
   DIALOG (file 148)
   Dow Jones News/Retrieval
   LEXIS-NEXIS (file ASAPII in NEWS Library and file ABI in BUSFIN Library)
   ProQuest Direct
   Wall Street Journal Interactive Publications Library

Ward's Automotive Reports
   DIALOG (file 148)

Ward's Communications (North American production and sales)
   http://wardsauto.com

Ward's Dealer Business
   Dow Jones News/Retrieval
   Wall Street Journal Interactive Publications Library

Rail

Association of American Railroads (freight railroad industry)
   http://www.aar.org

Federal Railroad Administration (accident statistics)
   http://www.fra.dot.gov

Railroad Reports (railroad industry)
   LEXIS-NEXIS (file RAI in TRANS Library)

Railroad WWWGraphy (worldwide rail facts)
   http://pavel.physics.sunysb.edu/RR/wwwgraphia.html

Railway Age
   DIALOG (files 15, 47, 148)
   Dow Jones News/Retrieval
   ProQuest Direct
   Wall Street Journal Interactive Publications Library

Urban

American Public Transit Association (finances, ridership, fares, vehicles, operations of mass transit systems)
   http://www.apta.com

Federal Transit Administration National Transit Database (transit agencies and their funding; also energy consumption, mileage, employment, safety)
http://www.fta.dot.gov/ntl/

Metasubway (length, year opened, number cars, number stations, gauge, etc.)
http://pavel.physics.sunysb.edu/RR/metasubway/

Motor Carrier Financial and Operational Statistics (Bureau of Transportation Statistics)
http://www.bts.gov/ntda/mcs/

National Transit Database (Bureau of Transportation Statistics) (profiles of U.S. transit agencies)
http://www.bts.gov/ntda/ntdb/

Water

Fleet Lists Project (world's naval ships, with specifications, number of crew, armament)
http://www.announce.com/~elmer/navy/fleets/

Lloyd's Register of Shipping (world shipbuilding)
http://www.lr.org

Shipbuilding/Water Transportation Reports (industry reports)
LEXIS-NEXIS (file SHI in TRANS Library)

Shipping Schedules (container shipping)
http://www.shipguide.com/

U.S. Maritime Administration (ship deliveries, insurance, ship operations and finances, employment, piracy)
http://marad.dot.gov/

Waterborne Commerce Statistics Center (U.S. Army Corps of Engineers) (inland waterways, ports, harbors, coasts—commerce)
http://www.wrc-ndc.usace.army.mil/ndc/wcsc.htm

CASE STUDY

Case Study 18-1: Airline Fatalities

Purpose: This case study illustrates how to use government agency Web sites to find transportation information. It also demonstrates how important it is that information be complete. In this case, a critical definition is missing.

Question: Track commercial airline fatalities over the past several years.

Likely sources: The Federal Aviation Administration (FAA), because it regulates and licenses air carriers; the National Transportation Safety Board (NTSB), because it tracks safety; the Bureau of Transportation Statistics (BTS), because it compiles a large array of transportation-related statistics.

Access points used: Links; titles

System: Web sites

The FAA was a logical place to start. This chapter includes a listing for the FAA Administrators Factbook, which covers accidents, at http://www.tc.faa.gov/ ZDV/FAA/administrator/factbook.html.

At the site, I found a section on Safety and a link to NTSB Comparison of U.S. Transportation Fatalities. Other links mentioned accidents, but not necessarily fatalities.

The link NTSB Comparison of U.S. Transportation Fatalities led to a table that compared the years 1994 and 1995. This was not a long enough horizon, but it was a start. The categories under Aviation were:

- General aviation
- Air taxi
- Commuter
- Foreign/unregistered
- Airlines

FIGURE 18-1
The FAA Administrators Factbook

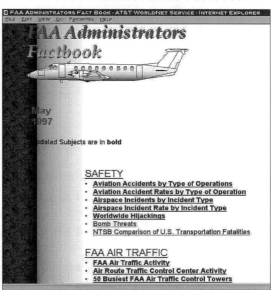

There was no definition for these categories. Airlines can run commuter operations and air taxis, so I lumped those two categories and the airlines category together to get a total for *commercial*. The total for 1994 was 327; for 1995 the total was 229. I also noted the numbers for Airlines alone (1994 was 239; 1995 was 168), which might ultimately be the category to use.

I needed to consult another source to get statistics going back further in time. The FAA also offers the FAA Statistical Handbook of Aviation at http://www.bts.gov/ oai/faasha.html; this source includes information on accidents. At that site, I found a category called Aircraft Accidents that presented a useful-looking list of tables. The best one was Table 9.4: Airlines: Scheduled and Non-scheduled Service Accidents, Fatalities and Rates (U.S. air carriers operating under 14 CFR 121) 1984-1993. I had my choice of text or spreadsheet. I chose text so I could read the table easily (see Figure 18-2).

FIGURE 18-2

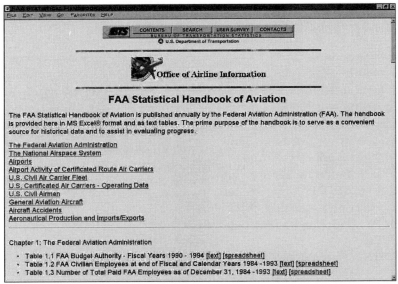

Choose the link to Aircraft Accidents in the FAA Statistical Handbook of Aviation

The table proved to have what I wanted—numbers of accidents, fatal accidents, and fatalities, as well as accident and fatality rates. The only remaining problem was that of definition: Was I getting the category of aviation I wanted?

FIGURE 18-3

TABLE 9.4
AIRLINES: SCHEDULED and NONSCHEDULED SERVICE 1/
Accidents, Fatalities and Rates
(U.S. Air Carriers Operating Under 14 CFR 121)
1984 - 1993

	1984	1985	1986	1987	1988	1989	1990	1991	1992 4/	1993 5/
Accidents										
Total	17	22	24	36	29	28	24	26	18	23
Fatal	1	7	3	5	3	11	6	4	4	1
Total Fatalities	4	526	8	232	285	278	39	62 6/	33	1
Aircraft Hours Flown (000) 2/	8,165	8,710	9,976	10,645	11,140	11,274	12,150	11,900	12,496	12,524
Aircraft Miles Flown (000,000) 2/	3,428	3,631	4,018	4,361	4,503	4,605	4,970	4,851	5,088	5,147
Departures (000) 2/	5,899	6,307	7,202	7,601	7,716	7,645	8,225	7,986	8,081	8,044
Accident Rate Per 100,000 Hours Flown										
Total	0.21	0.25	0.23	0.33	0.25	0.25	0.20	0.22	0.14	0.18
Fatal	0.01	0.08	0.02	0.04	0.02	0.10	0.05	0.03	0.03	0.01
Accident Rate Per Million Miles Flown										
Total	0.01	0.01	0.01	0.01	0.01	0.01	0.00 3/	0.01	0.00 3/	0.00 3/
Fatal	0.00 3/	0.00 3/	0.00 3/	0.00 3/	0.00 3/	0.00 3/	0.00 3/	0.00 3/	0.00 3/	0.00 3/
Accident Rate Per 100,000 Departures										
Total	0.29	0.35	0.32	0.46	0.36	0.37	0.29	0.33	0.22	0.29
Fatal	0.02	0.11	0.03	0.05	0.03	0.14	0.07	0.05	0.05	0.01

Source: National Transportation Safety Board
1 Includes accidents involving deregulated all-cargo air carriers

This table from the FAA Statistical Handbook of Aviation shows airline accidents and fatalities for large U.S. air carriers, though that's not exactly what the title says.

This table said that it included accidents involving "deregulated all-cargo air carriers and commercial operators of large aircraft when those accidents occurred during scheduled 14 CFR 121 operations." Too bad I didn't know what that meant—though I did know that CFR is the Code of Federal Regulations.

My next task was to find out what 14 CFR 121 is. Suffice it to say that I could find no definition within the source displaying the statistics—I had to go to the Code of Federal Regulations itself for the answer. 14 CFR 121 applies to "U.S. air carriers running domestic, flag, and supplemental operations using airplanes with passenger seating over 30 seats or a payload capacity of over 7500 pounds." In other words, the figures apply to large scheduled aircraft. (By the way, the citation refers to *Title* 14, *Part* 121 of the CFR.

Now I could add in the 1994 and 1995 figures from the first search in the FAA Administrators Factbook. Because I knew the definition, I added just the Airlines category: 239 fatalities in 1994 and 168 in 1995.

Lessons learned:

√ You may have to go to more than one source to gather the full data. (In this case, I had to go to multiple sources to cover the years I wanted.)

√ Publishers of statistics do not always furnish all the information you need to understand the numbers. You may have to go elsewhere for a fuller explanation.

√ Always question terms you don't understand.

Summary:
Now You're Ready!

I f you've read through this book to this point, you're in a great position to use the Internet and specialized online sources to find the elusive numbers and statistics you need on practically any subject. Here is a summary of the things you need to know to venture online when faced with a statistics question.

First, don't be faint-hearted! You know that finding a statistic can be like looking for a needle in a haystack. Use the sources and techniques outlined in *Finding Statistics Online* to help you plan your attack. Remember the three important steps involved in statistics-hunting:

1. Select the right place to look
2. Choose an effective strategy
3. Evaluate the data

THE RIGHT PLACE TO LOOK

No ideal source exists to answer all your questions. In the real world, you will have to use a variety of sources and adapt your search techniques to those sources.

Any source that consists primarily or wholly of statistics is a potential jewel. With such tools, you don't have to tell the system that you want statistics, since that's all you can get. You'll often find that almanacs, numeric databases, and statistical compendia— if such exist for your subject—are the best places to start. Other reference sources may be statistics-rich, even if they do not consist exclusively of numbers. So don't forget encyclopedias, fact books, databases composed of facts, handbooks, yearbooks, and rankings.

Just because sources are called *almanacs* or *statistical publications* does not mean they are not available at Web sites of associations, companies, and the like. In fact, you'll often find wonderful numeric data at fairly small Web sites.

Full-text and abstract databases are second best but necessary sources of statistical information, and they require different searching techniques from searching numeric and fact sources. The absolute best full-text databases are newspapers, major business magazines like *Forbes, Business Week,* and *Fortune,* and trade journals.

Tips for Choosing a Source

Define what you need to know in the form of a short question or statement. Use the Question section in each of the case studies in this book as an example.

Once you've defined what you're looking for, you should be able to consider it as a part of a general subject area. Look at the subject areas covered by chapters 5 through 18 of this book (see the Table of Contents or scan the Case Studies Table in Appendix B). Find the most likely looking chapter, go to it, and review the contents briefly. Pay special attention to the Best Places to Look directory that lists sources and locations for topical areas within that subject specialty.

Also check the clickable Directory of Online Statistics Sources. The Directory itself is on the World Wide Web at http://www.berinsteinresearch.com. The Directory contains additional categories more specific than those listed in the Best Places to Look directory in each chapter. The Directory links directly to more Web sites than are described in this book, and is updated on a regular basis.

If you still can't find a source that sounds as though it will meet your needs, experiment, using one of the Web search engines or directories; if that doesn't work, it's time to regroup. Get offline, go back and read the General Search Tips in Chapter 4 of *Finding Statistics Online*.

AN EFFECTIVE STRATEGY

In order to be able to search effectively, you have to know what the data looks like and which parts are searchable. Remember that statistics are found in many places and types of formats:

- Full text, with statistics within the text
- Abstracts, with statistics within the text
- Tables, standalone
- Tables within text
- Database records, usually fielded
- Datasets in machine-readable form
- Graphs and charts
- Handbook data
- Citations

These formats are illustrated in this book in Chapter 4 on pages 56-62. There are several "entry points" to any one of these source formats. (See the Access Points section in the case studies in Chapters 5 through 18 for examples in actual application.) Here's a checklist of entry points to the data:

- The text itself
- Titles
- Sponsoring organization
- Index terms, descriptors, and codes
- Captions

- Type of source
- Databases
- Fields
- Links

Your Search Weapons

Be sure to read several of the case studies in the subject-specific chapters of this book. They are real-life examples of what works (and what doesn't!) when doing down-and-dirty searching for statistics. Here are reminders from some of the lessons I've learned:

- Use search terms that indicate the possibility of statistical content. (Some of these terms appear on pages 62-66.)
- Don't be afraid of non-English text sources. There may be English-language abstracts, and numeric data can often be understood across a language barrier.
- Use one or more appropriate pathways into the sources. (A description of pathways appears on pages 55-56.)
- Be prepared to browse. Titles and indexing may be inadequate; the data you need may be buried in a report or table.
- Follow links to related data if the first source doesn't answer a question.
- Derive your own statistics by combining or massaging data you find in various sources. But be careful of mixing data arrived at through conflicting methodologies.
- Know when to stop. That point depends on your deadline, budget, and purpose.

EVALUATING DATA

Careful and thorough evaluation of data is necessary as and after you search statistics. If you need a review, see the section on Reading and Evaluating Data in Chapter 2: Statistics Basics, and check the Glossary of Statistics Terms in Appendix D. Be wary:

- Know, or become familiar with, the organizations that produce data in the field of your inquiry so you can judge their reliability.
- Use your own personal knowledge to question results that seem unlikely.
- Verify results that appear suspicious.
- Beware of unknown, unclear, or changing definitions or methodologies.
- Always read the footnotes! (Yes, they're boring, but they're put there for good reasons.)

Having reviewed, you should now be suited up and ready to tackle the wealth of online information that can give you the numbers you need to support an argument, wrap up a report, or make an important decision. Good luck on your journey, and let me know if you have problems—I *love* a statistics challenge.

—Paula Berinstein
paulab@berinsteinresearch.com

Vendor Information

Locations are in the USA unless otherwise stated. Telephone numbers are for North America unless otherwise stated. Country codes are preceded by +.

Autographics
3201 Temple Avenue
Pomona, CA 91768
(800) 776-6939
(909) 595-7204
(909) 595-3506 (fax)
info@auto-graphics.com
http://www.auto-graphics.com

BrainWave
N2K Telebase
435 Devon Park Drive
Suite 600
Wayne, PA 19087
(610) 293-4700
Help Desk: (800) 220-4664
(610) 293-4797
helpdesk@n2kbrainwave.com
http://alpha.n2kbrainwave.com

Brodart
500 Arch Street
Williamsport, PA 17705
(800) 233-8467 (U.S.)
(800) 265-8470 (Canada)
(800) 999-6799 (U.S. fax)
(800) 363-0483 (Canada fax)
http://www.brodart.com

Cognito!
Information Access Company
362 Lakeside Drive
Foster City, CA 94404
(415) 378-5369 (fax)

Support: (800) 227-8431
webmaster@cognito.com
http://www.cognito.com
http://www.iacnet.com

COMPanion Corp.
1831 Fort Union Blvd.
Salt Lake City, UT 84121
(801) 943-7277
(801) 943-7752 (fax)
Customer Support: (800) 347-4942
support@companioncorp.com
http://www.companioncorp.com

DataStar
The Dialog Corporation
(formerly Knight-Ridder Information, Inc.)
11000 Regency Parkway, Suite 400
Cary, NC 27511
(800) 326-9103 (Toll-free North America)
(919) 462-8600
(919) 468-9890 (fax)
Help Line: (800) HELP-388
http://www.dialog.com

DIALOG
The Dialog Corporation
(formerly Knight-Ridder Information, Inc.)
11000 Regency Parkway, Suite 400
Cary, NC 27511
(800) 326-9103 (Toll-free North America)
(919) 462-8600
(919) 468-9890 (fax)
Help Line: (800) HELP-388
http://www.dialog.com

Dow Jones Interactive
(formerly Dow Jones News/Retrieval)
Dow Jones & Company, Inc.
Business Information Services
P.O. Box 300
Princeton, NJ 08543-0300
Customer Service: (800) 369-7466
(609) 452-1511
support@bis.dowjones.com
http://bis.dowjones.com

Electric Library
Infonautics Corporation
900 West Valley Road
Suite 1000
Wayne, PA 19087
(800) 247-7644
http://www.elibrary.com

Encarta Online Library
Information Access Company
362 Lakeside Drive
Foster City, CA 94404
(415) 378-5369 (fax)
Support: (800) 227-8431
webmaster@encarta.cognito.com
http://www.encarta.com/library/intro.asp
http://www.iacnet.com

Endeavor Information
2200 E. Devon, Suite 382
Des Plaines, IL 60018-4505
(800) 762-6300
(847) 296-5636 (fax)
endeavor@endinfosys.com
http://www.endinfosys.com

FirstSearch
OCLC
6565 Frantz Road
Dublin, OH 43017-3395
(800) 848-5878
(614) 764-6000
(614) 764-6096 (fax)
http://www.oclc.org/oclc/menu/fs.htm
http://www.oclc.org
oclc@oclc.org

Gateway Software Corporation
P.O. Box 367
Fromberg, MT 59029
(800) 735-3637
gateway@gscweb.com
http://www.gscweb.com

IAC InSite and IAC InSite Pro
Information Access Company
362 Lakeside Drive
Foster City, CA 94404
(800) 227-8431
(415) 378-5369 (fax)
Content Support:
(800) 321-6388
(415) 358-4643
contentqa@iacnet.com
http://www.iacnet.com
http://www.iac-insite.com
http://www.insitepro.com

Innovative Interfaces, Inc.
5850 Shellmound
Emeryville, CA 94608
(800) 878-6600
(510) 655-6200
(510) 450-6350 (fax)
sales@iii.com
http://www.iii.com

LEXIS-NEXIS
9443 Springboro Pike
P.O. Box 933
Dayton, OH 45401
Customer Service in the U.S.:
Business (800) 346-9759
Government and law firms (800) 543-6862
Law Schools (800) 455-3947
http://www.lexis-nexis.com

A Matter of Fact
The Pierian Press
P.O. Box 1808
Ann Arbor, MI 48106
(800) 678-2435

(313) 434-6409 (fax)
pubinfo@pierianpress.com
http://www.pierianpress.com

NewsNet

Sadly, NewsNet ceased operations in August 1997, reducing access to a number of significant statistics resources.

NISC

Wyman Towers
3100 St. Paul St.
Baltimore, MD 21218
(410) 243-0797
(410) 243-0982 (fax)
info@nisc.com
support@nisc.com
http://www.nisc.com

Profound

The Dialog Corporation
11000 Regency Parkway, Suite 400
Cary, NC 27511
(800) 326-9103 (Toll-free North America)
(919) 462-8600
(919) 468-9890 (fax)
Help Line: (800) HELP-388
http://www.dialog.com

ProQuest Direct

UMI
300 North Zeeb Road
P.O. Box 1346
Ann Arbor, MI 48106-1346
Customer Service: (800) 521-0600
Sales (800) 521-0600, Ext. 2705
(313) 761-4700
http://www.umi.com

Questel•Orbit, Inc.

8000 Westpark Drive
McLean, VA 22102
Help Desk: (800) 456-7248
(703) 442-0900
(703) 893-4632 (fax)

help@questel.orbit.com
http://www.questel.orbit.com

SilverPlatter Information

100 River Ridge Drive
Norwood, MA 02062
(800) 343-0064 (U.S. and Canada)
(781) 769-2599
(781) 769-8763 (fax)
support@silverplatter.com
info@silverplatter.com
http://www.silverplatter.com

STN and STN Easy

Chemical Abstracts Service
P.O. Box 3012
2540 Olentangy River Road
Columbus, OH 43210
Customer Service: (800) 753-4227
(614) 447-3731
(614) 447-3751 (fax)
help@cas.org
http://www.cas.org

Vista II

Ameritech Library Services
400 Dynix Drive
Provo, UT 84604-5650
(800) 288-8020
(801) 223-5200
(801) 223-5202 (fax)
Vista II Support: (800) 978-4782
http://www.als.ameritech.com

Wall Street Journal Interactive Edition

Dow Jones & Company, Inc.
Business Information Services
P.O. Box 300
Princeton, NJ 08543-0300
Customer Service: (800) 369-7466
(609) 452-1511
support@bis.dowjones.com
http://interactive.wsj.com
http://bis.dowjones.com

Winnebago Software

457 East South Street
Caledonia, MN 55921
(800) 533-5430
(507) 724-2301 (fax, Sales)
Support: (800) 654-3002 U.S. and Canada
(507) 724-5530 (fax)
+1-507-724-5411 worldwide
support@winnebago.com
sales@winnebago.com
http://www.winnebago.com

Case Studies Table

The case studies in this book demonstrate practical dos and don'ts for searching statistics on numerous subjects and on a variety of online systems and World Wide Web sites. Use this table to find a case study on the topic or system of your choosing.

Case Study	Chapter Subject	Topic	Systems/Sources Used
5-1	Demographics and Population	City Population	Web: various sites
5-2		Religious Adherents	Web: Electric Library
6-1	Industry, Market and General Business	The Skates/Skateboard Industry	ProQuest Direct Data-Star PROMT
6-2		Book Returns	DJN/R
7-1	Financial and Economic	Non-U.S. Company Financials	DIALOG: Teikoku Databank
7-2		Insurance Losses	DIALOG: Trade & Industry
8-1	Health and Medical	Healthcare Spending	Web: Statistical Abstract ProQuest Direct
8-2		Incidence of AIDS	Web: Statistical Abstract
9-1	Scientific, Agricultural, and Environmental	Agricultural Water Use	Web: various sites
9-2		Boiling Points of Chemical Substances	STN
10-1	Historical	Military Casualties	DIALOG: Historical Abstracts
10-2		Fuel Prices	Web: USEIA
11-1	Public Opinion and Trends	Attitudes Toward Female Beauty	DIALOG: Public Opinion Online
12-1	Political and Government	Government Spending	LEXIS-NEXIS: MAJPAP
13-1	Sports, Entertainment and Arts	Movie Budget	Web: Internet Movie Database
13-2		Movie Attendance	LEXIS-NEXIS: AMDEM Web: American Demographics Web: WSJIE
14-1	Legal and Crime	Terrorism	Web: various sites
14-2		Number of Lawyers	LEXIS-NEXIS: AMLAWR Web: Statistical Abstract
15-1	International	Literacy Rates	Web: UNESCO
16-1	Technology	Number of 800 Numbers	Web: FCC
16-2		Laptop Sales	Web: CMPnet
17-1	Education	School Enrollment	Web: NCES
18-1	Transportation	Airline Fatalities	Web: FAA Web: NTSB

Glossary of Statistics Terms

See Chapter 2: Statistics Basics for more information about these common statistics terms.

Adjusted Numbers. Raw numbers that have been reworked by the gatherer before release, to account for seasonal variations or changes in the value of the dollar over time, for example.

Analysis. The determination of relationships among data. Analysis makes sense of the data and puts it in some context.

Average. A number that typifies a group of numbers. There are three common types of averages: mean, median, and mode.

Bell Curve. A graph in which the values are concentrated at the midpoint and taper out evenly in both directions from there. 68% of the data is within one standard deviation of the mean; 95% of the data is within two standard deviations of the mean; all of the data is within three standard deviations of the mean.

Census. A complete count of a thing or population to be measured.

Continuous Data. Measures, such as weights, heights, and other scaled data, that can always be subdivided just a little more.

Correlation. A method of data analysis in which the relationship between two measurements is explored.

Degree of Significance. An indication of the chances that data is correct. The higher the degree of significance, the greater the chances are that data is accurate.

Derivation. A methodology for producing statistics in which information is extracted or reformatted from raw data. Constructing an *index* is one form of derivation. Changing units of measurement is another, as when a daily rate is calculated by dividing a yearly rate by 365.

Discrete Data. Raw numbers that are counts of items that cannot be subdivided, such as people or cars.

Estimate. An approximation of an unknown value based on an extrapolation from a known value. Estimation may be used with current and future measurements.

Experiment. A methodology that involves the use of both a special study group upon which the experiment is conducted, and a control group where "business as usual" occurs. Experimenters examine the results obtained from the two groups for similarities and differences and may draw conclusions. An experiment is usually constructed around a hypothesis.

Forecasting. A methodology in which known measurements are used to predict the value of unknown measurements, which will be discernible at some future time.

Index. One number that summarizes multiple measurements and expresses them in terms of a common base. An index may represent measurements or counts of many things, or different aspects of one thing. One example is the Consumer Price Index.

Interval Data. A representation of the difference between two measurements. Interval data is best used when at least one of the measurements is known.

Mean. The arithmetic average in a group of numbers. The mean is derived by adding up all the values and dividing by the *number* of measurements. The mean may indicate hypothetical rather than real values.

Measurement. The use of instruments or devices to gather data.

Median. The midpoint in a group of numbers; a real or hypothetical value at which half the numbers in the group fall above and half fall below.

Mode. An average that represents the most frequently found numbers in a group. There can be more than one mode in a group. Unlike means and medians, a mode *must* reflect real values.

Nominal Data. A type of statistic that represents categories that are *not* assigned numerical values.

Observation. A methodology in which the subject is examined in its natural setting.

Panel. An ongoing survey. Panels provide more data than a single survey, and they allow follow-up over time.

Percentage. An expression of the relationship between a part and the whole that reduces counts to a common scale, based on 100.

Percentiles. An indication, based on 100, of how data is distributed. A percentile is a number below which a certain percent of the data falls. For example, the 90th percentile is the number below which 90 percent of the values occur.

Precision. The accuracy of a survey. The precision is proportional to the square root of the sample size.

Probability. An expression of the likelihood that something will occur. Probability is calculated based on the number of times an event occurs when a random experiment is run many times. A low degree of probability indicates less likelihood that the event will occur.

Probable Error. The chances that data are incorrect, and an expression of how well a survey measures what it's designed to measure. The lower the degree of probable error, the better the chances are that data is accurate.

Questionnaire. A measurement of attitudes, behavior or other values that produces a "snapshot" of them but does not measure against a standard. A questionnaire differs from a *test*, which does measure against a standard.

Random Sample. A methodology of sampling, or taking a representative portion of a group, in which the elements making up the sample are selected by chance. True random samples are so difficult and expensive to obtain that often variations on the random sample are used.

Ranking. A hierarchical comparison. Two kinds of numbers are involved in ranking: the *raw data*, and the *rank* or *rating number*. A searcher might seek the rank number, the raw data, or both.

Rate. An expression of a quantity or an amount in relation to another unit. For example, parts per million, used to measure pollutants, is a rate.

Rating. A subjective measure of something that has been assigned a numerical value. Scales such as "agree strongly," "agree," "agree somewhat," "disagree somewhat," "disagree," "strongly disagree" are examples of ratings (once the values have been converted to numbers). This kind of data is also called *ordinal data*, because it defines a relative position in a series.

Ratio. A type of statistic that expresses a relationship between two numbers. When ratios are given without presentation of the raw numbers behind them, interpreting them requires the same caution as when interpreting percentages: the situation can be overstated if small actual numbers are involved.

Raw Numbers. Pure data. A type of statistic that represents counts or measures.

Sample. A representative "taste" of a group. Samples may be used when censuses are too expensive or impossible to implement.

Significance, Degree of. *See Degree of Significance.*

Standard Deviation. A unit that measures the variability of data from an average. An item is said to be one or more standard deviations away from the mean. The farther away, the more unique and rare. The closer, the more common. Standard deviations are the most accurate when the data is distributed fairly evenly, as in a *bell curve*.

Standard Error. A way of measuring the chance that data is incorrect, and an expression of how well a survey measures what it's designed to measure.

Test. A measurement of the way something or someone performs compared to a standard. A test differs from a *questionnaire* because the questionnaire does not measure against a standard.

Validity. Truth or accuracy in statistical data and its representation. Degree of validity is affected by the methods for gathering, manipulating, and interpreting the data.

Bibliography

The following books were helpful to me in the research for this book and may be used for further reading:

Fuld, Leonard M. *Competitor Intelligence: How to Get It; How to Use It.* New York: John Wiley & Sons, 1985.

Haack, Dennis G. *Statistical Literacy: A Guide to Interpretation.* North Scituate, Massachusetts: Duxbury Press, 1979.

Halacy, Dan. *Census: 190 Years of Counting America.* New York: Elsevier/Nelson Books, 1980.

Huff, Darrell. *How to Lie with Statistics.* New York: W. W. Norton, 1954.

Lavin, Michael, et al. *Subject Index to the 1990 Census of Population and Housing.* Kenmore, NY: Epoch Books, 1997.

Lavin, Michael. *Understanding the Census: A Guide for Marketers, Planners, Grant Writers and Other Data Users.* Kenmore, NY: Epoch books, 1996.

Tanur, Judith M., et al., eds. *Statistics: A Guide to the Unknown.* 3rd edition. Pacific Grove, California: Wadsworth & Brooks, 1989.

United States Bureau of the Census. *Historical Statistics of the United States, Colonial Times to 1970.* Washington, D.C.: U.S. Department of Commerce, Bureau of the Census, 1975.

Zeisl, Hans. *Say It with Figures.* 5th edition, revised. New York: Harper and Row, 1968.

Index

F

research centers, 46-47
Researchline Database, 89, 107
Reserve Bank of India, 246
resource planning and deployment, 84
Responsive Database Services Inc., 4
Restaurants & Institutions, 114
Retail and Wholesale Trade Web site, 118
retail industry, market research, 117-119
Reuter Financial Service, 142
Reuters, 132
Reuters Insurance Briefings, 143
Reuters Media World, 108
Review of Particle Properties. *See also*
scientific databases
RiceWeb, 169
Riggleman, John R., 184
The Right Side demographic reports, 83
robotic technology, 260
Roll Call, 211, 212
Roper Center for Public Opinion Research,
43, 199, 201
Russia and the Commonwealth of
Independent States, international
statistics, 256

S

Sales & Marketing Management, 89
sample size, 27, 309
San Jose Mercury News, 265
Satellite TV Finance, 221
School Enrollment case study, 280-282
School Finance Data, 279
Science & Technology Data Canada, 261
science and technology research, 3
scientific databases. *See also* agricultural
statistics
numeric data, 72
resources, 166-177
types of data, 165-166
Scout Report Web site, 12, 54
Screen Finance, 222
SCRL French Company Financial Profiles,
137
search engines, 12, 43, 54. *See also names of
specific search engines*

search strategies. *See also* online database
systems; *specific names of online database systems*
data format considerations, 56-62
database characteristics and, 50-51
demographics data, 83, 85-90
economic research, 44
market research, 119
selecting resources, 51-55, 68, 296-298
tips, 11-12, 49, 55-56, 82, 119, 298-299
wording considerations, 23-25, 49, 62-67
SEC filings, 100
SEC Online, 135
second-tier sources, 51
securities. *See* investment information
Securities and Exchange Commission, 39
SEER (Surveillance, Epidemiology, and End
Results), 158
Segregation Data 1890-1990, 189
Selective Service System, 39
self-reports, 21-22
Service Annual Survey, 147, 156, 222
Shipbuilding/Water Transportation Reports,
292
SI Units, 168
SilverPlatter Information, Inc.
contact information, 303
DOSE, 171
EIU Country Forecasts, 130, 243
A Matter of Fact, 131, 155, 167, 208, 219,
234, 278
Search by Search system, 4
Simba Information, 44
Sistema Ditte Operanti con l'Estero/Italian
Trading Companies, 138
Skates and Skateboard Industry case study,
119-122
skewed data, 16, 20, 22, 27
Slovenia (Republic of), international statis-
tics, 250
Small Business Administration, 39
Snack Food, 114
Social Change Reports, 201
social issues, public opinion data, 199
Social Sciences Data Center, University of
Virginia, 88

international statistics, 254
Statistical Yearbook, 244
unfinished comparisons, 24
UNICEF (United Nations Children's Fund),
254
Uniform Crime Reports, Federal Bureau of
Investigation, 235
unions, 45
United Auto Workers, 45
United Kingdom
financial and investment information, 106,
138-139, 140
market research, 105, 106, 107
Times/Sunday Times, 252
United Kingdom Office for National
Statistics, 251
United Mine Workers of America, 45
United Nations
Demming Database, 254
Department of Humanitarian Affairs
(ReliefWeb), 254
Economic Commission for Europe, 254
Environment Programme, 251, 254
Food and Agriculture Organization, 253
High Commissioner for Refugees, 254
Industrial Development Organization, 254
International Drug Control Programme,
254
Population Division, 88, 189
Population Fund, 255
Statistics Division, 158, 242, 255
UNICEF (United Nations Children's
Fund), 254
World Crime Survey (UNCJIN), 235
United States. *See* demographics data;
government statistics; *names of specific
agencies, databases, and services;*
political statistics
United States Air Force Library Fact Sheets,
211
United States Navy Factfile, 211
United Steel Workers of America, 45
units/measures, 63-64
University of Michigan
Documents Center, Statistical Resources on
the Web, 55

Institute for Social Research, 199, 206
JSTOR database, 188
Population Gopher, 88
University of South Carolina, WWW Tide
and Current Predictor, 175
University of Virginia, Social Sciences Data
Center, 88
University of Wisconsin, Archival Data
Online Repository, 188
university-related research, 46, 154
Urban Institute, 43
Urologic Diseases—National Institute of
Diabetes and Digestive and Kidney
Diseases, 158
U.S. Banker, 133
U.S. Budget, 212
U.S. Bureau of Labor Statistics
demographics data, 85
described, 9
economic indicators, 37
financial and investment information, 128,
146
health and medical statistics, 155
historical statistics, 183
legal and crime statistics, 236
U.S. Business Cycle Expansions and
Contractions 1854-1991, 191
U.S. Census Bureau
demographics data, 84, 85, 277, 285, 290
described, 8, 12, 32
international statistics, 244
search strategies, 52, 55
U.S. Census of 1790, 184, 185
U.S. Coast Guard, 38
U.S. Coastal Tide Tables, 175
U.S. Commerce National Trade Data Bank
Market Reports, 147
U.S. Congress
Congressional Budget Office, 39
Congressional Committee Vote Report, 209
Congressional Committee Votes Archive,
209
Congressional District/State Profile Report,
209
Congressional Floor Votes Archive, 209
Congressional Honoraria Contributions, 211

Other Books of Interest from Information Today, Inc.

Finding Images Online: *ONLINE USER's* **Guide to Image Searching in Cyberspace**
Paula Berinstein
While text research has been done at the desk for years, finding images has traditionally meant either relying on professional stock image houses or engaging in long, often fruitless searches. Today, cyberspace is exploding with millions of digital images, many of them in the public domain. With a personal computer, a modem, and this book, you can learn to efficiently evaluate, search, and use the vast image resources of the Internet and online services, plus powerful databases designed specifically for image searchers.
357 pp/softbound/ISBN 0-910965-21-8/$29.95

The Internet Unplugged: Utilities and Techniques for Internet Productivity ... Online and Off
Michael A. Banks
Here is the first complete guide to the online and offline "extras" every Windows user needs to make productive use of the Net. Author Michael Banks demystifies all the important software tools, shows where to find them, and offers tips and techniques for using them effectively.
251 pp/softbound/ISBN 0-910965-24-2/$29.95

Naked in Cyberspace: How to Find Personal Information Online
Carole A. Lane
Now that so many types of personal records are searchable online, the bureaucratic red tape that used to protect our secrets from prying eyes has been stripped away ... and we're all naked in cyberspace. Without taking sides on the right and wrong of using online ingredients to compile a detailed dossier, this bestselling book tells you where to find personal information online and on CD-ROM.
544 pp/softbound/ISBN 0-910965-17-X/$29.95

Secrets of the Super Net Searchers: The Reflections, Revelations and Hard-Won Wisdom of 35 of the World's Top Internet Researchers
Reva Basch
Reva Basch, whom *WIRED Magazine* has called "The Ultimate Intelligent Agent," delivers insights, anecdotes, tips, techniques, and case studies through her interviews with 35 of the world's top Internet hunters and gatherers. The Super Net Searchers explain how to find valuable information on the Internet, distinguish cyber-gems from cyber-junk, avoid "Internet Overload," and much more.
340 pp/softbound/ISBN 0-910965-22-6/$29.95

The Online Deskbook: *ONLINE* **Magazine's Essential Desk Reference for Online and Internet Searchers**
Mary Ellen Bates
As the only desk reference to cover all the major online services and the Internet, this book helps you identify important online information sources and put them to immediate use. It includes the nuts and bolts of online searching, plus shortcuts, trouble-shooting guides, time and money-saving tips and techniques, directory of resources, and much more.
261 pp/softbound/ISBN 0-910965-19-6/$29.95

Electronic Democracy: Using the Internet to Influence American Politics
Graeme Browning
Award-winning journalist Graeme Browning, currently Communications Director for the Center for Democracy and Technology (CDT), provides real-world strategies for researching and advancing political causes online. Loaded with actual case studies of successful and failed online campaigns, this is a must-have guide for political activists and researchers.
186 pp/softbound/ISBN: 0-910965-20-X/$19.95

Electronic Styles: A Handbook for Citing Electronic Information
Xia Li and Nancy Crane
The second edition of the bestselling guide to referencing electronic information and citing the complete range of electronic formats includes text-based information, electronic journals and discussion lists, Web sites, CD-ROM and multimedia products, and commercial online documents.
214 pp/softbound/ISBN 1-57387-027-7/$19.99

To order directly from the publisher, include $3.95 postage and handling for the first book ordered and $3.25 for each additional book. Catalogs also available upon request.

Information Today, Inc., 143 Old Marlton Pike, Medford, NJ 08055 • (609) 654-6266

The Internet at a Glance
Susan E. Feldman and Larry Krumenaker
This handy, inexpensive beginner's guide is designed to be at your side while you're surfing the Net. It will help you perform the most common tasks and find information on the Internet, and gives the basic commands for e-mail, Usenet newsgroups, anonymous ftp, telnet, mailing lists, and more.
25 pp/spiralbound/ISBN 1-57387-024-2/$9.95

The Library Web
Julie Still, editor
Here's expert advice about Web page creation and maintenance from leading academic, special, and public librarians. Included are features on instructional materials, programs and software for building a Web site, how to involve all areas of the library in Web-based projects, and much more.
230 pp/hardbound/ISBN 1-57387-034-X/$39.50

The Evolving Virtual Library: Visions and Case Studies
Laverna M. Saunders, Editor
Access to remote resources that supplement or substitute for items owned locally is creating a transformation in libraries of all types. The virtual library is the phenomenon of the international system of electronic networks which enables a user at a computer terminal to search bibliographic citations, databases, electronic publications, and other types of information in digital format. Here is the first book to address the many issues involved in developing the virtual library.
154 pp/hardbound/ISBN 1-57387-013-7/$39.50

The Official Internet World Internet Security Handbook
William Stallings
Protecting personal and professional Internet-based data from damaging leaks and hacker attacks is vital in an age where more and more important information travels electronically. This practical guide, written by a leading Internet security expert, addresses the information security concerns of both individuals and businesses.
400 pp/softbound/ISBN 1-56884-700-9/$24.99

Electronic Image Communications: A Guide to Networking Image Files
Richard J. Nees
One of the latest buzzwords in the industry is "multimedia." And, of course, imaging is a basic element of multimedia. Whether looking to fill an immediate need or trying to find the direction the future may take, this book will provide a better understanding of the opportunities as well as the issues of image networking.
95 pp/hardbound/ISBN 0-938734-87-3/$39.50

Secrets of the Super Searchers: The Accumulated Wisdom of 23 of the World's Top Online Searchers
Reva Basch
Reva Basch, a super searcher in her own right, asks the questions that reveal the secret strategies and planning techniques of top online searchers in the fields of business, law, finance, communications, and the humanities. Learn how skilled searchers choose databases on professional online services, plan search strategies, cope with too many or too few hits, and know when the search is done.
235 pp/softbound/ISBN 0-910965-12-9/$39.95

The Online Manual
This is a unique reference tool for searching international business information online. The easy-to-use sections guide you through the available databases, helping you to locate the journal you need online, discover which databases cover your subject, identify important database hosts, find answers to specific queries, and much, much more.
659 pp/softbound/ISBN 0-904933-93-8/$250.00

The Online 100: *ONLINE* Magazine's Field Guide to the 100 Most Important Online Databases
Mick O'Leary
Here is a practical guide that evaluates the strengths and weaknesses of the top online databases. Concise descriptions of each database, typical search costs, advice on when and when not to use a certain database, and information on CD-ROM and Internet availability are all included in this essential reference for online and Internet searchers.
233 pp/softbound/ISBN 0-910965-14-5/$22.95

TCP/IP for the Internet: The Complete Buyer's Guide to TCP/IP Software
Marshall Breeding
The selection of the right TCP/IP package can be a daunting task, with differences among products involving many technical details. This is the first book to evaluate these disparate software packages and to offer the reader in-depth, descriptive reviews of the major products available for the Windows and Macintosh platforms.
305 pp/softbound/ISBN 0-88736-980-4/$24.95

To order directly from the publisher, include $3.95 postage and handling for the first book ordered and $3.25 for each additional book. Catalogs also available upon request.

Information Today, Inc., 143 Old Marlton Pike, Medford, NJ 08055 • (609) 654-6266